SG

Small Steps Beyond HTML

 # The Charles F. Goldfarb Series on Open Information Management

"Open Information Management" (OIM) means managing information so that it is open to processing by any program, not just the program that created it. That extends even to application programs not conceived of at the time the information was created.

OIM is based on the principle of data independence: data should be stored in computers in non-proprietary, genuinely standardized representations. And that applies even when the data is the content of a document. Its representation should distinguish the innate information from the proprietary codes of document processing programs and the artifacts of particular presentation styles.

Business data bases — which rigorously separate the real data from the input forms and output reports — achieved data independence decades ago. But documents, unlike business data, have historically been created in the context of a particular output presentation style. So for document data, independence was largely unachievable until recently.

That is doubly unfortunate. It is unfortunate because documents are a far more significant repository of humanity's information. And documents can contain significantly richer information structures than data bases.

It is also unfortunate because the need for OIM of documents is greater now than ever. The demands of "repurposing" require that information be deliverable in multiple formats (paper-based, online, multimedia, hypermedia). And information must now be delivered through multiple channels (traditional bookstores and libraries, online services, the Internet).

Fortunately, in the past ten years a technology has emerged that extends to documents the data base's capacity for data independence. And it does so without the data base's restrictions on structural freedom. That technology is the "Standard Generalized Markup Language" (SGML), an official International Standard (ISO 8879) that has been adopted by the world's largest producers of documents.

With SGML, organizations in government, aerospace, airlines, automotive, electronics, computers, and publishing (to name a few) have freed their documents from hostage relationships to processing software. SGML coexists with other data standards needed for OIM and acts as the framework that relates objects in the other formats to one another and to SGML documents.

As the enabling standard for OIM of documents, SGML necessarily plays a leading role in this series. We provide tutorials on SGML and other key standards and the techniques for applying them. Our books are not addressed solely to technical readers: we cover topics like the business justification for OIM and the business aspects of commerce in electronic information. We share the practical experience of organizations and individuals who have applied the techniques of OIM in environments ranging from immense industrial publishing projects to self-publishing on the World Wide Web.

Our authors are expert practitioners in their subject matter, not writers hired to cover a "hot" topic. They bring insight and understanding that can only come from real-world experience. Moreover, they practice what they preach about standardization. Their books share a common standards-based vocabulary. In this way, knowledge gained from one book in the series is directly applicable when reading another, or the standards themselves. This is just one of the ways in which we strive for the utmost technical accuracy and consistency with the OIM standards.

And we also strive for a sense of excitement and fun. After all, the challenge of OIM — preserving information from the ravages of technology while exploiting its benefits — is one of the great intellectual adventures of our age. I'm sure you'll find this series to be a knowledgable and reliable guide on that adventure.

About the Series Editor

Dr. Charles F. Goldfarb is the inventor of SGML and HyTime, and technical leader of the committees that developed them into their present form as International Standards. He is an information management consultant based in Saratoga, CA.

About the Series Logo

The rebus is an ancient literary tradition, dating from 16th century Picardy, and is especially appropriate to a series involving fine distinctions between things and the words that describe them. For the logo, Andrew Goldfarb, who also designed the series' "Intelligent Icons", incorporated a rebus of the series name within a stylized SGML comment declaration.

 # The Charles F. Goldfarb Series on Open Information Management

SGML *on the* WEB
S M A L L   S T E P S
B E Y O N D
H. T. M. L.

by
Yuri Rubinsky
and
Murray Maloney

Prentice Hall PTR
Upper Saddle River, New Jersey 07458
http://www.prenhall.com/

Library of Congress Cataloging in Publication Data

Cover Design Director: Jerry Votta
Cover Design: Talar Agasyan
Illustrations: Colin Moock
Editorial/Production Supervision: bookworks
Manufacturing manager: Alexis R Heydt
Acquisitions editor: Mark L.Taub
Editorial assistant: Kate Hargett

 Published by Prentice Hall PTR
Prentice-Hall, Inc.
A Simon & Schuster Company
Upper Saddle River, New Jersey 07458

The publisher offers discounts on this book when ordered in bulk quantities. For more information, contact:

Corporate Sales Department, Prentice Hall PTR
One Lake Street, Upper Saddle River, NJ 07458
Phone: 800-382-3419; FAX: 201-236-7141
E-mail: corpsales@prenhall.com

Printed in the United States of America
10 9 8 7 6 5 4 3 2 1

ISBN 0-13-519984-0

Prentice-Hall International (UK) Limited, London
Prentice-Hall of Australia Pty. Limited, Sydney
Prentice-Hall Canada Inc., Toronto
Prentice-Hall Hispanoamericana, S.A., Mexico
Prentice-Hall of India Private Limited, New Delhi
Prentice-Hall of Japan, Inc., Tokyo
Simon & Schuster Asia Pte. Ltd., Singapore
Editora Prentice-Hall do Brasil, Ltda., Rio de Janeiro

❧ DEDICATION

This book is dedicated to the memory of Yuri Rubinsky.

A Prayer About Prayer

I am beginning to understand that it matters less to whom I pray than that I pray.

That in praying for guidance, the real goal is to formulate questions so clearly that I can understand them. The external power that offers guidance comes from within me; the force of wisdom comes from my clarity; the strength of its convictions arises out of my choice to concentrate on this question or that call for help. All of these are requests for clarification.

That in praying for strength, the real goal is to recognize my strength. I have survived till now! I have done some of what I can do, but not all. I have understood all of what I needed to arrive here today and I accept that tomorrow I may need to learn more. My prayer for strength is a prayer for a moment of stillness in which to gather my resources.

I am not going into battle. I do not need the strength of ten. I do not need armour and a sword. All prayers are prayers for guidance and strength. I have what I need: I have the clear strength of one.

Yuri Rubinsky
(1952-1996)

✒ TABLE OF CONTENTS

❧ FOREWORD

A rich data type, HTML, has completely taken over.
— Bill Gates, Microsoft
(quoted in InfoWorld, March 18, 1996)

As the father of SGML, I'm also the grandfather of HTML, because it is an SGML application. As is nature's way in these matters, I achieved this status without being involved in either the act of procreation or the painful labor, but that doesn't impair my right to be proud of the progeny.

And I *am* proud of HTML — and of its inventor, Tim Berners-Lee, who, with his colleagues Dave Raggett and Dan Connolly, developed that invention into the remarkable tool that made the World Wide Web possible. They walked a careful line between the power and complexity of full SGML and the simplicity needed to achieve instant understanding and acceptance. Their success has made a profound change in the world of computing, as *Microsoft's* CEO has acknowledged.

But the World Wide Web has outgrown the original HTML. As Web site owners gain more experience, they seek the same facilities for Web publishing and document management that they currently enjoy elsewhere. These include more expressive formatting, better control of content and presentation, and *automatic* reuse of document content.

Now you can achieve the same benefits for yourself. With this book, you can create your own hypertext markup language just like Tim, Dave, and Dan did — with SGML. But you won't need to write your own browser or join a standards committee because the book includes a CD-ROM with everything you need to get started, using your favorite Web browser.

And you couldn't find better guides to creating your own HTML than Yuri Rubinsky and Murray Maloney. They are both founding members of the HTML working group of the Internet Engineering Task Force, and members of the *World Wide Web Consortium* (W3C) *Advisory Committee.* Murray is also a sponsor member of the *Davenport Group,* an industry consortium that produces widely-used SGML application standards. Yuri was instrumental in developing SGML markup for the visually disabled.

Yuri also invented the award-winning SoftQuad HoTMetaL HTML authoring tool, chaired the annual North American SGML conference series, and founded the SGML Open vendor consortium. He started this book and, after his untimely passing, Murray, his friend and colleague in these activities, finished it.

Together they lead you step by step in creating just the SGML markup language that you need for the Web — whether it's less than HTML, or beyond!

Charles F. Goldfarb
Saratoga, California
July 16 1996

Firmness, Commodity and Delight

HyperText Markup Language (HTML) is the world's best known application of Standard Generalized Markup Language (SGML), the International Standard language for open information management. But HTML taps only a small fraction of SGML's potential. This book will show you how to go well beyond what you could do with HTML. Naturally, a book whose subtitle is "Small Steps Beyond HTML" has to begin by asking: "Do we need more than HTML?"

Let's think first about architecture. The Roman architect Vitruvius, who lived at the time of Caesar Augustus, wrote a great and influential work called the *Ten Books on Architecture*. In those books, he expressed the opinion that architecture must offer "Firmness, Commodity and Delight". Two thousand years later, his advice still holds true for any form of architecture: Whether you are designing buildings or creating electronic structures for your information, you must take into account these characteristics of good architecture.

In a speech given at the North American SGML conference in 1989, architect Douglas MacLeod spoke about Vitruvius, and he explained the three characteristics in this way: "It is perhaps easier to understand these ideas in the context of buildings. *Firmness* is a good structure that holds up a building under all manner of conditions — during high winds, earthquakes, fires and snowstorms. *Commodity* is what makes a building comfortable — things are the right size, the heating and cooling systems work and you don't have to climb too many stairs in the course of the day. But *Delight* is what makes the building worth being in — Delight is what makes the building more than just a shelter. It may be an intellectual delight, a visual delight or even a delight to be in to listen to music, but it brings something more to the building than just functionality."

The World Wide Web is a form of architecture, *an architecture of information*, and accordingly, it must meet the criteria established by Vitruvius for good architecture. The World Wide Web expresses its architecture through the structures it gives us for expressing information, that is, through the HyperText Markup Language.

 At a high level, an architecture of information is the infrastructure we build to coordinate, take advantage of and make a coherent system out of our new ideas, tools, networks and capabilities. At a lower level, an architecture of information is the set of electronic structures we develop to create, edit, store, retrieve, manipulate, manage and make public our information content. In the case of the World Wide Web, we have been given a set of structures that includes paragraphs, titles, headings of various sorts, lists, images, links from one document to another, and so forth. *But is this enough?*

That question can be answered only by posing another: *Enough for what?* It is clear that HTML has provided enough capability for people to create tens of millions of documents. It has provided a common language of markup that lets those documents:

- be read by any kind of computer
- be read by various pieces of software
- be displayed in a meaningful screen presentation on all those computers
- be linked to one another
- be able to incorporate images, audio, video and animation
- be stored in databases and searched in rudimentary ways.

This is a great deal of significant functionality given that the only requirement is that the documents include a little bit of markup — a few extra words with angle brackets around them — that indicates paragraphs, titles, headings, and so forth.

So to get back to my second question: Is this enough? Does this degree of functionality balance the overhead of using the markup? Is this a cost-effective way of making information available?

As with any other business decision, the question of whether HTML works for you comes down to the business case.

Another, separate decision needs to be made first: Does the Web itself offer you something you cannot already get for less cost?

- Markets: Does the Web reach your readers and customers? Will it reach new ones?
- Speed: Does the Web reach them faster than other means? Does speed of delivery matter to you at all?
- Depth: Does the Web reach *enough of them* to be a worthwhile investment?
- Security and Payment Considerations: Can you do business on the Web with confidence? Alternatively, can you do business successfully on the Web without needing to collect money on the Web?
- Pro-Activeness: Is there value in giving your readers or customers a more active role in the acquisition of your contents than they might otherwise get? (That is, does the Web's interactiveness add value to your message? Does your data lend itself to hypertext path-making?)

If you are satisfied with enough of the answers to these questions, and you have decided that the Web is part of your future, then you have an opportunity to move to the second decision: Is HTML *enough*? Now you get to ask questions about capability.

- Display Capability: Is the appearance of a Web page good enough? Does it suit both your readers and your contents? Are there display distinctions you would like to make that HTML doesn't give you today?
- Functional Capability: Do the modes and means of interactivity work for your content and your readers? Could your data benefit from additional types of hypertext linking — (two-way links, for example, or links from one part of a graphic to part of another)?

Extending Capabilities in a Stable Framework

Part of HTML's success comes from the simplicity of Web. *Click!* And a file appears in your *browser* or your editor.

There's a reason for this immediacy — the software knows what to expect of the file you're sending it. It expects:

- plain text characters with no control characters or other unusual characters
- a specific set of markup, the stuff in angle brackets, that tells the software that <TITLE>This is a title.</TITLE> and that <P>This is a paragraph.</P>
- a small, finite set of known ways to interact with the markup and perform actions: traverse links, make headings bold, and so forth.

The secret is *No surprises*. The software knows the file will be HTML (the *.htm* or *.html* extension helps), or, to be more precise, *assumes the file will be in* HTML and acts accordingly.

A growing number of Web software-makers are inventing their own additional markup. Netscape Navigator and Microsoft's Internet Explorer are competing for market share with their proprietary extensions to HTML. This is fine in their own software, where they can pretend that their new markup is not a surprise. It does suggest that they want everyone who might read your documents to have their software.

This book suggests a slightly different approach. In a nutshell, I take the position that inventing new markup makes sense, indeed offers valuable new capabilities to both creators and consumers of information. But to be commercially viable in your business, markup must maintain the "No surprises" principle.

As luck would have it, there is *a standard way* of saying to software "This is the markup I use." To accomplish this, we let a document contain a "preamble" or "prolog", much like a book that defines the terms that it is going to use, or a computer program that defines the functions it then uses to run.

The document prolog can be in one of two forms. It could be:

- definitions of new markup, right there in the document, or
- a pointer to a separate file (or even a set of files, if you want to be fancy) that contains all the markup definitions.

This is, in fact, exactly what HTML does. It uses an internationally standardized mechanism — SGML — to create definitions. The Web browsers that you use, know about the definitions — more or less. HTML counts on the fact that browsers know the definitions. Accordingly, they don't use a prolog — they assume the definitions haven't changed — the standard one is "implied".

But there is a different class of software — software built to read and understand any prolog before it interprets the document itself — the prolog and the definitions it either contains or points to. Those definitions are written in SGML — the Standard Generalized Markup Language — and software that understands this mechanism for creating your own or extending existing markup is SGML software.

Using SGML as a *markup declaration language* allows you to create *any markup you want*, and have it clearly understood by any other SGML software that encounters it — now or in the future. SGML software will then let you assign display or print characteristics to that markup through style sheets: Do you want your headings bold and centered? Which markup do you want to use to indicate hypertext links?

That's what this book is about. What are the simplest steps you can take to invent the markup that makes sense for your information? What are the tricks that others have used to achieve certain capabilities? What are the basic principles that will let you assign both markup and characteristics?

Stability, Usefulness and Extensibility

I began this essay by talking about two-thousand-year-old precepts of good architecture. I'd like to end by updating those in the context of the World Wide Web:

Firmness:

If Vitruvius had designed the Web and the language of its information structures, he would have felt no differently than Tim Berners-Lee, its actual inventor, on the subject: To provide a real service to online readers, it must be robust. To be treated as a viable commercial medium, it must offer stability.

In these early, experimental days, we're all willing to put up with difficulties, downtime and a confusing competition for capability, but before long everyone who wants to conduct business of the Web will insist on firmness.

Commodity:

Usefulness. The Web must do what you need it to do, within the normal bounds of reason. (You can't expect it to replace all other forms of communications, for example, but you can insist that it do a good job at being a somewhat friendly means to publish and consume linked, global, digital data in a variety of media.) It must *accommodate* your reasonable requirements.

Delight:

I don't quite do justice to Vitruvius' request for delight when I suggest that the Web and its information structures must be extensible, but it is the case that without a built-in framework for extensibility (and, as luck would have it, a social environment that thrives on experimentation), we have no possibility of discovering pockets of the Web that do surprise and delight us.

The reason I insist on the full value of SGML on the Web is that it meets Vitruvius' requirements: SGML, an ISO standard with a ten-year history of successful implementation, certainly offers firmness and stability. As a language that enables you to define the new information structures you need, it is accommodating, meeting the commodity/useful criterion. And because it was designed as a tool for extensibility, its support for invention and delight is limited only by your imagination.

Yuri Rubinsky
Toronto, Canada
November 1995

❧ ACKNOWLEDGEMENTS

There are so many people who deserve acknowledg ment, not only for playing a part in the creation of this book, but for empowering and enabling Yuri and me, each in their own way.

- Anna and Andrew Rubinsky for bringing Yuri into our world.
- Holley Rubinsky for sharing Yuri with us, and for establishing the Yuri Rubinsky Insight Foundation.
- Joan Maloney, Andrea, Christopher and Brendan for their endless encouragement, steady support and endless patience.
- Peter Sharpe, Steve and Marian Downie, Bill Clarke, David Slocombe, Dave Gurney, Linda Hazzan, Roberto Drassinower and Bud Greasely for lifting and lightening the load. And to Lauren Wood, Liam Quin and Peter Sharpe for their help in creating the examples.
- Barb Burrows, for talking to me, listening to me, and writing for me, the two pages that were the most difficult to write in this entire book. And just for being the kind of close friend — to both Yuri and me — that I could turn to for help.
- Liam Quin for his masterful design of the printed book, his meticulous attention to detail, and his tireless effort in typesetting it for publication.
- Eliot Kimber, Charles Goldfarb, Hasse Haitto, Peter Lidbaum and Magnus Tobiason who each contributed to the HyTime examples.
- Paul Grosso, Melinda Stetina and the rest of ITEE for the ERD example.
- Wendy Freedman and Terry Sadlier for the GM example.
- Beth Micksch, John Dick and Robin Tomlin for the Datataker example.
- The ICADD committee and others who have contributed to making information accessible for the disabled: George Kerscher, Mike Paciello, Joe Sullivan, Jutta Treverarus, Jim Allen, Steve Edwards, Tom Wesley, Bart Bauwens, Jan Englen, Uli Strempel, David Holladay, Richard Jones and Jeff Suttor in particular.

- The book's editorial and production team at SoftQuad — Kay McCutcheon, John Turnbull, Colin Moock, Zvi Gilbert, Rodney Boyd, Nelson Adams, Cheryl Simpson and Ryan Germann — without whose technical assistance, artistry, hard work and dedication this book could not have been completed. (Not to mention giving up evenings, weekends and vacation time.)
- Bob Stayton and Henry Budgett at SCO, and Liam Quin and Ian Graham in Toronto for REL/REV.
- The members of the Davenport Group, the OSF, USL and X/Open DOC SIGs, the IETF HTML Working Group and the W3C HTML Editorial Review Board for the education gained by, and the pleasure of participating in their work.
- Jon Bosak, Eve Maler, Jeanne ElAndaloussi and Harvey Bingham for their technical guidance and encouragement.
- Dan Connolly and Dave Raggett, without whom the World Wide Web might never have become a truly exemplar case of SGML in action.
- Joseph Hardin at NCSA and Stu Weibel at OCLC for their very early enthusiasm for SGML on the Web, the Metadata workshop, and the Metadata DTD used in a simpler form in this book.
- Charles Goldfarb and Tim Berners-Lee, without whom the world would have neither Standard Generalized Markup Language nor the World Wide Web, respectively.
- Vanevar Bush, Douglas Engelbart, Marshall McLuhan, Ted Nelson and Vint Cerf, whose visions of the future paved the way to a better place than we had before.
- And to all of our dear friends, close colleagues, passing acquaintances and total strangers who deserve acknowledgment for fostering in us all the urgent belief that... "Life is a Daring Adventure, or it is nothing." — Helen Keller.

Yuri Rubinsky and Murray Maloney, 1996

❧ ABSTRACT

Here, you get to read a summary of this entire book in less than two pages.

HTML is *cool*! You can do lots of *cool* things with HTML. It is a language that enables publishing on the World Wide Web. The definition of that language is pretty much in the hands of a few companies and the *World Wide Web Consortium* (W3C). These companies are competing with each other to differentiate their products on features by creating versions of HTML that don't always get along. It is really hard to say what will happen to HTML next.

SGML is the international standard upon which the definition of HTML is based. SGML allows you to create languages like HTML. It also allows you to create languages that are very different and useful for entirely different purposes than HTML. SGML is being used to create and publish, in print and online, simple and sophisticated, small and large documents in the sciences, aerospace, telecommunications, government, education, electronics, computers, and pharmaceuticals. The vendors of SGML products are committed to interoperability.

If you are using HTML for any purpose today, you are already using SGML. Not only that, but you can add your own tags to HTML and use them for great effects in a full SGML browser. In fact, you can add your own phrase and paragraph tags to differentiate information such as part numbers, book titles, notes and warnings, or any type of information that you use. You can add additional hypertext linking capabilities, with greater precision and reliability, and with features such as group annotations and one-to-many linking.

This book will guide you through the fundamentals of working with SGML, step by step, with examples that are simple, easy to follow, and fun. You'll learn how to create hypertext documents that are even simpler than basic HTML. Then you'll explore how HTML applications work. After that, you'll learn how to develop more and more sophisticated applications, with style sheets, advanced hypertext capabilities, slides, tables, nested lists, revision control and more.

Murray Maloney
Pickering, Canada
September 1996

Talking the Talk

❧ CHAPTER 1

Why Go Beyond HTML?

The World Wide Web is in its infancy, doing its best to grow up quickly, but still fresh and new. HTML, the *markup* language that brought it to this stage, is limited and simplistic — characteristics that are both strengths and weaknesses.

Tim Berners-Lee, the inventor of the Web, gave the name HyperText Markup Language (HTML) to the simple angle-bracket markup that lets anyone publish on the Web. One types <TITLE> for the title, <P> (a paragraph *start-tag*) to begin a paragraph, and so on.

From an HTML first step, one can already move to whatever notation makes the most sense for the content: The Java language for small portable applications, the Virtual Reality Modelling Language (VRML) for 3D worlds, and the *Standard Generalized Markup Language* (SGML) for documents in which you want to place markup for greater control over the display, for sophisticated processing on a user's desktop, for a greater variety of hypertext link relationships, and for automatic generation of tables of figures or tables or contents.

This book concentrates only on HTML and SGML, the two languages devoted primarily to textual content (but each with appropriate procedures in place to incorporate non-text materials). Already, by lumping the two together in this paragraph, I do them both a disservice. They are as different as apples are — not from oranges — but from the entire category of fruit.

The Bottom Line Is Your Set of Requirements

If HTML gives you everything you need to build the World Wide Web pages you want, fine. (This book may show you techniques for maximizing what you can do with HTML.) If, on the other hand, you ever feel yourself being held back by the restrictions of HTML, full SGML may help.

The Four Fundamentals

You need only four pieces of information to understand the basics of HTML, SGML, and this book:

1. Whatever you're reading, from billboards to newspapers to your computer screen, every time you see a change in a typeface, you are seeing the effect of markup.

    For example, in the source file used to typeset this chapter, there is a code at the top that indicates that a new section begins, with a title:

    ```
    <SECTION>
    <TITLE>The Four Fundamentals</TITLE>
    <P>You need only four pieces of information
    to understand HTML, SGML, and this book:</P>
    ```

    The angle brackets set off the markup. The rest — the part you are familiar with (and have read twice) — is *data content*. In computer-based documents, *everything is either markup or data content*. You may not be used to seeing markup if you use a WYSIWYG (What You See Is What You Get) style of wordprocessor. But, all the codes needed to get the typographic effects you want *are there*, even if they are kept secret, hidden in whatever format the software uses to save files.

2. On the World Wide Web, you create files (or collections of linked files) consisting of data content and markup, and publish those as Web pages. To do this, you *simply put markup in and around the data content.* It is the task of HTML and full SGML software to recognize which is markup and which is data content, and to do the right thing.

3. HTML is markup that identifies a specific set of *element types* that are recognized by World Wide Web browsers. The browsers attach display characteristics and capabilities to that markup. For instance, <TITLE> and </TITLE> is the markup an HTML browser knows begins and ends the title of a document. Often that title is displayed in a separate window. Sometimes the title is used by "Back" or "History" mechanisms when they display a list of pages visited by the browser. What the browser chooses to do with a TITLE element is not expressed in the markup itself.

4. SGML is an internationally standardized language for creating sets of element types. HTML *is just one of the sets of element types that can be created using* SGML. You tell your software which element types you are using by defining them in a *document type definition* (DTD) using a formal, computer-readable *markup declaration.* You document them and add other relevant information to build an SGML *application,* for which you would then design *style sheets* telling a full SGML browser or viewer how to format the documents you create.

The Facts About SGML

SGML is not one of the many proprietary, wanna-be standards. It is the real thing. Here are the facts:

- SGML is an International Standard (ISO 8879), a European Community standard, a US Federal Information Processing Standard (#152), and a Canadian Government Treasury Board Information Technology Standard, among others.
- SGML is the result of user-driven consensus-building by participants from major and minor paper and electronic publishers, document owners, and vendors from a dozen or more countries.
- SGML is hardware, operating system and software independent.
- SGML is widely supported by vendors including major wordprocessing and electronic publishing tool suppliers.
- SGML is supported throughout the aerospace, automotive, defense, software, semiconductor, pharmaceutical, publishing and other industries.
- SGML is ten years old with a successful history of use and growth.

More documents have been created and stored in full SGML than HTML by many times because SGML:

- Separates the *form* (or display) of information from how its contents are *marked up*, allowing optimal reusability of the same contents among differing media and in different presentations.
- Allows an extensible language, for the creation of new information structures as needed.
- Uses reliable validation, the notion that software tools can tell you whether a document *conforms* to a specific SGML application.
- Provides the philosophical and technological underpinning for HTML, the language of the World Wide Web, the most widespread publishing application in the world.

A Good Time to be Using Full SGML

You picked up this book at just the right moment. This is A *Good Time to be Using* SGML (p. 425):

- New products are appearing with astonishing frequency, and many of them are coming from the largest software companies in the world. At the time of writing, there are more than 50 vendors of SGML software who are members of SGML Open, a consortium of SGML vendors and users.
- New industries are constantly exploring or adopting full SGML and, naturally, the decision to use full SGML is getting easier and easier every day.
- Considerable attention is being given to the World Wide Web, the most widespread SGML application imaginable, the application that shows that a little markup can go a long way.
- Those four initials — SGML — are starting to be used in mainstream computing magazines without an immediate explanation. Even more important, without an incorrect explanation. At the same time, mainstream book publishers are producing more and more SGML books. You have access to more print and online resources than ever before. There are also several conferences each year (sponsored by the *Graphic Communications Association*, a pioneering supporter of the standard), as well as newsletters and one-day and multi-day training courses offered by a large selection of suppliers.
- Attendance at the SGML conferences in Asia, Europe and North America is nearly doubling each year. Speakers are describing innovative, cost-efficient implementations of small and large electronic document systems meeting a wide range of needs — and likely overlapping, at least in some areas, with yours.

In practice, this body of supporting evidence means that those of you simply trying to get a job done now have more certainty than ever before. You can make a commitment to the world's first non-proprietary, rich document format without risk.

When HTML is Not Enough

In newsgroups and magazines, one reads frequently of the frustrations caused by HTML's limitations. Here is a purely subjective list, gleaned from newsgroups and conversations. It might be titled, *The Lists of Frustrations with HTML that I've Heard —* (*Eased or Solved by Full SGML*)

General Frustrations with HTML

- Too simple.
- Too complicated.
- *Tags* recognized by one browser but not the others.
- Not enough tags for what I want to do.
- Not enough intelligent control over formatting.
- Sense of chaos caused by so many HTML extensions.
- Inconsistent formatting by browsers.
- Poor quality of paper printing from Web pages.
- Web documents are less useful for other purposes, even publishing with other online tools or on CD, let alone on paper.
- Hard to find exactly what you're looking for.
- Broken links waste a lot of time.
- Lack of "link typing" — next, previous, up, down, back, forward, table of contents, index, glossary, etc.
- Too much formatting built right into the documents, and by extension...
- Limited access to Web content for the 15 per cent of the population that has visual (7 per cent) or other disabilities.

Detailed Frustrations with HTML

- Limited and awkward programmed control over formatting.
- Such small documents or such long waits.
- Lack of document-sensitive menu bars for better control over navigation and hypertext linking.
- No two-way links except through careful hand-crafting.
- You can't link to anything that was not prepared in advance for linking. On every object you want to link to, you require a NAME attribute value.
- Having to build whole pages whose only job is to connect longer documents back together.
- Inability to use company- or industry-specific markup (such as "PRICE" or "PARTNUMBER") for specialized processing, including end-user path tracking.
- Can't link part of a graphic to part of another.
- Lack of equivalent for footnote or pop-up note.
- Lack of automatic outlining for long documents.
- Lack of support for complex math and scientific symbols.
- No markup to encode the history of changes to a document.
- No way to express criticality of information — "WARNING" or "DANGER" markup.
- Lack of "author" or "date" or "publisher" means the only bounded searching is by TITLE or H1 or URL.
- No standardized concept of "expiry date" or "update by" or "last updated".
- Requires a database and scripts to include text portions on the fly, based on specified user requests.

The Web badly needs answers to many of these questions, and tools for Web site management — document control, hypertext link and anchor maintenance, revision history — and for search and retrieval of electronic information. The structures needed for these tasks can be readily expressed in full SGML. This book will show you how.

Read On

I hope that you enjoy reading this book and working with its examples. It is a step-by-step cookbook of some of the common SGML techniques that are used on and off the Web. What you learn here will be all you need to create and design your own documents, with markup that makes sense for you and your community of interest.

- See how HTML really works — under the hood.
- Learn full SGML in small, easy steps.
- Tame your element structures and attributes.
- Unleash your documents, information and design.
- Publish large or small documents.
- Enhance document formatting with publisher control.
- Create sophisticated hypertext linking on demand.
- Enhance HTML with your favorite extensions.
- Automatically build documents from boilerplate.
- Custom design personal views of any document.
- Navigate easily through documents and collections.
- Build collapsible tables of contents in a few keystrokes.
- Provide more sophisticated linking capabilities.
- Use pop-up windows for footnotes, graphics, video and more.

❧ CHAPTER 2
How to Use This Book

Getting a Quick Start

If you are new to HTML and SGML, we suggest that you start by getting an HTML browser, such as Microsoft Internet Explorer, NCSA Mosaic, or Netscape Navigator. They are available from your Internet Service Provider (ISP), at your local bookstore, and directly over the Internet. Browse a bit and familiarize yourself with the hypertext links, the design characteristics, and the utility of these tools and the accessibility of the documents that you see.

Once you are familiar with HTML on the World Wide Web and you become interested in learning about publishing full SGML documents, you have two paths that you could take.

- March straight ahead. This book steps its way through 40 examples that teach you what you need to know to publish HTML and full SGML documents. You'll start with simple examples and, before you know it, you'll be able to design sophisticated hypertext documents with tables, graphics, pop-ups, and active tables of contents.
- Jump right in to SGML! *The SGML Primer* (p. 379) offers an introduction to SGML markup — the stuff that adds *intelligence about itself* to content, and to document type definitions (DTDs) — the sets of declarations and strategies that application designers use to describe the structures of types of documents: memos, for example, or technical manuals, or corporate financial reports.

If you write HTML in your sleep and know the basics of SGML, you might want to brush up on *The* SGML *Primer* (p. 379) too.

If you're part of the SGML literati, don't take another step before reading SGML *Users, Start Here* (p. 415)

If you are wondering, "What's the big fuss?" You picked up this book at just the right moment. This is a A *Good Time to be Using* SGML (p. 425). There are new products from many companies, new industries are coming on board, the world's largest SGML application is serving tens of millions of users, the popular computer and business press are talking SGML, and the industry conferences keep getting bigger and better.

Organization of Parts and Chapters

Part One, containing the first three chapters, lays the groundwork for anyone with any experience creating HTML pages for the Web or for corporate intranets. It introduces the idea of SGML on the Web and highlights the relationships between HTML and SGML. You will learn or review the fundamentals of SGML, dip your toes into the syntax, and familiarize yourself with the tutorial approach of this book's first nine examples. They start you out with the simplest of SGML applications and quickly have you develop a mini-version of HTML.

Part Two, containing Chapters 4–6 and the next fifteen examples, guides you down the path to understanding HTML, enhancing the capabilities that are already built into it, and developing a useful mini-version of HTML. Before long you'll be creating your own HTML extensions — just like *Netscape* and *Microsoft.* Then you can develop our HTML application into the realms of library science, document management, editorial review, and change management, one step at a time.

Part Three, containing Chapters 7–9 and another fourteen examples, continues to explore SGML in more depth and develops new applications that will prove not only educational, but down right useful. They include advanced hypertext linking using *HyTime*, and applications that use structured tables.

Part Four, containing Chapters 10 and 11 and the final three examples, builds up your proficiency with parameter entities and general entities, and then ties SGML and network publishing together with a summary of document type declarations, public identifiers, and the SGML *Open* entity catalog.

The back of the book contains some useful and interesting appendixes, a bibliography that lists other books about SGML, and a complete glossary of SGML and HyTime terms used in the book. The book closes with a colophon, afterwords from the series editor and Murray Maloney, and brief biographies of the authors.

Organization of Examples

As you work your way through the examples, you'll discover that the structure of the individual exercises is intuitive and couldn't be simpler.

Goal of the Example: A brief introduction explaining which aspects of SGML philosophy, terminology, or technique you will encounter.

Goal of the Application: Describes the expected functions of the example application as you would find it implemented in HTML or in full SGML browsers.

Is Influenced by/Builds on: Then a bit of house-keeping: This section describes the formal or informal relationship of the example to other examples in the book, or to other HTML and full SGML applications that are being used in the world today.

Stored on the Accompanying Disk as: The names of the related sample DTD and document instance files on the accompanying disk. We include the name of the sample DTD even at the risk of intimidating first time users of full SGML. We expect that you will want to examine, copy and modify the sample DTDs and instances.

Step by Step: The section continues with step-by-step instructions for creating sample applications, sample documents, or both. Most examples also contain the full text of the SGML application you are creating, and a sample document that uses the markup declared in the sample application.

Bonus: What to look for on the accompanying CD-ROM, focussing on the display and navigation possibilities available to you when you examine that particular SGML application using the free software, SoftQuad Panorama. Note that the same examples will also work with other SGML software. On the disk are the files you need to use other tools too.

But wait, there's more... The final section of many examples hints at how that example relates to what's still coming in the book. Sadly, the linear nature of *any presentation medium* means that the evolutionary tree of the sample DTDs in this book is a lot more like that of the animal kingdom than I might have liked, with intertwining branches and dead ends. From many exercises, there are several plausible "next steps", each of which would bring you greater understanding of some interesting point.

Typing the Examples

In order to describe and demonstrate the value of various element types and attributes, I ask you to type in examples. (If you are too busy for that, there are completed examples on a CD ROM.) There is an expectation that you may choose, later, either to create your own documents using the SGML structures defined in the examples, or to copy relevant parts of the examples into other SGML applications.

But, this may seem a little odd because a great many people create HTML and SGML documents *not* by typing raw markup in and around their content, but by composing them in an HTML- or SGML-aware editor or wordprocessor. (For HTML only, you might use something like Front Page, Hot Dog, HoTMetaL PRO, HTML Assistant, Internet Assistant, or PageMill. For full SGML, you could use Arbortext Adept Editor, SoftQuad Author/Editor, or WordPerfect SGML Edition. And there are many others, in both categories.)

Such software, particularly SGML-aware software, makes a point of being help-ful. The software itself reads the *document type declaration*, and, for example, offers users a toolbar or scrolling pick-list of element types, inserting the markup and ensuring that no one can ever make a typing mistake in an element type *name*, or leave off an angle bracket or a slash. Some of the software inserts start- and *end-tags* simultaneously. The pick lists can be *context-sensitive*, suggesting element types only where they are allowed by the DTD. Similar support is available for attribute hand-ling, and for other SGML constructs such as *entities* and marked sections.

So my premise then is the same as the reason why we teach grade school chil-dren to do arithmetic even though pocket calculators are pervasive. Knowing what's being automated is fundamental to understanding what's really going on.

I encourage you to work with text examples directly, with a simple text editor, to create them "in the raw" if you find this approach helpful for the short *document instances* given here. However, all the examples perform in "SGML-friendly" software too. and I encourage you, just as heartily, to use SGML-aware software when you cre-ate real content — when you've moved out into *Life Beyond Examples*.

You'll notice that, throughout the examples, there is no formal analysis of the documents that are being created. The normal work that goes into creating an SGML application is being avoided for now. We simply say what is the absolute minimum number of structural element types that will give us some value for the least amount of work. Later on we look at some of the kinds of documents that need upfront anal-ysis before good DTDS can be written to reflect their structure. The examples have been chosen primarily to illustrate how to accomplish the creation of information structures that you know you want to create, not to figure out what you need to cre-ate your complex document.

Other books — see the *Bibliography* (p. 449) — cover methods and strategies for analyzing documents in order to design appropriate DTDS — appropriate to the requirements of existing and new documents, and to requirements imposed by cur-rent and hoped-for processing systems.

Instant Startup Using the Accompanying Disk

The overall architecture of the collection of exercises is more ornate. Some 40 SGML applications are shipped with this book. Sample files for each can be explored with the free SGML browser that accompanies this book.

If you wish to create your own samples, you can begin to see immediate results:

- Open one of the sample files (in the *startup* folder, ending with the *.sgm* suffix) and replace the existing content with new materials of your own. Be careful to avoid inadvertently tampering with the markup, that is, anything between angle brackets.
- Create content that uses the markup declared in the supplied document type definitions (DTDS). This means reading and understanding the applications that come on the disk, at least well enough to glean the element types whose names serve as markup in new files.
- Design and write your own SGML applications, including a DTD and *content* that do meet *your* requirements.

Of the 40 sample applications, many are simply slight variations of the previous one, altered to instruct you in a particular detail associated with a chapter or section. Of the 40, however, several are useful as standalone applications. Along with the names of their accompanying sample files and a brief description of each, these are:

plaintxt.dtd	How little markup can we add to a plain text file and still get interesting hypertext? This example answers that question. *Sample file: plaintxt.sgm*
plainbod.dtd	A handful of plain text applications grow in power slowly but steadily. This one is the pinnacle. In fact, it's no longer plain text at all. By now everything is marked up in some minimalist fashion. *Sample file: plainbod.sgm*
htmsimpl.dtd	Some people think, after close examination, that HTML itself is pretty complicated. This application is a simplified version of the markup language of the World Wide Web. Documents created using this markup will work in both full SGML and HTML-only browsers! *Sample files: htmsimpl.sgm and htmsimpl.htm*

minutes.dtd	A "real-world" application, this one combines, into one DTD, capabilities for marking up both an agenda and a set of minutes for any kind of meeting. Two style sheets show off the power of automatically generating headings and other text. *Sample files: agenda.sgm, minutes.sgm*
pressrel.dtd	Not a toy DTD, this application has been used for several years by at least a couple of companies and organizations to structure the releases they give to the media. *Sample file: pressrel.sgm*
slideset.dtd	Just for fun, a very simple DTD for creating a set of slides. There are three accompanying style sheets, so you can see the effect of applying differing styles to one document instance. *Sample files: slides1.sgm, slides2.sgm and slides3.sgm*
simptbl.dtd	You'd be surprised how much information you can convey in a well-constructed table. *Sample files: simptbl.sgm, simptbl2.sgm*

To begin working with these, move to the folder called *startup*. The content of this folder is a small subset of the full set in the parallel folder named *demos*, which includes every sample file used in the examples in the book.

The DTDs listed above may be found in the folder called *catalog*. They are also listed in the *catalog* file. Note that the DTDs in the *catalog* whose system names end in the suffix *.ent* are used by Panorama itself and may be ignored.

Typographic and Markup Conventions

Like most technical books, SGML *on the Web: Small Steps Beyond* HTML uses a variety of typefaces to distinguish between things. We've tried to keep it to a minimum, but if ever you should find yourself wondering why a phrase suddenly appears in italics, you can refer back to this page.

italics   Used to emphasis a word or phrase—that is, to *stress* its importance. Italics are also used for the names of files, and for the first time a term is mentioned if it's defined in the glossary.

                Some other things you'll see in italics include foreign words, names of software products, and book titles.

`typewriter font`   Used for exact text that you would type into a computer, or for computer output, generally in examples. An example of an SGML DTD or document instance is always shown in a typewriter font.

In addition, you'll find that the names of SGML element types are in CAPITALS, whereas the names of SGML attributes are in lower case (like normal text), with their values in quotes.

Sometimes we get a little carried away with all the excitement and **shout** at you, but not very often.

CHAPTER 3

Starting Simple

When HTML Is Too Much

Imagine that your task is simply to publish a collection of text files on the Web. If you're convinced that simple ASCII text is acceptable for display, there's no reason to move beyond the default display of any reasonable Web browser. Most will readily open up a text file — which might also be a news item or e-mail — and render it in a straight monospace font.

```
Memo to: Dave Gurney, CEO, SoftQuad International
From: Yuri Rubinsky, President, SoftQuad
Date: Oct 11, 1993
Here's a draft business plan for you to peruse.
Yuri
========================================================================
OBJECTIVES:
1. To foster a presence for our company in a brand new medium,
previously unexplored and unimplemented, based roughly on the
notions of vast, interconnected "hyperlinked" computer databases
that have hitherto been treated with skepticism by virtually
all serious computer scientists and engineers.
2. To encourage our marketing and public relations departments to
promote our products and services by learning to write press releases
and marketing information by typing in raw codes somewhat reminiscent
of mainframe computer batch typesetting languages but somewhat
less messy than Word Star or WordPerfect "reveal codes".
3. To promote our products and services by having individuals
around the world type into their computers an address for our
computer, a directory path and a filename, and thereby voluntarily
```

```
choose to read our promotional materials. Some of these people
may be paying a commercial provider of such access a fee per minute
to be able to read our materials and some of them, depending on
their location, may not even have access to our products and services.
4. To encourage arms-length third parties to promote our
promotional information by having them provide "links" to our
promotional pages based on how "cool" or "hot" our pages are,
but not to pay them for such promotion, expecting people simply
to find our materials, and, naturally, be interested in them.
5. To, in some senses, attempt to replace some of the functionality
of phone, fax, and postal and courier services in one fell swoop
with a new medium, and to do so by building on a decentralized,
anarchic network of computers put in place largely by academics
unconcerned by the cost of the medium.
6. In fact, to build this infrastructure without understanding
its economics, its transmission capabilities, its scaleability,
whether current or foreseen technologies can support it or whether
it can be made secure at all from the brilliant young hackers
whose keystrokes now roam the planet.
7. To do all this within 18 months.
+++++++++++++++++++++++++++++++++++++++++++++++++++++++++++++++++++++++++++
Memo to: Yuri
From: Dave
Date: Oct 15, 1993
Interesting idea. Time to take that holiday we've been discussing.
Dave
```

For people with a large legacy of content in simple formats, this text file presentation is good news, but it shouldn't be thought of as much more than a starting point. Nothing in such a display takes advantage of

- different formatting styles to identify importance
- choice of variable width fonts to enhance readability
- identification of document title for special treatment by a browser
- links to connect the displayed document to related information.
- other markup to support specialized functions such as table and form creation.

Of course, adding full markup to legacy text can be costly and time-consuming. Instead, let's see how to gradually increase markup, based on the most immediate uses for the content.

Adding markup = Adding value

Why the Title?

HTML has the reputation of being simple, but in fact has fairly complex rules about constructing hypertext links and anchors, establishing a base location for addressing, incorporating images, and so forth. Even HTML's less complex constructs have strict markup requirements. (A major strength of HTML is how very useful it is when used sparingly.)

The examples begin with a simple SGML application — plain text — and move through a gradually increasing complexity and richness in the markup. The sample applications in this chapter demonstrate that one can create meaningful Web pages when using markup that's even simpler than the simplest HTML —.

As you read through this chapter you'll discover that you can slowly but surely build richness and usefulness into content by adding more and more markup to plain text documents until you create a viable structure for hierarchical browsing, hypertext linking, and content-based searching. And indeed, plain text will even allow us to support markup layered on from the outside, as we will see in the discussion of link types that point into a document. That is to say, we can point at the internal contents of a plain text file using markup constructs that we will see in later chapters. We'll create a core file with absolutely no markup that can nonetheless have hypertext anchors and provide a surprising amount of functionality.

❧ EXAMPLE 1

Plain Text in SGML

Goal of the Example:

The example introduces or demonstrates:

- the use of the document type declaration to let an SGML application know that the document instance is associated with a particular document type definition
- start-tags and end-tags to contain content
- the *element type declaration* and *parsed character data* (PCDATA).

Goal of the Application:

- To provide a foundation for the display of any text document on the Web in a full SGML browser — allowing it to exploit the browser's capabilities, such as control over the document's look and feel.
- To provide such a foundation in a way that allows its value to be extended incrementally.

The universal usefulness of this DTD (as simple as it is) shouldn't be underestimated. We can take any plain vanilla ASCII text file we want, surround it with minimal markup and use a full SGML browser to explore it. We can establish a style that works for this format, perhaps assuming that plain text, because of its origins in e-mail or newsgroups should, in fact, be displayed in a mono-spaced font. We then use this look and feel to present files for which we have neither the time nor the reason to add sophisticated markup.

Is Influenced by/Builds on:

Almost any software can open a plain ASCII file, including Web browsers. This simple application builds on that basic capability but puts it into the context of SGML, allowing us to add value to any number of documents over time by adding markup, either automatically, or by hand.

Stored on the Accompanying Disk as:

Sample DTD: *plaintxt.dtd*

Sample Instances: *plaintxt.sgm*

Step by Step:

The document type declaration associates the *document element* (name shown in bold below) with a specific *document type definition* (DTD).

```
<!DOCTYPE plaintxt PUBLIC "Plain Text">
```

Here the highest level element of the document — PLAINTXT — is associated with the DTD whose *public identifier,* that is more specifically, the DTD's , *system-independent name,* is "PLAIN TEXT". (These names are, by default, case sensitive in SGML: it matters whether they appear in lower case or capital letters. SGML literati will recognize that the reference concrete syntax is used in all examples, except for changes in the quantity set.)

Note that *markup declarations* begin with <! and end with >. As we continue with the example, we see that the markup begins with the left angle bracket (<) and ends with a right one (>).

```
<!DOCTYPE plaintxt PUBLIC "Plain Text">
<PLAINTXT>Here we are inside plain text.
```

The start-tag for the PLAINTXT element type uses angle brackets as *delimiters,* setting the markup apart from the rest of the content. (At least that is true for SGML's *reference concrete syntax* used in this book. SGML does provide a way to change the

Example 1 — Plain Text in SGML

delimiters if that is required.) Notice that in tags, you may use upper or lower case characters. Everything from the <PLAINTXT> to the </PLAINTXT> is considered the content of a PLAINTXT *element*. That content could contain other markup. The tags contain the formal name of the element type, called the *generic identifier*. This name is often, but not necessarily, a word. As in this example, it may be an abbreviation or nickname for the element type.

The end-tag looks like the start-tag except that it begins with the left angle bracket immediately followed by the *slash* character (</). Like the start-tag, it ends with >.

```
<!DOCTYPE plaintxt PUBLIC "Plain Text">
<PLAINTXT>Here we are inside plain text. This is
the first text that appears within the plain
text document. It has no structure except what
we assume based on its built-in visual presentation.
That is to say perhaps there is a centered head,
perhaps paragraphs, lists and so forth but there
is no markup at all to suggest these.
We create new visual paragraphs in plain text with just
a blank line. To make a subheading, we use
any of the tricks that we've learned through
years of diligence. For instance, we make some
phrase upper case and centered and figure it's
a heading.

                THIS IS SUCH A HEADING

At the end of the document we simply close off with
the end-tag for the plain text element.
</PLAINTXT>
```

This sample file may be found on the companion disk under the name *plaintxt.sgm*. The document type definition is stored on the disk as *plaintxt.dtd*. It contains the following element declaration:

```
<!ELEMENT plaintxt (#PCDATA)>
```

Bonus:

Figure 4. If you're looking at the sample files in Panorama, be sure to choose the Styles menu and select from the various available display formats listed at the top of the menu. Sadly, this is the most fun you can have with no markup. The fun really begins with the next example.

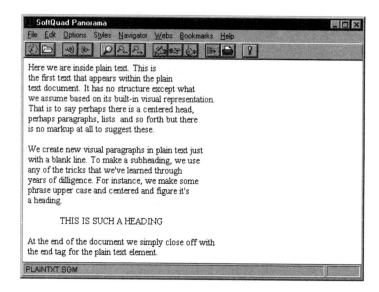

A side effect of the functionality differences between most Web browsers and Panorama is immediately apparent when you open the file for the first time. Panorama recognizes the semantic notion of what it calls "verbatim" text. That is, you can tell the software that the contents of a certain type of element — any element type you want, in fact — is to be treated as if all the carriage returns are meaningful. That is what is happening here with the PLAINTXT element type. In HTML (and therefore in Web browsers), certain element types automatically display those carriage returns.

The advantage in the HTML browsers is that you don't have to tell them which element types are to be treated that way. The advantage in full SGML browsers: You can tell them when you want this to work, and for which element types. In the case of the sample files for this chapter, obviously, your demonstration version of the software has the appropriate set-up file to make this happen.

Adding Simple Anchors and Links to Plain Text

Goal of the Example:

The example shows how to add *subelements* to the document element that was created in the first example, and introduces.

- the use of *attributes* and *attribute definition list declarations*
- the use of the ID and IDREF keywords (one small way to exploit the capabilities of an SGML *parser*)
- the use of #REQUIRED and #IMPLIED keywords.

An attribute of an element, loosely defined, is a characteristic of that element, and there is no limit to the sorts of characteristics you might want to associate with a specific element: a *unique identifier* (discussed in this example), levels of secrecy or security, status of a document ("draft", "revised" or "final", for example), creator, version number, date of posting, date of expiry, effective date, source of a graphic, destination anchor of a link, and so forth.

Goal of the Application:

- to create the simplest possible anchors and links using the basic capability provided by full SGML for use in an SGML document.

Is Influenced by/Builds on:

This application builds directly on one of the built-in functions of SGML, the capability to uniquely identify any specific instance of an element type — that is, an element. This in turn means that software can readily access that unique element for display, for indexing, for hypertext linking, for manipulation that's the result of any combination of factors, including the type of element being identified, its context (the elements enclosing it), and so on.

Note   Before we carry on, I need to make an important distinction between HTML and SGML hypertext linking; any HTML hypertext link element type represents "an anchor that points to another uniquely named anchor" — it is a one-way link — but the *processing semantics* of the link, that is, the action associated with the string of characters, comes from the rules of HTML, not from any capability intrinsic to SGML. That is, the value of the href attribute of the <A> element type uses an addressing scheme that is defined and understood by HTML user agents, but it is not a notation that SGML applications in general understand unless, or until, the programs that work with them are trained to do so. I mention this because not all SGML applications do understand Web processing semantics.

Stored on the Accompanying Disk as:

Sample DTD: *plainlnx.dtd*

Sample Instance: *plainlnx.sgm*

Example 2 — Adding Simple Anchors and Links to Plain Text

Step by Step:

This DTD offers a simple way to read plain ASCII files and include very basic hypertext linking within them. Before we begin, let's examine what we mean by hypertext linking. A hypertext link is *a relationship between two or more objects*. The linked objects are referred to as the *anchors* of the link. Going from one anchor to another is called *traversing the link*. In a binary link, there are two anchors. For the purposes of this example, these two anchors are represented with two element types (ANCHOR1 and ANCHOR2), and one of them (ANCHOR2) also represents the hypertext relationship itself.

On with the example. To the top of any text file, add the following two lines:

```
<!DOCTYPE plaintxt PUBLIC "Plain Text Plus Links">
<PLAINTXT>
```

and at the end of the file, add: </PLAINTXT> At this point you've gone no further than we did in the very first example in this chapter.

To markup text so that it can be linked to as an anchor, type <ANCHOR1 ID="MYANCHOR"> in front of it (where *myanchor* is a unique identifier that starts with a letter from A–Z and is followed by letters, digits, hyphen and period) and after the anchor's text, type </ANCHOR1>.

In addition to identifying text so that it can serve as an anchor of a link, it is also necessary to have markup for the link relationship itself. For convenience, in a binary link, we can simply add that information to the markup of one of the anchors. Therefore, to markup text as an anchor that also represents a link to the <ANCHOR1>, type <ANCHOR2 IDREF="MYANCHOR"> before the linking text, and </ANCHOR2> afterwards. The unique identifier, *myanchor* or whatever you chose to use on the <ANCHOR1>, must be the same for the hypertext link to work. You can have any number of <ANCHOR2> elements pointing to the same <ANCHOR1>, but each <ANCHOR1> must have a unique ID.

```
<!DOCTYPE plaintxt PUBLIC "Plain Text Plus Links">
<PLAINTXT>
The secret to dealing with masses of data is in touch, how we
reach out and <ANCHOR2 IDREF="MYANCHOR">touch information</ANCHOR2>.

Touch affects our decisions and touches our lives. There is an actual
moment of contact, when you need to access a computer on the network
to grab the data you need to draw the graph to accompany the text that
comes from the draft that comes from the memos that Lou, down the hall
in engineering, wrote.

After twenty or thirty years of quiet simmering,
hypertext capability is now treated as a reasonable requirement
for information retrieval. Automated methods of establishing the
connections between information will enable people to gain
<ANCHOR1 ID="MYANCHOR">instant sensory access to what they need.
</ANCHOR1>
</PLAINTXT>
```

First of two likely declarations

Here are the element type and attribute definition list declarations as given in the DTD:

```
<!ELEMENT plaintxt (#PCDATA | anchor1 | anchor2 )*>
<!ELEMENT (anchor1 | anchor2) (#PCDATA)>

<!ATTLIST anchor1 id    ID    #REQUIRED>
<!ATTLIST anchor2 idref IDREF #REQUIRED>
```

The vertical bar ("|") in the element type declarations above means "or." That is, we can read the first declaration as saying that a PLAINTXT element can contain #PCDATA or an ANCHOR1 element or an ANCHOR2 element. The asterisk (*) at the end means that there can be any number of these, including zero. So we could now have a document that contained any mixture of text and ANCHOR1 element or an ANCHOR2 elements.

Example 2 — Adding Simple Anchors and Links to Plain Text

The *keyword* #REQUIRED — the pound sign tells us that "REQUIRED" is an SGML keyword and not an actual *attribute value* — informs the SGML parser that whenever one of these element types appears, it *must* be accompanied by a value for this attribute.

The *validating* SGML *parser* (frequently simply called the "parser" when you're among friends) is software that is commonly used to read an SGML document and report whether it conforms to the rules given in a DTD. That reporting of errors, called validation, can be very helpful in determining whether a document or set of documents is ready to be published.

Possibility two:

You can readily adjust the rules about whether or not users of your application *must* create the unique ID and the IDREF attribute values or simply *may*. From the point of view of our example, we have an opportunity to determine what it means if we loosen up the rules a bit:

```
<!ATTLIST anchor1 id   ID   #REQUIRED>
<!ATTLIST anchor2 idref IDREF #IMPLIED>
```

Now the DTD recognizes that in creating a document instance, you may not always know what a ANCHOR2 will point to, you may simply know you want a certain word or phrase to *potentially* act as one anchor in a hypertext link relationship. The #IMPLIED keyword effectively says that filling in the IDREF is optional; the SGML application will *imply* a value in the absence of actually seeing one there.

This notion of *implying* a value is very powerful: It means that different full SGML systems could set different "default" running behavior, and values that are implied might be implied by one set of rules for paper publishing system, and another set of rules for electronic delivery.

Hypertext Anchors

It is worth reinforcing that each element that is part of this example's binary hypertext link relationship is an "anchor." The element that references the other anchor, although very commonly thought of as the link itself, is also one of the anchors in the relationship. The anchor that the user traverses to is often referred to as the "linkend". This terminology, however, does not do justice to the full hypertext linking model that is described in this book. The term "linkend," while convenient when thinking about a binary link that can only be traversed in one direction, is actually misleading. It creates the impression that all hypertext links have a single starting point and a single destination. Nothing could be further from the truth.

The element types that are used in this and many other examples in this book are merely syntactic representations of anchors and hypertext link relationships. That is, the markup identifies the anchors and the link relationships. While the distinction between anchors and links may seem unnecessary at first, it will become essential when we explore hypertext link relationships among three or more anchors. In the meantime, we'll try to expose hypertext linking gradually and with consistent terminology as we continue through the examples in this book.

A word about IDS and IDREFS

The values assigned to ID and IDREF attributes as explored in this example are limited to the document in which they reside. That is, an SGML parser will tell you whether or not an ID is unique to a document, but the parser *cannot* determine whether the name is unique among a group of documents. As we step through the examples in this chapter, the basic hypertext links and anchors introduced here will evolve, with much more powerful and expressive hypertext capabilities.

Example 2 — Adding Simple Anchors and Links to Plain Text

Bonus:

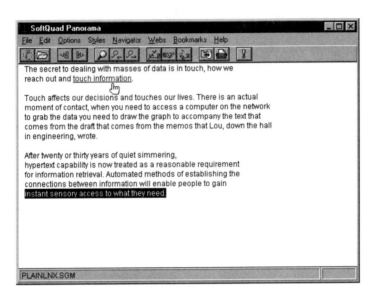

Figure 5. Try the sample file plainlnx.sgm in Panorama to witness firsthand the utility of the ID/IDREF capabilities of full SGML.

Admittedly, this is a very simple and trivial example of hyperlinking in action. But that is also the point of the example. Here we are, at the end of the second example in the book, and we have already composed two documents using a total of three element types.

But wait, there's more...

This hypertext thread continues in this chapter with Example 4 (*You Can Empower Anything You Can Identify*) on page 39 and Example 7 (*A Rose by Any Other Name Would Smell as Sweet*) on page 59. Later, in Chapter 8 (*You Can Get There From Here*) on page 263, we'll explore hypertext linking even further with entertaining and educational six examples.

A Little Bit of Structure in Our Plain Lives

Goal of the Example:

In this section we include enough structural elements to display a meaningful hierarchy of headings and subheadings on the screen but still without doing complex analysis of the documents that we are trying to create.

Goal of the Application:

- To build upon the simple foundation provided in the PLAINTEXT DTD to exploit the browser's capabilities such as control over the document's look and feel and automatic display of certain elements as navigational tools.
- To provide such a foundation in a way that allows it to be extended incrementally.

Is Influenced by/Builds on:

Could anyone disagree with the notion that the real value of a DTD with headings is that it more accurately reflects how we intuitively think of documents than the plain text DTD? This DTD builds on the human brain's natural instinct for order — which is greatly assisted by breaking anything down into smaller more comprehensible units.

Stored on the Accompanying Disk as:

Sample DTD: *plainhds.dtd*

Sample Instance: *plainhds.sgm*

Step by Step:

For this application, we've begun with the plain text DTD that we used in our first example and added a few more component pieces to it. (The hypertext links and anchors that we explored in the previous example will be back later.)

```
<!ELEMENT plaintxt (#PCDATA|head|subhead)*>
<!ELEMENT head      (#PCDATA)>
<!ELEMENT subhead   (#PCDATA)>
```

As you can see, we start to get a bit more expressive power in our DTD by adding two types of heading to our plain text document type. The sample document still starts with a PLAINTXT element, but now it contains HEAD and SUBHEAD elements in among the plain text paragraphs:

Example 3 — A Little Bit of Structure in Our Plain Lives

```
<!DOCTYPE plaintxt PUBLIC "Plain Text with Headings">
<PLAINTXT>
<HEAD>Pushing the Edges
of the Plain Text DTD</HEAD>

In this example, we use heads and subheads to break up the document
into meaningful sections. Later we will go even further. Well, you
could argue that since these are just very simple examples, the
sections aren't really all that meaningful.

<SUBHEAD>Many Uses for the Plain Text DTD</SUBHEAD>

These examples are particularly exciting because there is so little
markup in them, and yet they have potentially so much capability
when displayed on the World Wide Web... or in any full SGML browser.

<SUBHEAD>Subheads Really Pay off in Outline Mode</SUBHEAD>

It's only natural that if, when you're writing, you decide something
deserves to be treated as a heading or subheading, then the software
should make a big deal about that. You've already made the decision.
And your readers deserve to reap the benefits of that decision.
</PLAINTXT>
```

Bonus:

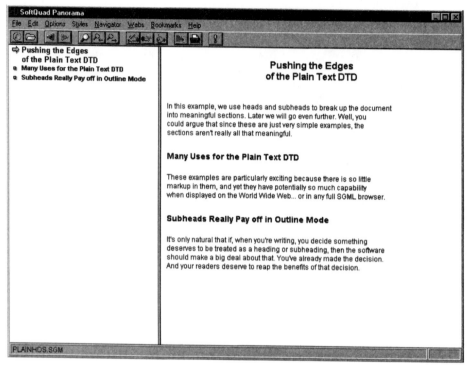

Figure 3. *Open this file using SoftQuad Panorama (on the included disk) and you will see immediately the advantage of having headings in the document. Notice too that the screen is divided vertically. The left side is reserved for the navigator, an outline view created on-the-fly by the software.*

It should be clear that the added advantages of the outline view and the styles to set off the important parts of the document come to you from that very small amount of additional markup.

❧ Example 4

You Can Empower Anything
You Can Identify

Goal of the Example:

We know that a specific attribute defined for a certain element type can be used to enable specific capability, such as hypertext links. In this example we see the beginnings of a very rich field of endeavor. The notion that the *same attribute (or attributes)* when associated with different element types, can provide common functions to element types which otherwise meet very different goals.

Goal of the Application:

- To continue to layer functionality onto the PLAINTEXT DTD in such a way that we now offer hypertext linking not only through ANCHOR1 and ANCHOR2 elements, but through any other elements we choose to enable.
- To enable linking to work with any heading or subheading in the document.

Is Influenced by/Builds on:

In the previous example, we began to examine the value of structure. In this example, we'll tie together the power of hypertext linking with the expressiveness of structured headings.

Stored on the Accompanying Disk as:

Sample DTD: *plainlah.dtd*

Sample Instance: *plainlah.sgm*

Step by Step:

This DTD is almost identical to the one we worked with in the previous example. Notice that we have brought back the ANCHOR1 and ANCHOR2 element types, and added the id attribute to the headings:

```
<!ELEMENT plaintxt           (#PCDATA|head|subhead|anchor1|anchor2)*)>
<!ELEMENT (head|subhead)     (#PCDATA)>

<!ELEMENT (anchor1|anchor2) (#PCDATA)>

<!ATTLIST (head|subhead) id    ID #REQUIRED>
<!ATTLIST anchor1        id    ID #REQUIRED>
<!ATTLIST anchor2        idref IDREF #REQUIRED>
```

It would be valuable to type in the full sample file (*plainlah.sgm*), as printed on the next two pages, in order to get a good feel for the way the attribute values work. Some attribute values need to be unique, to uniquely identify an element so that you can go to it through a hypertext reference. Other attributes need not be unique because any number of them may be referring to a given heading or anchor.

However, it would be nearly as valuable to type in all the markup in the example, and just paste in dummy text to create a sample file of your own to load into the browser. In fact, by an interesting coincidence, the sample file is *about* dummy text!

A secondary function of this example is to introduce the famous *Paradox of Hypertext*, as you'll discover while reading the sample document.

Example 4 — You Can Empower Anything You Can Identify

```
<!DOCTYPE PLAINTXT PUBLIC "Plain Text with Links and Headings">
<PLAINTXT><HEAD ID="HEAD1">The Greek Borges Document Incident</HEAD>

Each of these paragraphs may contain anchors that are linked to
any of the elements that have unique IDs. This means that
we can put an anchor in right here
--<ANCHOR2 IDREF="SUBHEAD1">click here</ANCHOR2>--
to get to a subheading in the next section

Here in this second paragraph we will put in an anchor that
is linked back to the head at the beginning of the article.
<ANCHOR2 IDREF="HEAD1">Click here</ANCHOR2>
to go back to the top of the article.

<SUBHEAD ID="SUBHEAD1">Introducing Borges and Greek</SUBHEAD>

One could editorialize here for a little while about the nature
of the "Click here" phrase. There is a strong school of thought
that this is the one phrase that should never appear in a
hypertext document, that it's a kind of admission of defeat of
style if you actually have to tell someone to do this. (This is a
variation of the riddle posed by the Argentine writer Jorge Luis
Borges: In a riddle whose answer is "Chess", which word must never
appear? Of course that doesn't seem to be true for the riddle
you've just read.)

<ANCHOR1 ID="RIDDLE">
Our variation: In a riddle whose answer is "Hypertext",</ANCHOR1>
<ANCHOR2 IDREF="TARGET1">which phrase should never appear?</ANCHOR2>.

Now let's change the subject.

Here's a little piece of history for you. In certain days gone by,
we would fill out dummy pages of things with what was called
Greeked-in text, Greek for short. The idea was that it was
gibberish, but was less distracting in examples like this one
than those infernal paragraphs that just went on and on filling
space and never really saying anything, paragraphs whose
only purpose was to be an example or a space-filler.
```

Greek text was fun because it used non-Greek letters, in fact,
pure, unadulterated gibberish whose primary value was that the
words looked and felt about the right length and texture to match
English-language gibberish. You could mock up a page, add the
Greek text, and get a pretty good feel -- right down to the number
of words on the page -- for how the thing would come out.

<SUBHEAD ID="SUBHEAD2">The Second Subhead: It's All Greek</SUBHEAD>

Ah, those were the good old days.

Where are the neiges d'antan? For auld lang syne, then, we'll
use Greek text for the rest of this sample file. You see, it has to
be long enough to show you the benefits of using SGML elements
as navigational aids.

Lorem ipsum dolor sit amet, consectetuer adipiscing elit, sed diam
nonummy nibh euismod tincidunt ut laoreet dolore magna aliquam erat
volutpat. Duis autem vel eum iriure dolor in hendrerit in vulputate
velit esse molestie consequat, vel illum dolore eu feugiat nulla
facilisis at vero eros et accumsan et iusto odio dignissim qui
blandit praesent luptatum zzril delenit augue duis dolore te feugait
nulla facilisi.

Lorem ipsum dolor sit amet, consectetuer adipiscing elit, sed diam
nonummy nibh euismod tincidunt ut laoreet dolore magna aliquam erat
volutpat. Duis autem vel eum iriure dolor in hendrerit in vulputate
velit esse molestie consequat, vel illum dolore eu feugiat nulla
facilisis at vero eros et accumsan et iusto odio dignissim qui
blandit praesent luptatum zzril delenit augue duis dolore te feugait
nulla facilisi.

Here is the answer of <ANCHOR2 IDREF="RIDDLE">the riddle:</ANCHOR2>
<ANCHOR1 ID="TARGET1">Click here.</ANCHOR1>

And here is a quick way to get to the very
<ANCHOR2 IDREF="HEAD1">top of the document</ANCHOR2>--one which never
uses the word "click".

Well, almost never.
</PLAINTXT>

Example 4 — You Can Empower Anything You Can Identify

Bonus:

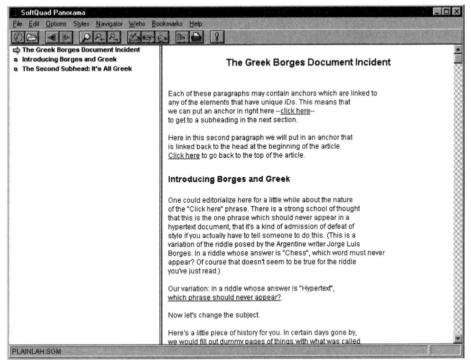

Figure 7. *When you load the example file plainlah.sgm, the "Table of Headings" navigator is shown. Go to the Navigator menu and choose "Table of Links" to see a listing of each link in the document. Next, choose "Table of Links and Headings" for a merged view of the links against a background of headings. For more complex documents, your ability to navigate using any element in the* DTD *will prove to be very valuable.*

Let's not lose track of the *Navigator* capability in Panorama amidst all this excitement. If you ever create large HTML documents, you know how much time you spend building other documents whose only purpose is to give you a "table of contents" for the rest of the collection. If you spend a lot of time building HTML pages, you may have even built a small program to do this for you.

There are many reasons why we specifically tell our software what a chunk of content is — that is, why we actually do markup — but one of the most useful is in creating automatic navigational tools. In full SGML browsing you get this capability for free — or nearly.

But *wait, there's more...*

We have demonstrated the use of straightforward hypertext linking in our plain-talking Plain Text DTD. This hypertext thread continues in Example 7 (A *Rose by Any Other Name Would Smell as Sweet*) on page 59, when we build on this and the previous linking example to transform our "anchor" element types (ANCHOR1 and ANCHOR2) into the HTML equivalent, using only one element type.

❧ EXAMPLE 5

The Names Can Be Changed to Protect the Innocent

Goal of the Example:

This DTD is virtually identical to *plainhds.dtd* but has been included to show that identical structures can be accomplished with different names for the element types — for all or some of the element types in a DTD.

Naturally, when structures are this similar, simple software programs can be used to *transform* a document marked up according to one DTD into conformance with another.

Goal of the Application:

To build upon the simple foundation provided in the Plain Text DTD to exploit the browser's capabilities such as control over the document's look and feel, and automatic display of certain elements as navigational tools — and to do so using element type names that are familiar to users of HTML.

Is Influenced by/Builds on:

Slowly but surely, we're wending our way towards HTML. The new names come from traditional HTML, which came from the first SGML DTD, "General Document", which came from IBM's GML starter set. They were there in the beginning, and will live on forever.

Stored on the Accompanying Disk as:

Sample DTD: *plainhx.dtd*

Sample Instance: *plainhx.sgm*

Step by Step:

The example DTD is identical to *plainhds.dtd* except that the names of the heads have changed.

```
<!ELEMENT plaintxt (#PCDATA|h1|h2)*>
<!ELEMENT h1       (#PCDATA)>
<!ELEMENT h2       (#PCDATA)>
```

So, effectively, we've re-begun with the plain text DTD and added a few more component pieces to it. We could keep going like this and slowly recreate all of HTML.

```
<!DOCTYPE plaintxt PUBLIC "Plain Text with HTML Headings">
<PLAINTXT>
<H1>Pushing the Edges
of the Plain Text DTD</H1>

In this example, we use heads and subheads to break up the document
into meaningful sections while using names for them that will
be familiar to users of HTML. Well, I suppose you could argue that
since these are just very simple examples, the sections aren't really
all that meaningful.

<H2>Many Uses for the Plain Text DTD</H2>

These examples are particularly exciting because there is so little
markup in them, and yet they have potentially so much capability
when displayed on the World Wide Web... or in any full SGML browser.

Note that traditional Web browsers will ignore the PLAINTXT start-
and end-tags, and will display this file correctly just as they are.
They won't produce the outline view however!
```

Example 5 — The Names Can Be Changed to Protect the Innocent

```
<H2>Subheads Really Pay off in Outline Mode </H2>
```

It's only natural that if, when you're writing, you decide something deserves to be treated as a heading or subheading, then the software should make a big deal about that. You've already made the decision. And your readers deserve the reap the benefits of that decision.

```
</PLAINTXT>
```

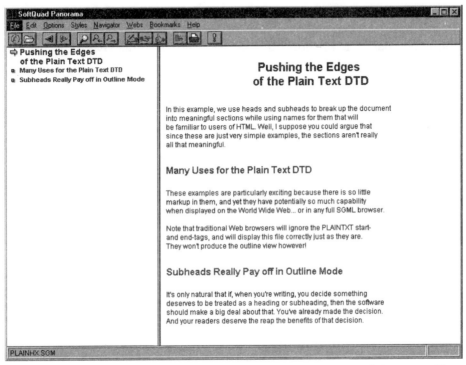

Figure 8. When you open plainhx.htm in an HTML-only browser, you'll see exactly what you expect to see. The document is formatted according to the settings that are built into this browser, or the settings that you can establish in another browser's options or preferences dialogs.

Bonus:

Take a look at *plainhx.sgm*. When you open *plainhx.sgm* in Panorama, you can select from an extensive set of style sheets in the "Styles" menu. In fact, any document that uses the same public identifier can automatically use the same set of style sheets.

An interesting trick starts to be revealed here. Although the style sheets are mapped to a public identifier, they can, in fact, specify styles for arbitrary elements. In other words, the style sheet does not have to limit itself to the element types from a single DTD. In fact, it is conceivable that a single style sheet could serve for an entire collection of DTDs. How else could we explain the same style sheets working for this example and the previous ones?

But wait, there's more...

Transformation of documents from conformance with one DTD to another is a vital part of full SGML use today. We discuss it again when we get to enriched hypertext linking through *architectural forms* in Example 31 (*Cranking up the Power*) on page 287.

❧ EXAMPLE 6
Trcks o' Shrthnd

Goal of the Examples:

The examples introduce or demonstrate:

- the use of *parameter entities* as a shorthand for repeated phrases in a DTD both for convenience (particularly in ease of typing and re-typing complex structures), and as a way of storing element type declarations (or *attribute definitions* — we'll get to those later) in one place so they can easily be revised or maintained
- where parameter entities make sense for elements, and where they don't.

Goal of the Application:

To introduce lists and paragraphs that may appear anywhere in the document where a heading is allowed, and to add additional headings.

- Lists can be ordered (OL) or unordered (UL) but both can have a similar structure.
- Lists have items (LI).
- Another list type is unique. Definition lists (DL) expect to have matching pairs of defined terms (DT) and definitions (DD).
- Paragraphs (P) are just paragraphs.

Is Influenced by/Builds on:

These three types of lists have been available since the invention of *Generalized Markup Language* in 1969. They were later built into IBM's Generalized Markup Language starter set, the predecessor of SGML — the same markup language used at CERN, where Tim Berners-Lee was working when he created HTML for the Web.

Stored on the Accompanying Disk as:

Sample DTD: *plainuol.dtd*

Sample *Instance:*   *plainuol.sgm*

Step by Step:

First Step: Understanding the parameter entity

There are only three things that you have to know about the parameter entity:

- A parameter entity must be declared with a unique name and replacement text
- A parameter entity, once declared, is referenced by name, with a percent sign as a prefix and a semicolon as a suffix; %entity; is an example
- A parameter entity reference, when it is encountered by an SGML parser, is replaced by its replacement text.

Note   The use of parameter entities is almost exclusively within DTDs. We include sample instances with these DTDs, but they show off the DTD itself, not the specific capabilities of the parameter entities. Obviously there are advantages to entities outside of DTD creation. We'll discuss the *general entity* in Example 27 (*Turn off the Lights!*) on page 253.

The best way to learn about parameter entities is to see one applied in practice, simplifying the development of two DTDs. Let's review two sample DTDs that used identical structure for headings, but different names. The first one was *plainhds.dtd*:

Example 6 — Trcks o' Shrthnd

```
<!ELEMENT plaintxt (#PCDATA | head | subhead)*>
<!ELEMENT head    (#PCDATA)>
<!ELEMENT subhead (#PCDATA)>
```

The second one was *plainhx.dtd*. We had already seen by now that two element types with identical content models could be declared simultaneously:

```
<!ELEMENT plaintxt  (#PCDATA | h1 | h2)*>
<!ELEMENT (h1 | h2) (#PCDATA)>
```

The parameter entity lets us declare a shorthand name for text that we're going to re-use. For example:

```
<!ENTITY % heading     "h1 | h2">
<!ELEMENT plaintxt     (#PCDATA | %heading;)*>
<!ELEMENT (%heading;)  (#PCDATA)>
```

Everywhere in the DTD that %heading; appears, it stands for the replacement text that has been declared for it. That is, when we see the *entity reference* %heading; anywhere, we can substitute the declared *replacement text* parameter, "h1 | h2".

The real payoff in using this clean style of declaration is in how readily we can re-declare the nature of any appropriate element types. In the example, we may wish to re-declare all the headings in the DTD. We can easily switch to other names by making a change in only one part of the DTD:

```
<!ENTITY % heading "head | subhead">
```

or just as readily extend the declaration to include one or two more types of headings.

```
<!ENTITY % heading "h1 | h2 | h3 | h4">
```

Let's move to the list examples.

Second Step: Adding lists

At first glance, given the description in the *Goals of the Application*, the following declarations might appear sensible:

```
<!ENTITY % heading      "h1 | h2 | h3 | h4">
<!ENTITY % list         "ul | ol | dl">

<!ELEMENT plaintxt          (#PCDATA | %heading; | %list;)*>
<!ELEMENT (%heading;)       (#PCDATA)>
<!ELEMENT (ul | ol)         (li)>
<!ELEMENT dl                (dt | dd)>
<!ELEMENT (li | dt | dd)    (#PCDATA)>
```

There is a simple clue that something may be wrong: We've declared the parameter entity %list; but only used it once — a probable sign that it's not acting as an especially useful piece of shorthand.

Step Three: Getting the entity right

In this case, the *content model* for the ordered and unordered lists is the same, but that of the definition list is unique. Although the three types of lists may appear in the same places (and are therefore a plausible candidate for use of a parameter entity), on closer examination, the definition list should not be included here. A better form would be:

```
<!ENTITY % heading      "h1 | h2 | h3 | h4">
<!ENTITY % list         "ul | ol">

<!ELEMENT plaintxt       (#PCDATA|%heading;|%list;|dl)*>
<!ELEMENT (%heading;)    (#PCDATA)>
<!ELEMENT (%list;)       (li)*>
<!ELEMENT dl             (dt | dd)*>
<!ELEMENT (li|dt|dd)     (#PCDATA)>
```

Example 6 — Trcks o' Shrthnd

Step Four: Getting the lists nested

Let's go a bit further, adding nested lists and an additional level of complexity . We'll have to modify the content model for list items to include nested lists.

```
<!ELEMENT (%list;)    (li)*>
<!ELEMENT dl          (dt | dd)*>
<!ELEMENT (li | dd)   (#PCDATA | %list; | dl)*>
<!ELEMENT dt          (#PCDATA)>
```

Step Five: Adding the paragraph

Let's finish up by declaring a paragraph.

```
<!ENTITY % heading    "h1 | h2 | h3 | h4">
<!ENTITY % list       "ul | ol">

<!ELEMENT  plaintxt   (#PCDATA|%heading;|p|%list;|dl)*>

<!ELEMENT  (%heading;) (#PCDATA)>
<!ELEMENT  (%list;)   (li)*>

<!ELEMENT  dl          (dt | dd)*>
<!ELEMENT  (li | dd)   (#PCDATA | p | %list; | dl)*>

<!ELEMENT  dt          (#PCDATA)>
<!ELEMENT  p           (#PCDATA)>
```

Now our documents contain a mix of text, headings, lists and paragraphs.

Step Six: The Instance

```
<!DOCTYPE plaintxt PUBLIC "Plain Text with Lists">
<PLAINTXT>
<H1>Pushing the Edges
of the Plain Text DTD</H1>
<P>In this example we introduce very simple examples
of ordered lists, unordered lists, and definition lists.</P>

<H2>Lists</H2>
<H3>Ordered Lists</H3>
<P>An ordered list is more commonly known as a numbered list.
But, as we all know, numbered lists sometimes aren't numbered;
they can often use the letters of the alphabet, roman numerals,
or even words like "First" and "Second". So, using the term
"ordered" makes it clear that sequential ordering is intended.</P>

<H3>Nested lists:</H3>
<P>Putting lists inside of other lists starts to create a
little depth in your documents.  Having ordered lists
adjust their numbering type depending on how deeply
they are nested seems like a reasonable and worthwhile
reaction from a browser.</P>

<OL>
<LI>Wet hair
  <OL><LI>Turn on faucet</LI>
      <LI>Adjust temperature</LI>
      <LI>Stick head under tap</LI></OL>
</LI>
<LI>Wash hair
  <OL><LI>Apply shampoo to wet hair</LI>
      <LI>Lather shampoo</LI>
      <LI>Rinse shampoo off of hair</LI></OL>
</LI>
<LI>Groom
  <OL><LI>Towel dry</LI>
      <LI>Brush into place</LI>
      <LI>Blow dry</LI></OL>
</LI>
</OL>
```

Example 6 — Trcks o' Shrthnd

```
<H3>Unordered Lists</H3>
<P>An unordered list is more commonly known as a bullet list.
But, as we all know, bullet lists sometimes aren't bulleted
they can often use dashes or other symbols. So, using the term
"unordered" makes it clear that no sequential ordering is intended
or required.  This can leave a browser free to reorder items
into columns or alphabetical order if it knows how.</P>

<UL>
<LI>Bread</LI>
<LI>Milk</LI>
<LI>Coffee</LI>
<LI>Juice</LI>
<LI>Tea</LI>
</UL>


<H3>Definition Lists</H3>
<P>A definition list is just what you would think it is.
You use it to declare terms and provide definitions
for them.  Typically, the terms are words or phrases
that need clarification. But definition lists might also
be used to present a list of features, or even a menu.</P>

<DL>
<DT>Jumbo Hot Dog</DT>
<DD>A succulent all-beef frankfurter,
steamed delicately in a maple syrup-coated
bamboo casing, and garnished to your liking with
honey mustard, seasoned ketchup, diced onions,
and banana peppers. Served on a sourdough bun.</DD>

<DT>Hamburger</DT>
<DD>A quarter pound of tender ground chateaubriand,
baked to your liking in a hickory-fed brick oven
and garnished with hot mustard, seasoned ketchup,
sliced onions, red hothouse tomatoes, and lettuce.
Served on a seven grain bun.</DD>

[...and so on...]
</DL>
```

Bonus:

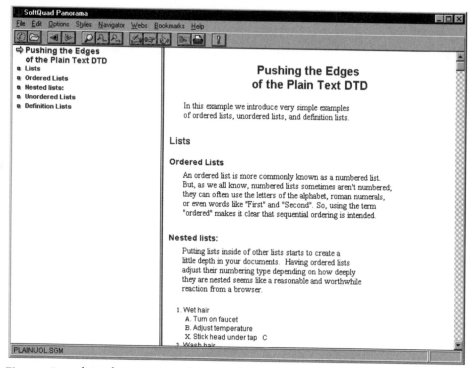

Figure 9. *Open plainuol.sgm to witness the ease with which the numbering of nested lists is accomplished. The autonumbering is made possible because of the simple structure that was introduced by declaring* LI *and* DD *to be containing elements for any of the element types named in* %list;*. Clever software and style sheets can set and increment counters easily when there are clear signals that the count should change in number or in depth.*

Example 6 — Trcks o' Shrthnd

Note　Notice in these simple DTD examples how important it is that all the new element types that we declare have two common details:

- they must appear in the same model groups, and
- they must have the same content model.

It is a frequent mistake in DTD creation to rely too heavily on parameter entities. You may find yourself assuming that a set of element types do share identical content models *only because they appear in the same places.* It's very important to create the DTD — at least in a draft or sketch form — in a way that resolves all the parameter entity references.

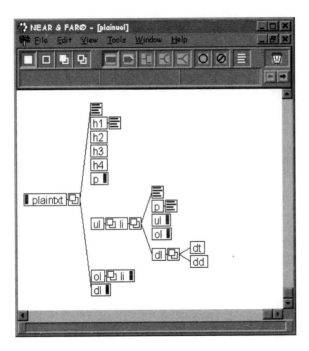

Figure 7. *Microstar's Near and Far Designer, shown here, is a tool for DTD visualization and design.*

But wait, there's more...

Later, in Example 13 (*What Was That Link I Saw You With?*) on page 113, we'll see that parameter entities may be used to declare sets of *attribute specifications*.

In Example 11 (*This Element is Half Full*) on page 99, we'll also see that parameter entities can be nested; you can declare one parameter entity to include several others. One of the most powerful capabilities of parameter entities is that they can be re-declared in the *declaration subset* in the document entity itself, thereby *preempting* the declaration in the DTD. We'll do some tricks later, in Example 16 (*Striding off into the Subset*) on page 139, where we re-declare the structure of the HTML DTD without ever touching the file that contains it.

A Rose by Any Other Name
Would Smell as Sweet

But What if You Called both a Rose and a Pansy by the Same Name?

Goal of the Example:

The Rose/Pansy example has three unrelated goals:

- To show that there is a relationship between names that describe what something is (such as "anchor" or "heading"), and the names by which they're known in an SGML or HTML application — such as "A" or "H2". These are formally called generic identifiers or element type names and they are akin to people's proper names and their nicknames.
- To introduce the problem of "overloading" an element type — of making it do more than one poor element should have to.
- To introduce a new attribute value type, CDATA.

Goal of the Application:

To fold into one element type (A) the functions we have previously associated with both ANCHOR1 and ANCHOR2. If you've used HTML, you may have noticed how very hard-working the A element type is:

- <A> is the anchor that you click on to traverse a hypertext link. That is, when the href attribute is set, an <A> element represents an anchor and the anchor's hypertext link relationship with another document or object.
- <A> may also act as an addressable anchor — an anchor that's being pointed *at*. That is, when the name attribute is set, <A> is an object that can be addressed as an anchor in any HTML hypertext link relationship.
- <A> has an href attribute that contains the address of an object that is the other anchor of a one-way hyperlink. The address is a Uniform Resource Locator (URL), which includes a transport protocol, the name of a machine, and the the folder and filename of the destination document.
- If necessary, the address also includes the unique identifier of the other anchor within the file (the *fragment identifier*), if the other anchor happens to be a specific object within a file rather than the whole file.
- In some cases, the URL contains a query to be run on the server
- Sometimes the address contains a pointer to a map that the server or the browser uses to resolve clicks on a graphic in order to turn those into regular URLs.

This is a heck of a lot of capability for any one element type to have to support!

Is Influenced by/Builds on:

This example brings together the element type naming conventions of HTML with the hypertext links, anchors and headings we have been building over the last few examples. It builds directly on the *plainhx.dtd* that we met earlier in this chapter, but concentrates on what happens when we change the names of the ANCHOR1 and ANCHOR2 element types.

Example 7 — A Rose by Any Other Name Would Smell as Sweet

Stored on the Accompanying Disk as:

Sample DTD: *plainhtm.dtd*

Sample Instance: *plainhtm.sgm*

Step by Step:

Let's start by merging the declarations from the *plainuol.dtd* in the previous example and *plainlah.dtd* from several examples back:

```
<!ENTITY % heading    "h1 | h2 | h3 | h4">
<!ENTITY % list       "ul | ol">
<!ENTITY % anchor     "anchor1 | anchor2">

<!ELEMENT plaintxt    (#PCDATA|%heading;|p|%list;|dl|%anchor;)*>

<!ELEMENT (%heading;) (#PCDATA)>
<!ATTLIST (%heading;) id  ID  #REQUIRED>

<!ELEMENT (%list;)    (li)+>
<!ELEMENT dl          (dt | dd)+>
<!ELEMENT (li | dd)   (#PCDATA | p | %list; | dl)*>
<!ELEMENT dt          (#PCDATA)>
<!ELEMENT p           (#PCDATA)>

<!ELEMENT (%anchor)   (#PCDATA)>
<!ATTLIST anchor1     id    ID    #REQUIRED>
<!ATTLIST anchor2     idref IDREF #REQUIRED>
```

As you can see, we are continuing to use the parameter entities introduced in the previous example, adding %anchor; for the two anchor element types — the part of content *being pointed at* and the part *doing the pointing.* Both can appear almost anywhere in the PLAINTXT document instance, and both can contain any kind of character data for content.

Each of the anchor element types has an attribute value that makes it clear which is the pointer and which is the "pointee". The ANCHOR1 element type has an associated attribute value of id that is intended to carry a name or that has to be unique identifier throughout that document. (The same attribute is also used on the headings in this document type.) The ANCHOR2 element type has an attribute named idref to make it obvious that it is referring to something by providing the address of an anchor. In addition, both of those attributes are REQUIRED so that we can count on those attributes being there to be pointed at (in the case of ANCHOR1 and the headings) and to make it clear that it makes no sense to insert an <ANCHOR2> without actually telling the system what it is pointing at.

Note In real life — *life beyond examples* — you would rarely force writers to declare unique identifiers for element types that might rarely be pointed at. That is, you'd more likely use the keyword IMPLIED for the id attribute of the two heading types.

Morphing our hypertext anchors

Now we start changing the names to match HTML. The most commonly used anchor in HTML is the A element type. The attribute name, that corresponds to what we called idref previously, is href in HTML. Let's re-declare these first by simply changing the names:

```
<!ELEMENT a (#PCDATA)>
<!ATTLIST a href IDREF #REQUIRED>
```

But let's look at how HTML declares the *attribute definition list* for this element type:

```
<!ATTLIST a href CDATA #IMPLIED>
```

Understanding why REQUIRED has been replaced with IMPLIED is easy: Because this element type is performing so many functions, it would be unreasonable to force users to always put in an href attribute value. They may not be using <A> as a link, in which case having an href value wouldn't make sense.

But notice too that the IDREF keyword has been replaced with CDATA. CDATA is the most "liberal" of the *declared value* keywords, telling the SGML parser that the value to be filled in may be zero or more valid SGML characters. Obviously, IDREF is much stricter — it can only refer to an ID value and therefore must match one elsewhere in the document. But this would never work in the world of HTML. Certainly it makes sense that you would still want identifiers (for anchors, headings, or *anything* you're pointing to) to be unique, but in the world of the Web, you can point *anywhere*! You can't expect an SGML parser to race off and determine whether the IDREF you've inserted matches an existing ID on a document you may not even own.

Example 7 — A Rose by Any Other Name Would Smell as Sweet

How does the browser know what to do?

The use of the href attribute *must be established by application conventions*, by a specification outside the capabilities built into SGML. And this is indeed how it works. There is much in HTML — and indeed in *most* SGML applications — that is conveyed by documentation or specifications or means other than simply through the DTD. The definition of an SGML application from the ISO standard makes this clear:

> SGML application: Rules that apply SGML to a text processing application. An SGML application includes a formal specification of the markup constructs used in the application, expressed in SGML. In can also include a non-SGML definition of semantics, application conventions, and/or processing.
>
> ISO 8879: 4.279

The relevant sections of the HTML 2.0 *Specification* describes what an HREF must do:

> The A element indicates a hyperlink anchor... At least one of the NAME and HREF attributes should be present... HREF gives the URI of the head anchor of a hyperlink. [...] Once the address of the head anchor is determined, the user agent may obtain a representation of the resource. [...] An HTML user agent allows the user to navigate the content of the document and request activation of hyperlinks denoted by A elements... To activate a link, the user agent obtains a representation of the resource identified in the address of the head anchor.

Note The term "head anchor", used by the HTML 2.0 *Specification*, corresponds to an addressable anchor. The term "user agent", for our purposes, is an HTML browser.

Back to our example

The attribute value list declaration for <A> uses href and CDATA because it counts on HTML browsers knowing what the specific semantics of those values are. Web browsers know how to process hypertext links and anchors because an understanding of those semantics is built right in to the browser.

Remember that our original premise was to show how HTML folds, into one element type, the functionality that we associate with both anchors of a binary, unidirectional hypertext link. This was our original attribute definition list declaration for the ANCHOR1 element type in our previous examples:

```
<!ATTLIST anchor1 id ID #REQUIRED>
```

Naturally, if the A element type is also to fulfill this role, it needs to have a unique identifier so that it can be found by any browser. The HTML DTD adds this capability when it declares the attribute definition list for the <A> element type:

```
<!ATTLIST a name ID    #IMPLIED
            href CDATA #IMPLIED>
```

Two details have changed. Our term, id has been changed to name, which is similar in connotation, suggesting, I think, that the value of the name attribute should be a unique identifier. If the suggestion weren't strong enough, the SGML keyword ID does the job. Any SGML validating system will check that the value of this attribute is unique to the document in which it resides. That's good enough for us, because the application convention in HTML is to point to the document first, and then to point to the unique name within that document, which is called a fragment identifier in the HTML specification. If you can be certain that a document name is also unique (and to a great extent, the URL convention of machine name, directory path and filename ensures that), then the combination of the document filename and the name attribute value will also be unique.

Note   An ID attribute value must be unique across *all* elements in a document. When a parser looks for a unique identifier, it will not check the name of the element type — it looks *only* at the values of attributes whose declared value is ID in the DTD.

Example 7 — A Rose by Any Other Name Would Smell as Sweet

Notice that the keyword REQUIRED has been replaced with IMPLIED. As with the href attribute, the DTD cannot force it to exist since it won't be needed if nothing is going to point to the <A> element in which it resides — that is, if the anchor does not also represent the hypertext link relationship.

Bonus:

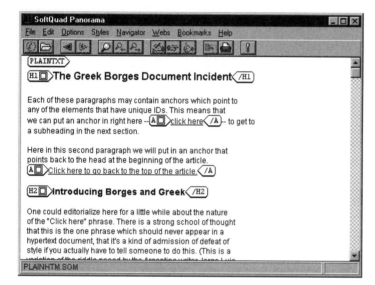

Figure 11. *Example files created with this* DTD *work with both the full* SGML *browser that accompanies the book, and with any popular* HTML *browser — a clear indication (if you still needed convincing) that* HTML *is really an application of* SGML.

An *afterthought...*

A moment ago I said that HTML browsers have built into them an understanding of the processing semantics of href values. By now you will certainly have gathered that one of the big differences between HTML and other SGML applications is that you can change names of element types or of attribute values to anything you want in full SGML applications. But the big question remains: *How do you let a processing system know the processing semantics of the element types and attributes you've created?* Much much more on this later.

In the meantime, a slight variation of this DTD will give us a chance to explore semantics for a moment.

As the Ancient Philosophers Say: Semantics Happen

All HTML documents are expected to have a title. That title is used in special browser windows that don't scroll with the rest of the document, appears in "History" lists, or may appear in a list of open windows if your browser lets you keep several files around at once. Some Web crawling applications gather up titles from collections of documents and either draw diagrams of their connections or perform other analysis on their relationships. The only reason they can do this is that somewhere in each HTML document is a phrase marked up as a TITLE:

```
<TITLE>
As the Ancient Philosophers Say:
Semantics Happen
</TITLE>
```

Functional capabilities like those listed above are cases of the *semantic information* associated with the element type TITLE. This example simply shows some different ways in which software applications express the *processing semantics* of titles.

Goal of the Example:

- To introduce two more indicators for element type declarations: the comma (a connector that means "followed by"), and the question mark (an occurrence indicator that means "optional").
- To support the markup requirements for recognizing paragraphs within our documents.

Goal of the Application:

- To introduce the notion of sequence in a DTD.
- To introduce the TITLE element type as used in HTML.

Is Influenced by/Builds on:

This application builds directly on the previous DTD and adds to it the HTML TITLE element type.

Stored on the Accompanying Disk as:

Sample DTD: *plainttl.dtd*

Sample Instance: *plainttl.sgm*

Example 8 — As the Ancient Philosophers Say: Semantics Happen

Step by Step:

Here's the declaration for the document element type PLAINTXT:

```
<!ELEMENT plaintxt (#PCDATA|%heading;|%list;|dl|p|a)*>
```

You will remember that the vertical bar (the | symbol) means "or" and the asterisk (the * symbol) means "zero or more, in any order". The declaration says that PLAINTXT consists of character data that may be parsed, or any of the anchor, heading, or list elements, any number of times, and in any order.

But now we want to enforce the identification of each document with a title. We do so with the following declaration:

```
<!ELEMENT plaintxt (title, (#PCDATA|%heading;|%list;|dl|a|p)*)>
```

Pretty straightforward — the parentheses provide grouping, just as they do in arithmetic. The content model consists of a group that begins with a TITLE element type, followed by the group with which we are now familiar. The comma following the word "title" has the meaning "followed by". There are no other characters associated with the TITLE (such as the asterisk), so there must be *one and only one* instance of a TITLE element in each document. Once that requirement has been fulfilled, then members of the other *model group* may be inserted — the character text, headings, unordered and ordered lists, definition lists, paragraphs and anchors.

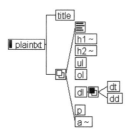

Figure 12. The tree view illustrates the structure of the DTD. A plaintext document starts with a title, and then contains character text, headings, unordered and ordered lists, definition lists, paragraphs and anchors.

Let's say we wanted to let the document creators decide if they wanted to include a TITLE element or not, but we wanted to indicate that it must appear first if there is one. We would do that with the question mark, or "optional" indicator, as in the following example declaration:

```
<!ELEMENT plaintxt (title?, (#PCDATA|%heading;|%list;|dl|a|p)*)>
```

Here is a list of all the indicators that you might want to use in a content model and their meanings:

Indicator	Description
?	Optional — element type or model group appears once or not at all.
,	Sequential — (*e.g.* a, b, . . . a must be followed by b; b is followed by . . .) Note: In "love,marriage?", love *may* be followed by marriage.
*	Optional and Repeatable — element or model group may appear zero or more times (*i.e.*, not at all or any number of times).
+	Required and Repeatable — element or model group must appear once, and may appear more than once (*i.e.*, "p+" is the same as "(p,p*)") .
&	"AND" — all the elements must occur, but may appear in any order (*e.g.*, "a & b & c" and "c & b & a" are allowed).
|	"OR" — only one of the elements or model groups must appear (*e.g.* "naughty | nice" means either naughty or nice).

Example 8 — As the Ancient Philosophers Say: Semantics Happen

plainttl.sgm, the sample file that accompanies this DTD doesn't have a lot to do:

```
<!DOCTYPE PLAINTXT PUBLIC "Plain Text with HTML Title, Anchors and Headings">
<PLAINTXT>
<TITLE>Philosophers Wax Poetic about Semantics</TITLE>

<H1>Semanticists Wax Poetic about Philosophy</H1>
<P>The body of this document plays no role whatsoever in the point
of the example. Everything that is going to happen already has.</P>

<P>That's philosophy.</P>

<P>Titles have more to do with what a document is really about than
H1 elements do. That's semantics. If you open this file in various
browsers, you'll find that the TITLE element acts in different ways.
You'll probably even find that the paragraphs are treated quite
differently among the Web browsers and Panorama. It's all in the
application interpretation of the element semantics. Aren't you glad
you asked?</P>

<P>By the way, when I say "Everything that is going to happen already
has", I mean only in this example. I wouldn't want to give you the
impression that I was taking poetic license where only semantic license
was warranted.</P>
</PLAINTXT>
```

As you can plainly see, the body of this document contains the usual assortment of paragraphs along with an H1 and a TITLE element. The fun starts when you see how a brower and a style sheet express a semantic distinction between the title and the heading.

Bonus:

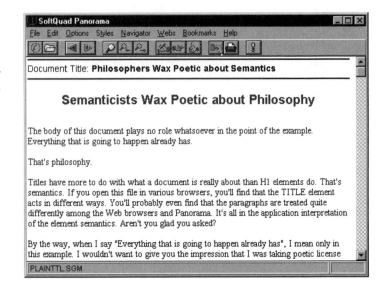

Figure 13. This example works in several ways. Using the version of Panorama that accompanies the book, open the plainttl.sgm file. Notice that, in the default style, all the text is much the same.

Move through all of the styles that come with the sample. The final one, called *Emboldened Monospace*, really gets carried away with making sure you know that the H1 and TITLE element types are to be treated differently.

But wait, there's more...

Speaking of semantics, there is a corollary to the notion that the SGML browser has to be told how you want to treat TITLE elements. SGML applications also need to be told what to do when they run into: <A HREF="WHATEVER">. As you will have gathered by now, only HTML browsers know *intuitively* (speaking anthropomorphically) how to act on these. It is worth spending a few moments exploring how full SGML browsers learn these semantics.

Example 8 — As the Ancient Philosophers Say: Semantics Happen

There are really only three pieces of information that an SGML browser would need in order to duplicate the functionality that comes built into a Web browser for handling the A element type:

- What are the names of the element types whose attributes receive the special functionality? (Alternatively, one could establish a mechanism that says "Any element with these special attribute names is to be treated as an HTML anchor.")
- What is or are the names of attributes that store the addresses of the other anchors in a hypertext link relationship? That is, where is the address stored to which the browser goes if someone clicks on a link? In HTML, a number of named attributes can carry this kind of information. For example, href, which we've talked about already, and src, action or script, which point to actions or scripts associated with forms. We need to identify all of these as having special meaning for a browser.
- If a unique identifier is *not* given the SGML declared value ID in the DTD, what is the name of the attribute that carries the identifier? For the HTML anchor, for instance, it's the name attribute that lets other anchors link to it.

❧ Example 9

Final Small Steps on the Road to a Useful Mini-Version of HTML

Goal of the Example:

I have a theory that for many purposes HTML is more than you need. As evidence of this assertion, I urge you to look at the vast majority of the pages on the Web today. They use only a tiny subset of the types of elements that are available to them in HTML.

Admittedly, the element types that most people *don't use* in HTML are there for historical reasons. HTML grew out of a computing environment. Naturally, therefore, there are several element types that exist only to satisfy requirements that grew out of writing computer programs or writing about programs.

But there are some that we haven't yet discovered that make a serious and significant contribution. We'll continue to explore one of the most obvious — the *paragraph* — and what it means to mark it up. Then we'll look at just a few of the subelements that make sense within paragraphs (and headings, and elsewhere, for that matter).

Goal of the Application:

- To provide a useful subset of the functions of HTML in a vastly simpler application.
- To build a foundation of element types that will support us as we explore bits and pieces of more complex HTML functions throughout the next chapter.
- To support the markup requirements for recognizing *emphasized* text within our paragraphs.

Is Influenced by/Builds on:

This is the moment of confluence. HTML is meeting PLAINTXT and they are finding their common ground. It will be a small step indeed to go from this final plain text application to something that really has the look and feel of HTML.

Stored on the Accompanying Disk as:

Sample DTD: *plainbod.dtd*

Sample Instance: *plainbod.sgm*

Step by Step 1: The DTD

Let's look first a few lines of the DTD and then move on to create the *plainbod.sgm* sample file from scratch.

First we'll pick up the parameter entities that we've been using thus far, and then declare the PLAINTXT document element type.

```
<!ENTITY % heading "h1 | h2 | h3 | h4">
<!ENTITY % list    "ul | ol">

<!ELEMENT plaintxt (title, (#PCDATA|%heading;|%list;|dl|p|a)*>
```

Bold and italic together again for the first time

In our newest DTD, the element type P, standing for paragraph, can occur anywhere that the other "body" element types can occur. That is, anywhere after the TITLE. Any number of them may appear, in any order. We won't declare all the element types here, but let's look specifically at the new content model for the paragraph:

```
<!ELEMENT p (#PCDATA | b | i)*>
```

No longer happy to declare an element type's content simply as PCDATA, we've now added two subelements to the model group, and allowed B and I (standing for "bold" and "italic") to appear in and among the character data. This type of content for the paragraph is called "mixed content" because it mixes character data with subelements.

Be true to your paragraph

If you look closely at the allowable content for a PLAINTXT element, you'll notice that, if you chose to, you could still use PCDATA within PLAINTXT mixed in with the paragraphs, headings, lists and anchors. The effect of this flexible content model really means that you could get away with never using paragraph tags, and you wouldn't really have solved the problem we've set ourselves here. Accordingly, let's re-declare the content model for PLAINTXT:

```
<!ELEMENT plaintxt (title, (%heading;|%list;|dl|p|a)*)>
```

This gives the model some "teeth", and now that the PLAINTXT element can no longer contain PCDATA, it is no longer "mixed content", but is called "element content".

Text arcana

Let's move on to declare content for the bold and italic element types. We won't allow a bold element to contain an italic element, and vice versa, although some applications do. So the B and I element types will contain only character data:

```
<!ELEMENT (b | i) (#PCDATA)>
```

You will recall that we've accumulated headings and various list element types from DTDs in previous examples. Let's allow the new emphasized element types, the bold and italic, in headings, list items, definition terms and the definitions themselves.

Clearly, we want to change the entire DTD in one step, so this is a job for a new parameter entity declaration. As we continue through the examples in this book, we'll define and use the TEXT parameter entity in any content model that calls for mixed character data and special phrases, and PCDATA anywhere that only character data is permitted:

```
<!ENTITY % text "#PCDATA | a | b | i">
```

Cleaning the Nest

While we're at it, let's go a bit further, by cleaning up the nested lists we created earlier. We'll have to modify the content model for list items to avoid mixing character data with element content, encouraging the use of paragraphs inside list items and definitions:

```
<!ELEMENT (%list;)    (li)+>
<!ELEMENT dl          (dt | dd)+>
<!ELEMENT (li | dd)   (p | %list; | dl)*>
<!ELEMENT dt          (%text;)>
```

Targeting the Title

While we're in here adding useful bits, we should probably make the title address-able. We only have to add the id attribute to the TITLE element type and use the IMPLIED keyword:

```
<!ATTLIST title id ID #IMPLIED>
```

Now a reference can be made to the main title of the document, from a table of contents or perhaps a bibliography.

Here then is the complete DTD

```
<!ENTITY % heading    "h1 | h2 | h3 | h4">
<!ENTITY % list       "ul | ol">
<!ENTITY % text       "#PCDATA | a | b | i">

<!ELEMENT plaintxt    (title, (%heading;|%list;|dl|p|a)*)>

<!ELEMENT title       (#PCDATA)>
<!ATTLIST title       id   ID  #IMPLIED>

<!ELEMENT (%heading;) (%text;)>
<!ATTLIST (%heading;) id   ID  #IMPLIED>

<!ELEMENT p           (%text;)>

<!ELEMENT (%list;)    (li)+>

<!ELEMENT dl          (dt | dd)+>
<!ELEMENT (li | dd)   (p | %list; | dl)*>
<!ELEMENT dt          (%text;)>

<!ELEMENT (b | i)     (#PCDATA)>

<!ELEMENT a           (#PCDATA)>
<!ATTLIST a name ID   #IMPLIED
            href CDATA #IMPLIED>
```

Figure 14. This tree view makes it clear that we still have a very flat structure for our evolving DTD. This DTD is also tidier because it does not allow mixed content.

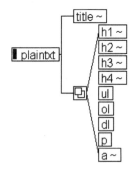

Step by Step 2: The Instance

Now let's work with this DTD in a sample instance. We won't use the definition list or anchor element types, but just enough of the new and old elements to experiment.

As always, this sample file (in this case *plainbod.sgm*) is available on the disk accompanying the book. Notice that the document element, PLAINTXT, is still with us. Because the document instances created with this DTD have no internal *structure* to speak of, I've chosen to draw the line separating the PLAINTEXT DTD from HTML one step further in the sequence — at the top of the next chapter. We'll examine just a couple of pieces of the instance:

```
<!DOCTYPE PLAINTXT PUBLIC "Plain Text with Body Elements">
<PLAINTXT>
<TITLE>The Last of the Plain Text Applications</TITLE>

<H1>Just Enough Structure to be Dangerous</H1>
```

When you open this file you will rediscover what we learned from the previous example, *plainttl.sgm*: TITLE and H1 dramatically highlight the notion of *information semantics*, what the element *means*. Many people, in their HTML documents, make the contents of the two elements identical, knowing that the contents of the TITLE element will not appear on the screen. It's more likely to appear in a separate title box, or at the top of the software application window, and to reappear in lists of visited sites, and so forth. The first H1 in a document will be the largest, boldest phrase to appear on the screen when the document opens. So it too acts as a kind of title. HTML tradition gives us the chance to use both, either to accomplish two different roles, or to carry one specific content chunk, the thing we think of as "the title".

```
<P>The major difference between a file created in accordance with
<I>plainbod.dtd</I> and one that conforms to its predecessors is
that now <I>everything</I> is marked up in some way. No decisions
are being left up to default browser behavior. For example, when
you display this file in any Web browser you'll see that the length
of the lines in all the paragraphs changes according to how wide
you set the display window. All the examples have always done that,
but now, for the first time, the same happens in <I>Panorama</I>
too.</P>
```

These are the first italic tags that we've used in the Plain Text series. They raise a critically important issue for users of SGML: When do you decide what the screen (or paper) presentation of a piece of content should be? In the example above, we've chosen to wrap the name of a piece of software with italic tags. That reflects a common, paper-oriented background in representing product names, book or movie titles, and so forth. But it might be more dramatic to have names of software appear in *red* or *blinking* or *larger than the surrounding text*.

There is a more generic way of dealing with our reasonable desire to give ourselves some flexibility in the display of that software name. The creators of HTML chose to include two tags in their original suite of tags that are much more generic than the <B> or <I> that I've included here. HTML includes <EM> for *emphasis*, which is usually interpreted as *italic*, but may not be, and <STRONG>, which is usually interpreted as **boldface**, but may not be.

It might have been wiser to include EM and STRONG in this DTD rather than B and I since I feel very strongly that the more general solution gives you far more power. At the same time, I appreciate that the bold/italic approach may seem more natural, and it's certainly more common.

```
<P>Previously, the way <I>Panorama</I> distinguished paragraphs
was actually just an optical illusion. Because the PLAIN TEXT
application was set by default to preserve carriage returns,
you thought you were seeing paragraph breaks. <I>Panorama</I>
didn't really know that the information object you saw as a
paragraph was special in any way. The Web browsers felt the same,
but because they had no way to be told to treat carriage returns
as generally meaningful, they ran all the paragraph content
together.</P>

<P>Now of course, with this full, rich markup, all the browsers
know what to do.</P>
```

The content of this example brings out a very subtle point — perhaps too subtle to worry about this early on in the book. The advantage of having meaningful line breaks and, or carriage returns is that you can control the final display in yet another useful fashion. Think of computer program listings or poetry.

In standard HTML there are several element types that count on the software interpreting them as if the carriage returns really are there. They also count on the software *not* to interpret other element types in the same way. You can experiment with this phenomenon by changing the width of your display window in any browser which re-wraps the text to fit, that is, that re-wraps any text that is contained within the majority of element types (such as paragraphs, headings, list items), but which does *not* re-wrap element types that have been defined as being "pre-formatted". The "definition" as to which element types wrap and which do not is beyond the scope of an SGML DTD, but is part of the accompanying set of application conventions which is considered part of the full SGML application as a whole.

```
<H2>We <I>Still</I> Have a Hierarchy of Heading Types</H2>
<P>In fact, we could make a list of what we now have:</P>
<OL>
<LI><P>We still have our four types of headings--H1, H2, H3, and H4--
except that now they can contain our two new element types,
<B>bold</B> and <I>italic</I> emphasized text.</P></LI>
<LI><P>The different list types are still with us, but now they are nested:
<OL>
<LI><P>ordered,</P></LI>
<LI><P>unordered and</P></LI>
<LI><P>definition lists.</P></LI>
</OL></LI>
<LI><P>We still have our anchor element, complete with the
attribute values that let us point to it or use it to point
to another anchor, any heading or the title.</P></LI>
<LI><P>The new enforcer on the block is the P element type, the
paragraph. Paragraph start- and end-tags wrap the contents of each
paragraph, allowing for no confusion as to what is or isn't a
paragraph.</P>
</LI></OL></PLAINTXT>
```

Bonus:

If you're looking at *plainbod.sgm* in Panorama, be sure to choose all the available style sheets from the Styles menu. You'll see that we chose to follow a very abstract route in some of the style sheets, displaying <B> with italic, and <I> as either bold or purple.

Figure 15. For a dramatic display of the semantic attachment associated with even the slightest change of markup, make a copy of this file, changing the <OL> *and the* </OL> *to* <UL> *and* </UL>. *Suddenly the items in the list will have bullets or squares instead of being numbered.*

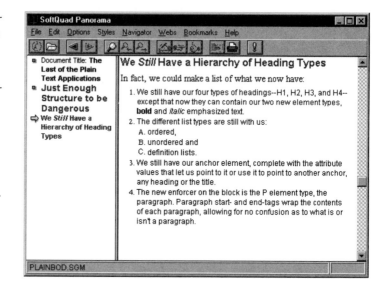

How Far We've Come in this Chapter

The DTD is complete. We have defined a subset of the HTML element types that will let us create files that will work instantly on the Web, in any Web browser. At the same time, we have built up this set of declarations formally and carefully, creating a fully *conforming* SGML *application* that can be used with any SGML browser, editor, or other SGML system.

You've experienced first-hand the creation of a formal specification for an SGML application — the exact same process (albeit far, far simpler) that countless others have used while building full SGML applications for:

- traditional publishers, under the aegis first of the American Association of Publishers Electronic Manuscript Project, which later evolved into ISO 12083
- the aerospace industry, under the wing of the Air Transport Association (ATA)
- computer systems software documentation writers, architects and publishers, who work together developing and maintaining the DOCBOOK DTD, as the Davenport Group
- the defense industry in many countries around the world, under the acronym CALS
- HTML, of course, created by Tim Berners-Lee, shepherded along by Dan Connolly and Dave Raggett, with the help of the HTML Editorial Review Board (ERB) and the International Engineering Task Force IETF
- representatives of the world-wide community of blind and other visually impaired readers under the International Committee for Accessible Document Design (ICADD) activity
- the news industry — newspapers, wire services and press agencies — under the News Industry Text Format (NITF) working group
- the semi-conductor manufacturers who are part of the Pinnacles initiative
- the computational linguists and other representatives of academia who are part of the Text Encoding Initiative (TEI)
- and many others.

You've learned to read and to declare element types, to establish names for information objects and to formally specify where and how they may appear in a document instance.

You've learned to read and declare basic attribute values, to appreciate the functional distinctions among three SGML keywords:

- ID (checked for uniqueness)
- IDREF (checked that it matches an ID)
- CDATA (checked for common characters and length).

You've learned to recognize a vocabulary that includes element types, document instance, attribute value and other terms that are part of a carefully thought-through approach to specifying electronic publishing applications, and that will survive to work for you in applications far more sophisticated than those covered by this book. The same vocabulary will act as a foundation for any further exploration that you do of HTML and full SGML.

You've built up, step by step, a skeletal version of an HTML application. It's very basic, admittedly, but it does at least enough to build a small-but-mighty Web presence for your information.

You've also run into the heavily-loaded term *semantics*, and managed to keep reading.

You're ready for the next chapter, if you'd like. Or you're ready to start putting files up on the Web or on local filesystems for use either with HTML or full SGML browsers.

The variety of available SGML systems is far greater than the software currently available for just HTML. Ensuring that HTML is a formal SGML application — which is a large part of the activity of the World Wide Web Consortium's HTML Editorial Review Board — gives HTML users access to all that SGML software. From the point of view of creators of HTML, SGML conformance may appear to mean a concern for adding bits of markup that sometimes may seem like more work than casually sprinkling just a handful of tags. In fact, SGML conformance means the freedom and flexibility to use any full SGML software, from any vendor or shareware source, on any operating system. And it means conformance to an International Standard that guarantees that information content you create will outlast the tools you've used to create it, and be readable by generation after generation of new tools.

Later, as we further explore hypertext linking in HTML, SGML, and HyTime, we encounter new and different terminologies and models that allow us to describe much more sophisticated and powerful hypertext relationships. There's a variety of SGML software that manages inter-document hypertext links — software that conforms to HyTime handles inter-document links in an internationally standardized way as you will see in Chapter 8 (*You Can Get There From Here*) on page 263.

PART II

Walking the Walk

◆§ CHAPTER 4

Exploring HTML with a Flashlight

Sometimes HTML is just right for your purposes, although you may not need all or even very much of its capability.

This short chapter continues to explore SGML constructs by walking you through portions of the HTML application, edited out from the full-blown HTML DTD, and presented as mini-applications, any one of which can stand on its own.

When HTML Is Just Right

The creation of an SGML application normally follows a fairly rigorous path beginning with a careful analysis of:

- the documents that will use the markup
- the corporate and inter-corporate information-sharing that will be affected
- the production system(s) that an SGML system will either feed or replace
- the available off-the-shelf or customized software tools
- the anticipated costs and savings in both time and dollars.

This analysis is conducted against a backdrop of current and future uses of the data (including potential publications based on the repackaging of existing content), requirements for conversion of existing information resources ("legacy data"), for document management and for display or processing, impact on staffing, training and support, importance of conformance to international, national or industry-wide standards.

In summary, implementing SGML has always been considered a *Big Deal*, with an impact on an organization's competitiveness, strategic direction and bottom line. *Suddenly HTML turns all that on its head.* Suddenly, this SGML application says:

- Don't bother analyzing your data — a set of supported markup codes exists.
- Forget cost-benefit analysis — it's all happening too fast. Just dive in and try it. Run a few Web pages up a flagpole and see who salutes.
- Ignore corporate buy-in and sign-off. Set up a Web site, tell everyone about it, be a hero or heroine, and then try to determine corporate policy.
- Don't plan any further out than you have to. Heck, don't even bother to figure out how you're going to update your pages until you have to.

In short, here's an SGML application that seems to be built on the principle that everyone's an expert, just as everyone's new at this. There are no rules — or at least very few. This is heady stuff. It gives everyone who's willing to experiment or to take a few risks an advantage in positioning themselves, their company, their organization or government department, as bold, innovative, and technologically sophisticated. These are times akin to the days of any historical Gold Rush, where people who weren't millionaires a year ago now are, where you or your company may now be paying a lot of money to someone to advise you about technology that didn't exist six months ago. You may be the person they're paying!

So what's my point? What is this chapter about, really?

Even at this early moment in its history, HTML has a lot of innovation encircling it, as well as a lot of experience behind it. An active community of thinkers and doers is contributing to its development and formalization. Tens of millions of network documents use HTML to get information across to the millions of readers. Tens of millions of pages is not a lot of pages, by the way, compared to all the other major SGML applications. What makes the HTML application particularly interesting, however, is how widespread those pages are, how disparate their authors, and how much has been accomplished with so little infrastructure and technology. Other SGML applications have taken years (and in some cases small fortunes) to design and implement. There is, in HTML, an exhilarating balance between a minimal set of element types, and a maximal collection of capability and power for the small amount of markup that you use. All in all, nuggets of capability within HTML deserve a closer look. This chapter offers those.

Nice Body. Nice Head.

Goal of the Example:

In our last episode, we left *plainbod.dtd*, which, if the truth were to be known, was no more than a mechanism to allow us to surround text with some start-tags and end-tags and thereby add value, primarily for display in browsers of various sorts. Admittedly, there was also a notion that by surrounding phrases with <A> and </A>, we could add *semantic* value to those phrases. In that way, we indicated to our browsers that someone could click on one anchor and be transported to another anchor at the other end of a hypertext link.

Those kinds of capability represent just a small portion of what markup can do for us. Before we get to other similarly dramatic examples, however, let's catch our breath and examine a subtler notion — the idea and value of containing elements in markup.

Goal of the Application:

- To become a true subset of the HTML application, so completely as to allow document instances that conform to this DTD to conform, as well, to the HTML 3.2 DTD. (This would allow an author to create documents according to this simple application knowing that they are *guaranteed* to work in any Web browser. The reverse, of course, would not be true, since HTML includes element types and attributes that this DTD knows nothing about.)
- To enable a browser to distinguish between elements that are to be displayed as the contents of a document, and those that are not.
- To start to build a useful hierarchy for a document, such as an outliner might offer, for moving easily through it and, while editing, moving whole chunks of that document.

Is Influenced by/Builds on:

This application takes the final example of the last chapter, *plainbod.dtd*, and *wraps* the element types that comprise it in the containing elements from HTML — HEAD and BODY.

Stored on the Accompanying Disk as:

Sample DTD: *htmsimpl.dtd*

Sample Instances: *htmsimpl.sgm* and *htmsimpl.htm*

Example 10 — Nice Body. Nice Head.

Step by Step:

We begin with the same set of parameter entity declarations that we developed for the plain text set of DTDs:

```
<!ENTITY % heading "h1 | h2 | h3 | h4">
<!ENTITY % list    "ul | ol">
<!ENTITY % text    "#PCDATA | a | b | i">
```

Now comes the most dramatic moment. We're going to change the document element from PLAINTXT to HTML. So our first declarations set the stage:

```
<!ELEMENT html (head, body)>
<!ELEMENT head (title)>
<!ELEMENT body (%heading; | %list; | dl | p | a)*>
```

The declarations are straightforward. The element type HTML consists of a HEAD element type followed by a BODY. In this DTD, just as in the formal specification for HTML 3.2, both elements are required to be present. (Later we'll discuss *minimization*, a technique that, under some circumstances, allows you to leave off start-tags or end-tags or both.) The HEAD might have a TITLE, and the BODY contains the familiar grouping from the previous examples. Everything else in the DTD remains as it was.

Let's look at the top of the sample file, *htmsimpl.sgm*.

```
<!DOCTYPE HTML PUBLIC "Simplified HTML">
<HTML>
<HEAD><TITLE>A Simple Title Contained in the Head</TITLE></HEAD>
<BODY>
<H1>The First Heading Is Contained in the Body</H1>
<P>On an entirely unrelated topic, have you noticed that all
the examples begin with the H1 element? ...
```

The <HEAD> and <BODY> are serving as containing elements, or *containers*. We're already familiar with the concept of containers because we've been using the list elements all along. These two containers are doing both a social and a technical job.

The Social Role of These Containers

The idea is that the HEAD of a document contains information pertaining to the whole document, information which is considered to be *part of the document* but not considered part of the *document content* itself. The document content is contained within the BODY element.

This is a very significant concept. We are used to thinking of the document as *being what you see* on the printed page. But of course, there's much more to it than that. At a more abstract level, the document can be thought of as being the sum of the information it contains *and* the information *about* that document. That information set may contain some or all of the following data, or various other pieces of information:

- its title (which might also appear within the document)
- its creator, or editor, or other responsible party (information which might also appear in the "visible" content)
- its date (or a suite of dates including revision and release dates and other important milestones)
- its ownership or copyright holder
- its keywords that may be used for finding it
- its relation to other documents (and the next section of this chapter will explore this)
- its role — whether it acts as a table of contents or an index or a glossary
- its base location on a file system, in the case of HTML, from which all link addresses and relative paths are calculated instead of fixed paths (the BASE element type)
- its cost, if it's to be sold in an electronic form
- its authentication (a checksum of some kind), if a browser is to determine whether anyone has changed any of its contents without permission
- its list of readers who have specifically requested that they be kept informed of updates to it
- and any other characteristics that may be worth keeping around.

All this is called metadata and we'll talk about it in later chapters. In fact, we'll build small SGML applications to handle some of the cases outlined above.

That is the *social* job description that I mentioned above.

Example 10 — Nice Body. Nice Head.

The Technical Role of These Containers

The *technical* role that the containing elements play is the simpler one, and it was introduced earlier. According to the HTML specification, nothing in the HEAD should be visible in the main document display window of a browser (and therefore nothing should be printed out when you print the document). Everything in the BODY would be, by default, visible. There may be occasions when you would want to render other content invisible, but that's a matter between you and your style sheet. If that's want you want to do, you'll probably want to be using a full SGML browser, rather than an HTML browser. (Typical uses for such capability would be questions and answers, with the answers hidden, or technical instructions with expert-level detail hidden from novice users.)

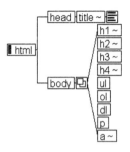

Figure 16. This tree view illustrates the structure of the DTD. In any document that uses this DTD, a HEAD element contains a TITLE, while the BODY contains the headings, lists, paragraphs and anchors.

Bonus:

We have seen that there is special value in dividing documents up into separate parts, just as this book, for instance, is divided into:

- the front matter: title pages, table of contents, and so forth
- the body of the book: the chapters
- the rear matter: the glossary and the index.

We've also seen that the HTML TITLE element type fits neatly into a HEAD element with other "front matter" element structures, while the other elements that we've been exploring (so far intuitively) work well within a surrounding BODY element, completely analogous to the body of this book.

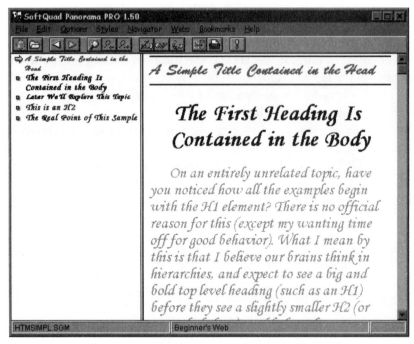

Figure 17. *Notice the Navigator that displays with the sample file if you're using Panorama: Click on the plus sign to see what's enclosed. Navigators can be selected from the Navigator menu. With the commercial version of Panorama, you can create new navigators, using any element type at all as a navigational aid.*

Three style sheets for Panorama illustrate distinctions between possible *presentation semantics* of HEAD and BODY element types. Choose "Standard HTML" from the Styles menu to see the HEAD and its content disappear. Choose "Red Head" to have color act as the primary distinction. Choose "Pretty Faces" to let the choice of typeface and certain other typographic features change. Notice that *all* the style sheet effects you're seeing are based entirely on associating stylistic attributes with either HEAD or BODY. The subelements inherit from those two elements. Admittedly this would all be a little more dramatic if there were more contents to the HEAD than simply TITLE.

Example 10 — Nice Body. Nice Head.

Added Bonus:

As an added bonus, let's count up the terms I seem to have felt compelled to use in these last paragraphs when talking about what you're seeing on the screen:

- semantic distinctions
- typographic features
- style sheet effects
- stylistic attributes
- what you're seeing on the screen.

For the purposes of this example, we'll assume that these all share a common meaning. From now on we'll try to be a bit more careful about the terms that we use and the important distinctions among these ones in particular.

But wait, there's more...

In the next chapter, Example 18 (*Put a Little Hierarchy into Your Life*) on page 153, carries the container idea one step further, wrapping containing elements around headings and the text they relate to, imitating completely the standard publishing notion of sections and subsections.

❦ EXAMPLE 11

This Element is Half Full

Goal of the Example:

- To show additional uses for the element type declared content keyword EMPTY, particularly:
  - to carry non-display (or non-printing) meta-information (which we've seen in previous sections)
  - to act as a marker for "display objects" such as horizontal rules or line breaks.
- To illustrate the use of nested parameter entities.
- To demonstrate the use of *comments* within declarations.
- To continue to explore HTML functionality, step by step.
- To resume the discussion of how semantics get attached to new element types.

Goal of the Application:

To support control over line breaks and the inclusion of horizontal rules.

Is Influenced by/Builds on:

The example continues to explore the HTML 2.0 DTD by adding incremental functionality to previous examples. In this case, HTML element types which are declared as EMPTY are declared in the sample application.

Stored on the Accompanying Disk as:

Sample DTD: *empties.dtd*

Sample Instance: *empties.sgm*

Step by Step:

Let's begin by looking at the parameter entities that begin the sample DTD:

```
<!ENTITY % heading "h1 | h2 | h3 | h4">
<!ENTITY % list    "ul | ol">

<!ENTITY % font    "b | i">
<!ENTITY % text    "#PCDATA | %font;">
```

We remember the first two declarations for element types which are our old friends. But the FONTdeclaration is new and the TEXT declaration has been modified — making a distinction between character data and its markup. We quickly see the benefit of nested parameter entities in other places. Here %text; will automatically pick up the replacement text included in %font;. If we want to re-declare %font; at any time in the future, we can comfortably presume that everywhere %text; appears, the new element types will be allowed.

```
<!ENTITY % brules  "hr | br">
<!ENTITY % empties "%brules;">
```

Example 11 — This Element is Half Full

The declarations that follow recognize that there is a category of element types that may be declared as EMPTY:

- the "rules and breaks", which includes <HR>, whose job is to draw a horizontal rule across the screen, and <BR>, which forces a line break wherever it appears.

The exact wording of the parameter entity declarations goes a little bit further in explaining the relationship. By declaring the entity reference %empties; as incorporating %brules; there is an implication that the list of rules and breaks may be extended (carefully, of course) to include related element types, and that the new ones will automatically find their way into the same legal contexts as HR and BR.

```
<!ENTITY % block "(a | p | dl | %list; | %empties;)">
```

By now, we're triply nested: %block; includes %empties; which includes %brules;. There is, theoretically, no limit to how complicated you want to be in exploiting this construct. One caution, however; even if you understand the complex nestings of a DTD you've written, others (ranging from users to whoever has to maintain the application when you move on to other tasks) will need to be able to make their way through it too.

Note   *Use of parameter entities — especially nested ones — can be dangerous if not managed properly. If you use them, recognize that you need to follow them around, to resolve them with paper and pen to be sure that the parameter entities have the intended effect everywhere you wish to allow (or disallow) certain element types.*

In the element type declaration portion of the DTD, we use the parameter entities normally. You'll notice that despite what I told you previously, %block; is used only once. Here we're using the construct more as a method for building reusable, easily-modifiable structures than as a shorthand form of typing. Accordingly, we're less concerned about a parameter entity that appears only once. It's busy making a subtler contribution.

```
<!ELEMENT html   (head, body)>
<!ELEMENT head   (title)>

<!ELEMENT title (#PCDATA)>

<!ELEMENT body   (%heading; | %block;)*>

<!ELEMENT (%heading;) (a | %text;)*>
<!ATTLIST (%heading;) name          ID  #IMPLIED>

<!ELEMENT (%list;)    (li)+>

<!ELEMENT (li|dd)     (p | %list | dl)*>
<!ELEMENT dt          (a | %text;)*>
<!ELEMENT p           (a | %text;)*>

<!ELEMENT (%font;)    (#PCDATA)>

<!ELEMENT a           (%text;)*>
<!ATTLIST a name ID   #IMPLIED
            href CDATA #IMPLIED>
```

Note   I've re-simplified the DTD only to make for a clearer sample application for the empty element types.

Example 11 — This Element is Half Full

In the next three declarations you run into something you've not seen previously in the sample applications, but which may be somewhat obvious from the usage: Comments. The phrases that are set off from the rest of the declaration with the double hyphens before and after (comment delimiters) have no effect on the formal declaration of the element types, or any other declarations in which they might appear. In this form they may be used only in declarations; there is a slightly different form — a *comment declaration* — in which they may appear both in DTDs and in document instances. The samples show a typical use of comments, explaining something which might otherwise seem a bit cryptic:

```
<!ELEMENT hr  EMPTY -- horizontal rule -->
<!ELEMENT br  EMPTY -- forced line break -->
```

This is the crux of the example. For all intents and purposes, the two new element types seem much the same, with cryptic names and declared content of EMPTY. They even appear in all the same places in the content models of other element types.

Obviously, the interpretation of the element types by browsing or other software holds the key to understanding what's going on here. When display software sees <HR>, it will draw a rule automatically adjusted to the current width of the screen. When display software sees <BR>, it will force a line break. This allows you to publish poems, for example, inside a paragraph:

```
<!DOCTYPE HTML PUBLIC "Empty Elements">
<HTML>
<HEAD><TITLE><H1>Empty Display Objects</TITLE>
<BODY>
<H1>Empty Display Objects</H1>
<HR>
<P>I think that I shall never see<BR>
A poem as lovely as a tree.</P>
<HR>
</BODY>
</HTML>
```

The first thing you notice is that there are no end-tags for the BR and HR elements. This is a rule in SGML: *Empty elements are indicated with start-tags but no end-tags.* This is completely logical — they don't contain anything. In a sense, they really are *markers* in the text to indicate where a break occurs, where a rule should be drawn, where an image is placed. The appearance in a file of the start-tags <HR> and <BR> says "At this point something happens."

Bonus:

The only trouble with putting what I've called "display objects" directly into the file —
 and <HR>, for example — is that by doing so you risk locking yourself into one version of a display if you rely solely on them to control presentation. With a style sheet approach, in which *to the greatest extent possible* all display or formatting decisions are delayed until the "moment of display", you allow for negotiation between the publisher (as represented by the server, perhaps with a set of style sheets) and the reader (who may have personal sets of style sheets).

A classic example of the necessity of this approach is the use of large type for people who have difficulty seeing. It is not reasonable to expect that everyone in the world would build the large font sizes into their source file. But how could you make sure that *every* text that you read is enlarged if you have difficulty seeing?

While the use of the BR and HR element types are less obviously rife with difficulty, one can readily imagine the advantages in being able to say, "All sections begin with a horizontal line", under circumstances where that makes sense. Fixing the <HR> markup directly into a file means never being able to say you'd like to change the display based only on immediate conditions.

Example 11 — This Element is Half Full

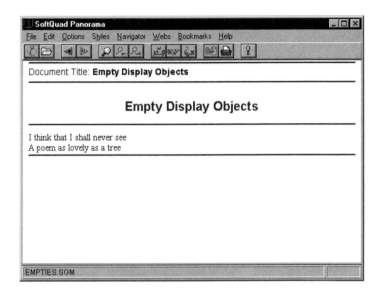

Figure 18. The sample file emp-ties.sgm shows the use of the empty elements.

But wait, there's more...

In the next section, we continue to explore the separation of display characteristics from the markup. In particular, we challenge the idea of B and I, the bold and italic element types.

Let's Emphasize Text, He Said Boldly

Goal of the Example:

Here's an exaggerated typical paragraph:

```
<P>The <I>Pickering Picayune</I> says that <I>SGML: The Movie</I> is an
<I>absolutely</I> masterful <I>piece de resistance</I> in the classic
genre of a latter day Douglas Adams.</P>
```

Perhaps the problem has become obvious through overkill. *Each of the italic elements in the paragraph means something different.* In this short example, we see italic used to:

- identify the title of a newspaper
- identify the name of a movie
- draw attention to or emphasize a word, phrase or sentence.
- make a French expression appear in italic

Imagine that you'd written an 800-page book sprinkled with references to other books. At the end of the project, one of the many things you might want is to be able to automatically generate a bibliographic list of all those titles. Now imagine further that you had carefully marked up each book title as italic, just as in the example above. *There's nothing you can do.* You can't really do a worthwhile search for everything in the book that's italic because your book titles are mixed with other italicized information.

In the same vein, the word "absolutely" in the example has been marked up as italic, but the author's actual intent was simply to emphasize the word. In a Web browser, the notion of emphasis might be achieved through italic, but instead could have been accomplished through blinking text, through the use of color or a larger type size, or other methods limited only by one's imagination. On paper too, many methods exist to represent emphasis.

In the best of all worlds, then, we might have been much better off with markup that doesn't limit us to the I element type, or even to I and B. (Bold face text suffers from exactly the same limits as italic. You may want to represent an idea in many ways in many media. To mark it up as bold limits the presentational possibilities.)

Goal of the Application:

- To free the author from having to mark content up as bold or italic;
- To offer the author two new element types which are less constraining in appearance and more general.

Is Influenced by/Builds on:

As do all the examples in this chapter, this topic comes directly from the HTML 2.0 DTD.

Stored on the Accompanying Disk as:

Sample DTD: *boldlygo.dtd*

Sample Instance: *boldlygo.sgm*

Example 12 — Let's Emphasize Text, He Said Boldly

Step by Step:

This is the shortest "Step by Step" section in the book. We could start with the previous DTD simply replace:

```
<!ENTITY % text    "#PCDATA | %font;">
```

with

```
<!ENTITY % text    "#PCDATA | em | strong">
```

That would be the bold way. However, I recognize that some people have a sentimental attachment to using <B> and <I> in their documents, so I will be gracious. Let's re-declare the parameter entity to include both the traditional element types and the general ones. The HTML 2.0 DTD distinguishes %font; element types from what it calls %phrase; (in which it includes EM and STRONG). We'll make the same distinction in our examples:

```
<!ENTITY % font   "b | i">
<!ENTITY % phrase "em | strong">
<!ENTITY % text    "#PCDATA | %font; | %phrase;">
```

Bonus:

Naturally we can have a bit of sport with this in Panorama. Try out *all* the style sheets accompanying the sample file called *boldlygo.sgm*. Stop at nothing. Take no prisoners.

Figure 19. Open boldlygo.sgm and choose HTML with Frills from the Styles menu for a dexterous look through our Welcome to a Demo of Various Styles. A veritable cavalcade of technicolor dream pages.

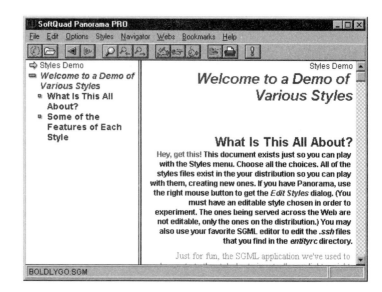

Figure 20. Choose Large Type for the big picture. This style, which we hope to make available for all our Web pages, will allow people with visual disabilities to read the screen.

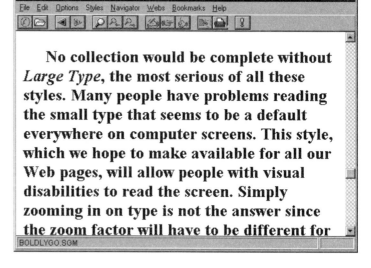

Example 12 — Let's Emphasize Text, He Said Boldly

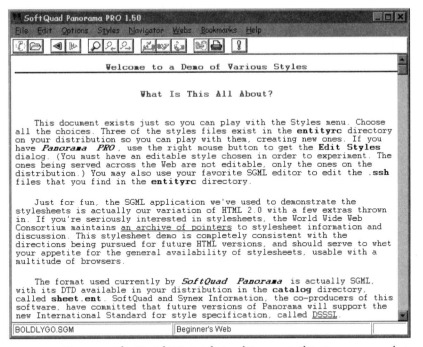

Figure 21. The Straight Text style is a bit more staid in its appearance, but highly readable and probably more practical for that reason alone. With Panorama, you can use this style in order to print straight ASCII representations of simple HTML files.

But wait, there's more...

We didn't really have to re-write the DTD to add EM and STRONG. In Example 16 (*Striding off into the Subset*) on page 139, we'll see that, had we wanted to make this change on a temporary basis, we could have simply *re-declared* the entities at the top of our file:

```
<!DOCTYPE HTML PUBLIC "Empty Elements" [
<!ENTITY % text "#PCDATA" | b | i | em | strong">
]>
<HTML>
<HEAD><TITLE>Tools to Boldly Emphasize</TITLE></HEAD>
<BODY>
<H1>To <STRONG>Boldly</STRONG> Emphasize Strong <EM>Italic Text</EM> </H1>
<P>At first glance, the effect of swapping strong and emphasis
for bold and italic is invisible to the naked eye.
Later, though, as soon as you want to <EM>re-purpose</EM> the content,
suddenly it turns out to be easier to re-assign an emphatic
element type to be bold and red and huge than an italic one.
The latter seems to always carry around the notion that
<I>once italic, always italic</I>.
</P>
```

When I said "on a temporary basis", however, I meant what I said. If, in fact, we wish to make this change for all our documents, and for everyone sharing a specific DTD, then make the change directly in the DTD. Otherwise, sometime, someone will forget to add the new *entity declaration* to their document instance, and they won't know what hit them.

❧ EXAMPLE 13

What Was That Link I Saw You With?

Goal of the Example:

What can you really do with an element type called LINK? People have been confused by its use within the HTML HEAD element since, as you've seen, there is already an anchor element type that represents a hypertext link. In fact, we shall see that there many types of elements that can represent a hypertext link. The element type that is actually named LINK in HTML has a very specific task to accomplish. It is used to describe the nature of the relationship that a whole document has to another document, or fragment of a document.

In part, then, this example, is about naming, pointing out that you should consider the impact of the name you choose on the clarity or confusion surrounding your application. In small part, it is about using parameter entities in attribute definition list declarations, just as we did previously for element type declarations.

For the most part, the example is about the SGML reserved word NAMES, and what it does and doesn't support in an SGML application.

Goal of the Application:

- To provide suitable markup for a browser to offer special services based on the nature of the relationship that one document has to another. For example, a browser that saw a hypertext link relationship of "index", could place a button on a toolbar that would take users to the index any time they clicked on the button.
- To provide markup where editing software can leave a record of relationships established among documents during their creation. For example, that a linked document is the "next" or "previous" one to read in a sequence.
- To provide suitable markup for other SGML software to offer special services that go beyond simply browsing.

Is Influenced by/Builds on:

This application, like all the others in this chapter is a true subset of HTML. Files that conform to this DTD will all conform to HTML itself. In fact, this application is influenced by an application developed at the *Santa Cruz Operation* (SCO) to deliver extensible online documentation and context-sensitive help. That application uses the LINK element type, along with the rel attribute, to link together hundreds of thousands of HTML files into books, collections, and, ultimately, a library.

Stored on the Accompanying Disk as:

Sample DTD: *htmlink1.dtd*

Sample Instance: *htmlink1.sgm*

Example 13 — What Was That Link I Saw You With?

Step by Step:

The value that this example adds to the DTDs we've been building thus far occurs in the two parameter entities referenced in the attribute value list for the LINK element type.

```
<!ENTITY % relType "NAMES">
<!ENTITY % revType "NAMES">
```

In the previous chapter I said that parameter entities are useful in places where the same text — their replacement text — appears in several places in a DTD. In the case of these two declarations, however, they appear only once. Why then would we use this parameter entity? Only one reason: to be able to change it readily. (In the next example, you'll see why we declared these as parameter entities instead of simply typing the keyword NAMES directly into the attribute definition list declaration.)

The keyword NAMES indicates that the value that a user assigns must be a list of SGML NAME strings. For our purposes, a NAME value may be a string of 1 to 8 characters (8 is a "default" limit imposed by the SGML *declaration* and can be changed there) that starts with a-z or A-Z, followed by a-z, A-Z, hyphen or period. A NAME list is a list of NAMES; each string must be separated by one or more spaces, tabs or returns (*separators*).

Once we've declared the attribute below, we'll examine an example of its use.

```
<!ELEMENT html    (head, body)>
<!ELEMENT head    (title, link*)>

<!ELEMENT title   (#PCDATA)>
<!ATTLIST title   name ID #IMPLIED>

<!ELEMENT link    EMPTY>
```

The HEAD element type still has the required TITLE, but that is now followed by zero or more LINK elements. As you read on, you discover that the LINK element type has declared content that uses the keyword EMPTY. Don't be surprised: EMPTY says precisely what you would imagine. This element, when you use it, is not allowed to have content. *All the information it carries is carried in attribute values, and the element type name itself.*

Your software exploits the fact that we're carrying this information in attributes instead of as content. The value of this choice is that it's easy for SGML software to recognize where that information is, what it's called, and whether it conforms to one of the attribute value types allowed in full SGML.

```
<!ATTLIST link name ID        #IMPLIED
               href CDATA     #REQUIRED
               rel  %relType; #IMPLIED
               rev  %revType; #IMPLIED>
```

The use of the LINK element is as follows — you can insert any number of LINK elements into the document (including zero), and each instance of a LINK element type carries two vital pieces of information:

- the href value, which is the address of another object, and
- usually a rel or rev value, which contains the name assigned to describe the relationship between the two anchors.

The rel value can be used to describe the relationship of the other document to this one, while the rev value describes the relationship of this document to the other.

In the following example, the LINK elements connect a chapter in a book to the next and previous chapters, a table of contents, and an index. A browser that recognizes these values of the rel attribute can use the information to offer particular access to the contents. For example, it can use a suite of toolbar buttons across the top of the page to connect to the linked documents:

```
<!DOCTYPE html PUBLIC "Simplified HTML with Link">
<HTML>
<HEAD><TITLE>What Was That Link?</TITLE>
<LINK HREF="TOC.SGM"   REL="TOC">
<LINK HREF="EX12.SGM"  REL="PREV">
<LINK HREF="EX14.SGM"  REL="NEXT">
<LINK HREF="INDEX.SGM" REL="INDEX">
</HEAD>
```

Note   Element types that have been declared as EMPTY *may not have end-tags.*

Example 13 — What Was That Link I Saw You With?

There is a great deal of freedom associated with any attribute value of NAMES. You may create valuable and interesting relationships among sets of documents, and you have a place to store that information for posterity, and, presumably for any browser that can be made to recognize the new "keyword" that you've invented. At the same time, for the more ordinary situations, the same freedom may become a bit troublesome. For example, someone else in the office right next to yours could be working on a similar project, and might have used the `rel` attribute in a book too:

```
<!DOCTYPE html PUBLIC "Simplified HTML with Link">
<HTML>
<HEAD><TITLE>What Was That Link?</TITLE>
<LINK HREF="TOC.SGM"    REL="ISTOC">
<LINK HREF="EX12.SGM"   REL="ISPREV">
<LINK HREF="EX14.SGM"   REL="ISNEXT">
<LINK HREF="INDEX.SGM"  REL="INDICE">
</HEAD>
```

You insist that TOC stands for "table of contents". Your neighbor insists on using "ISTOC" to mean the same thing. We hope you work out a compromise, and users need only have one browser to deal with both of your document sets. In worst cases, the neighbor is actually on the other side of the world, and can't be convinced to do it your way.

Bonus:

Figure 22. One could construct another, very similar example that points to a glossary, and then watch in Panorama as that specific attribute value makes for specialized handling. Load the sample file, htmlink1.sgm and choose "Buttons" from the Styles menu.

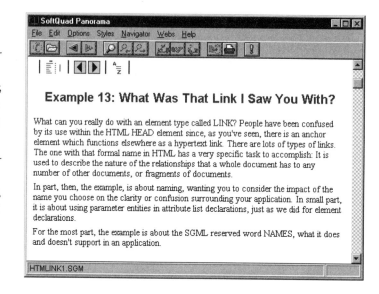

But Wait, There's More...

If you examine *htmlink1.dtd* and *htmlink1.sgm*, you'll discover that I have included some additional declarations beyond what is explained in this example to make the icons appear. What I neglected to tell you was how the icons are generated for the LINK elements — using external entities and a data content notation, which will both be explained in Example 27 (*Turn off the Lights!*) on page 253. This example and the next one are the only examples in the book in which I use something in the sample files that isn't explained immediately.

❧ EXAMPLE 14

On Being Specific

Goal of the Example:

This example illustrates an editorial position. In the previous application, you could choose any names you wanted for the keywords in the attribute values of `rel` and `rev`. Allowing any names at all means everyone can create their own special `rel` and `rev` attributes, and of course do interesting things with them. However, for any software application that interprets those names, having a fixed set makes life considerably easier than having to somehow interpret *any* term that comes along. Enforcing a strict *and closed* list of potential attribute values means that all browser makers can interpret them the same way, knowing precisely what they can expect to run into in the documents they'll meet. This example serves to show that you can control the possible attributes of `rel` and `rev` by declaring a set of fixed names for them.

Which brings us to Murray's third law of open information management: *Developing and observing standards is the way to help everyone share the information infrastructure with dozens, hundreds, thousands, or millions of people.*

Goal of the Application:

- To provide suitable markup for a browser to offer special services based on the nature of the relationship that one document has to another.
- To provide markup so that editing software can leave a record of relationships established among documents during their creation.
- To provide suitable markup for other SGML software to offer special services that go beyond simply browsing.

Is Influenced by/Builds on:

This example changes only two parameter entities from the previous example, *htmlink1.dtd*. The rel and rev values that are used in this example are taken from an Internet Draft written by Murray Maloney and Liam Quin as part of the HTML Working Group. The draft expired in 1996, but its content is being used by the W3C HTML ERB for new work on HTML.

Stored on the Accompanying Disk as:

Sample DTD: *htmlink2.dtd*

Sample Instance: *htmlink2.sgm*

Example 14 — On Being Specific

Step by Step:

We begin by redeclaring the parameter entities that were at the core of the previous example. This time we give each of them specific names or keywords. A clever browser is presumed to have an understanding of these terms and to act upon them in differing ways.

```
<!ENTITY % relType "INDEX | TOC | NEXT | PREV">
<!ENTITY % revType "BIBLIO | SUMMARY">
```

These parameter entities are used in the attribute definition list declaration for the LINK element type:

```
<!ATTLIST link name  ID       #IMPLIED
               href  CDATA    #REQUIRED
               title CDATA    #IMPLIED
               rel   %relType; #IMPLIED
               rev   %revType; #IMPLIED>
```

The first example from the previous section conforms to this DTD:

```
<!DOCTYPE html PUBLIC "Simplified HTML with Link 2">
<HTML>
<HEAD>
<LINK HREF="TOC.SGM"      REL="TOC">
<LINK HREF="EX13.SGM"     REL="PREV">
<LINK HREF="EX15.SGM"     REL="NEXT">
<LINK HREF="INDEX.SGM"    REL="INDEX">
<LINK HREF="GLOSSARY.SGM" REL="GLOSSARY">
<LINK HREF="SUMMARY.SGM"  REL="SUMMARY">
```

Admittedly, this instance is exactly like the previous example. The difference is subtle but crucial. In this example, an application that works with this document type (whether a browser or publishing system) can be programmed to treat the target document as a table of contents if the value of the rel attribute is "TOC". The processor can act accordingly, popping a "Table of Contents" button onto a toolbar, for example. Similarly, the toolbar can show buttons for the next and previous chapters, and a button for the book's index.

Hypertext link relationships

Here is a new attribute definition list declaration that provides a more extensive set of useful `rel` and `rev` values — with a bit more expressive power:

```
<!ENTITY % relType "FIRST  | LAST     | NEXT    | PREV
                    |CHILD  | SIBLING  | PARENT  | TOP
                    |BIBLIO | GLOSSARY |INDEX    | TOC
                    |COPYRT | TRADEMK  | TRANS   | SUMMARY">

<!ENTITY % revType "FIRST  | LAST     | NEXT    | PREV
                    |CHILD  | SIBLING  | PARENT  | TOP
                    |BIBLIO | GLOSSARY |INDEX    | TOC
                    |COPYRT | TRADEMK  | TRANS   | SUMMARY">
```

You've seen a few of these already. Let's review them briefly and speculate on the ways that a useful browser could assist a curious reader.

The first set of values — FIRST|LAST|NEXT|PREV — are links through a sequence, such as the chapters in a book. Presumably a busy reader might want to extract the gist of a book from the introduction and summary — for example, the first and last nodes in a book. The next set of values — CHILD|SIBLING|PARENT|TOP — are links to nearby nodes in a tree-like structure of information.

The next set — BIBLIO|GLOSSARY|INDEX|TOC — are links to components that contain related information. The bibliography and glossary might be a part of the current document, or they might be shared among a set of documents on the same subject or from the same publisher. The index and table of contents are navigational tools that are usually tied closely to the document.

The penultimate set — COPYRT|TRADEMK — are links to information that wants to say something about the information in the document. The copyright notice asserts authority over the document, the disclaimer limits responsibility, and the trademark notice assigns fair credit for trademarked terms or icons.

Finally we come to the last values in our list — TRANS|SUMMARY — which are links between one document and a translation into another language (natural or otherwise), and a summary of the document. The utility of a link to a translation is obvious to any non-native language speaker who has been faced with an unintelligible document. A clever hypertext system would alert the reader to the existence of a translation in their first language. And a summary is what you have just read.

Example 14 — On Being Specific

Bonus:

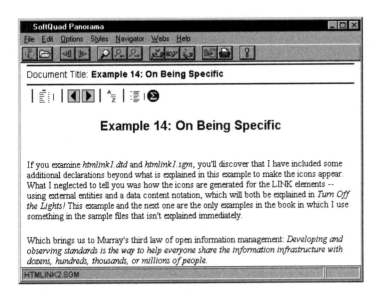

Figure 23. The demo file, htmlink2.sgm, shows off a small set of button functions built on the attributes of the LINK element type.

As I mentioned at the end of the previous example, if you examine *htmlink2.dtd* and *htmlink2.sgm*, you'll discover that I have included some additional declarations beyond what is explained in this example to make the icons appear in Panorama. What I neglected to tell you was how the icons are generated for the LINK elements — using external entities and a data content notation, which will both be explained in Example 27 (*Turn off the Lights!*) on page 253.

But wait, there's more...

One of the proposals for HTML (after HTML 3.2) is the addition of a class attribute to many of the element types. The goal is to allow certain element types to perform multiple roles in a document (that is, to allow certain markup to be reusable even when the elements it is demarcating are clearly quite different from one another).

This is a practical approach for HTML browsers, given their inherent difficulty with extensions. Its intention, in part, is to make HTML more useful without having to accommodate as many declared element types as are really useful. For example, instead of creating <FOOTNOTE>, <WARNING>, and <NOTE> element types, the suggested approach encourages the use of <P CLASS="FOOTNOTE">, <P CLASS="WARNING">, and <P CLASS="NOTE">.

The proposal does *not* anticipate a fixed set of defined classes. This means, of course, that anyone can invent a class for an element type, and build a style sheet for the browser to support that class, and not really care or notice whether other people support the same or any other interpretation of that class attribute.

❧ EXAMPLE 15

No Anchor is an Island

Goal of the Example:

Here we go further with the attributes introduced in the previous section, demonstrating the processing semantics involved with having the same attributes associated with a different element type (<LINK> in the previous example, <A> in this one).

At the same time, we continue to extend the HTML capabilities of the sample DTDS, picking up and explaining other attributes for the A element type.

Goal of the Application:

- To allow individual anchor elements to demonstrate and act upon *their* relationships to other objects by adding the rel and rev attributes to the HTML A ("anchor") element type.
- To use additional attributes on the HTML anchor element type to allow you to know the title of a linked document without having to retrieve it; to record the machine- and system-independent unique identifier (the Uniform Resource Name) for the target of a one-way link; and to record the name of any display or functional operation that may act upon the link (the *methods*).

Is Influenced by/Builds on:

The example continues to explore the HTML DTD by adding small pieces of incremental functionality to previous examples. In this case it adds a useful set of HTML attributes to the anchor element type.

Stored on the Accompanying Disk as:

Sample DTD: htmlanch.dtd

Sample Instance: htmlanch.sgm

Step by Step:

Everything in the DTD stays the same as the previous example except that we augment the attribute definition list declaration for HTML "anchors" (the A element type) with the rel and rev attributes previously associated only with the LINK element type, and with three other attributes, urn, title and methods.

```
<!ATTLIST a name    ID       #IMPLIED
            href    CDATA    #IMPLIED
            rel     %relType #IMPLIED
            rev     %revType #IMPLIED
            urn     CDATA    #IMPLIED
            title   CDATA    #IMPLIED>
```

Example 15 — No Anchor is an Island

Some Attributes You Can Use on an Anchor

name

Name of this anchor. We've met this one before. Our DTD differs from the standard HTML 3.2 in that it uses the SGML keyword ID to ensure that it is unique within the bounds of its document.

href

Address of hypertext anchor. The basic HTML hypertext addressing mechanism, which all Web users know and love.

rel

Describes the relationship of the target anchor to the current anchor. As with the previous examples, rel lets us announce that the current anchor links into part of a set, or that it leads to the next or previous member in a sequence, or has a special semantic relationship. For example, in the following anchor, the target anchor is the complete copyright notice:

```
<A [...] REL="COPYRIGHT">Copyright 1996</A>
```

rev

Describes the relationship of the anchor to the destination. The value of the rev attribute may seem redundant, since it is simply used to describe the relationship in the opposite direction. However, the inverse relationship may be helpful in further qualifying a complex set of relationships. The utility of this becomes apparent when you consider managing dozens, hundreds or even thousands of documents in a set. For example, if you kept all of your footnotes in separate documents, without a link to point back a document could become orphaned. The following anchor is declaring that it contains the footnote content of the target anchor:

```
<A NAME="FN107" REV="FOOTNOTE" HREF="...">
```

urn

Permanent address of the target anchor. Much work is going on in research circles trying to solve a very basic problem: the Web's URL mechanism is inflexible and direct. Using a URL has been likened to telling someone to get a book from the library's seventh floor, on the third stack to the left, on the middle shelf, fourth book from the end of the row. The book may be there, but there is no certainty that it will be, or even that library will.

The URN is intended to solve this problem much the same way that ISBN and ISSN numbering schemes do for books and magazines, by creating a machine- and location-independent unique identifier for the document in question. When the URN research task is complete, implementors will be faced with getting agreement on a URN "resolution" service — a mechanism to translate a unique identifier into a particular URL that gets the closest copy of a document, or one in a language you want, or one that otherwise answers the question "Which copy of Shakespeare's *Hamlet* do you want?"

title

Title of the target anchor. Today the only way to find out the name of the target document is to click on a link and go there. Alternatively, the `title` attribute lets the author of a document also offer its readers a hint (beyond just the URL) of the target by incorporating it's title into the source link. This is not widely implemented, but one can imagine browsers displaying the title of a document you can traverse to in addition to or in place of its frequently-cryptic URL.

Example 15 — No Anchor is an Island

Classy Links

In the following sample document, we'll see two different uses of these anchor attributes:

```
<!DOCTYPE HTML PUBLIC "Simplified HTML Anchor-with-REL/REV">
<HTML>
<HEAD>
<TITLE>Just a Busy Busy File</TITLE></HEAD>
<BODY>
<H2>Start with an H2 Head for Genteel Classiness</H2>
<P>Designers, in an article in <IT>Working Web</IT> magazine entitled
<A NAME="DESIGN" HREF="HTTP://WWW.EXAMPLE.EDU/PAPERS/DESIGN_STRAT.SGML"
REV="BIBLIOENTRY" URN="ISSN//135-3453-443//VOL7 ISSUE12//PP 102-110//EN"
TITLE="DESIGN STRATEGIES FOR PAGES THAT ZING">Design Strategies for
Pages that Zing</A>, claim that the H1 heading is simply too large
for use with the other default type sizes in most browsers and
therefore too jarring to use in a well-designed page. Accordingly,
they suggest (and naturally I've therefore used), the subtler H2.</P>
```

In the sample anchor above, the name attribute allows other links (either in the current document or others) to point to this specific anchor. The href attribute is the pointer to the target anchor. The rev attribute explains that this link has a bibliographic entry relationship to the target article — that is, this link contains all the information you need to refer to the "Design Strategies…" article. This information includes the urn attribute value (which is non-functional here, and written using a fictional syntax, but which expresses the notion that pieces of the permanent record, such as published articles, deserve a better address than a transitory and fragile URL).

The value of the `title` attribute, the name of the target anchor's document, is duplicating the name in the actual text, but might not always do so. People frequently refer to anchors without including their names, as in the continuation of the example:

```
<P>They use the term <A NAME="ZEIT1"
HREF="HTTP://WWW.EXAMPLE.EDU/GLOSSARY.SGML#ZEIT"
REL="GLOSSARY" URN="ISBN//1234-2341-1234//FIX THIS//EN"
TITLE="THE DESIGNER'S GLOSSARY" METHODS="SEARCH">zeitgeist</A> to mean
the full-blown sensation that comes from an exquisitely created Web
site, comparing that sensation with the subtle but powerful way in which
every issue of a well-designed magazine lets you know that it is part of
a sequence of other issues. Even though they may contain completely
different content, somehow you know that they're part of the larger,
breathing entity that makes up that magazine over time.</P>

<P>Strictly speaking, this example article, as interesting as it is,
has gone on long enough to make its point, which is simply to show off
two different uses of the anchor element type andits attributes.</P>
</BODY>
</HTML>
```

In the anchor for "zeitgeist", the name attribute is again serving as the unique identifier so other anchors can point here. The `href` attribute now takes us not just to another file, but to the element with the unique identifier "zeit" which presumably is the glossary definition for the term "zeitgeist". The `rel` attribute makes it clear that the document at the other end of the link is a glossary; the urn is another unique name. The value of the `title` attribute (the name of the target document) does not appear anywhere else in the document, so could be displayed as a useful notification to a reader, technology permitting.

Example 15 — No Anchor is an Island

Bonus:

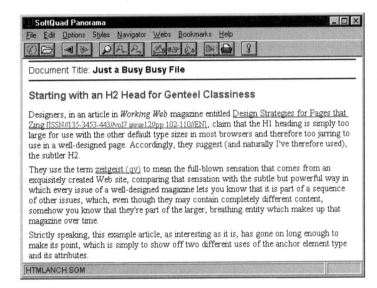

Figure 24. Comparing the use of the htmlanch.sgm file in Panorama and the identical (except for file extension) htmlanch.htm in a Web browser, you'll see that I've tried to show off a little of the functionality you might associate with the additional knowledge you get from the new anchor attributes.

Of course the hyperlinks won't work with this sample file because the URLs are fictional.

But wait, there's more...

You've already been promised that we will revisit the whole business of metadata later in the book. The relationships among sets of documents are a critical part of that picture. Similarly, there is a strong tie between the metadata research work and URN research. The URN is recognized as a vital piece of metadata that must be designed, supported technologically, and exploited widely.

How Far We've Come in This Chapter

In the next chapters, we take for granted the use of the EMPTY keyword. More importantly, we recognize that allowing *non-SGML data entities* into a document gives us an extraordinary flexibility: we can locate and provide processing attributes for *any kind of content* we want, knowing that the processing system can call for third-party software (a "helper" application as they're often called on the Web) to perform the required display, or action, or other functionality.

This very general capability is what allows us to embed graphics formats, audio-visual and video clips, scripts in programming languages such as Sun's Java, and three-dimensional images stored as Virtual Reality Markup Language (VRML). It's not up to the SGML markup to somehow "deal with" those foreign formats; rather we can use SGML constructs, such as attributes, to store, dimensions, durations, cropping and scaling values, pointers to the source file and a keyword to indicate the type of format — all aspects of multi-media objects that sorely need consistency in their storage and presentation.

We were introduced to simple phrases used as comments inside a DTD. In fact, they can be quite complex, multi-line, and carry very useful information. They can also be used to separate a DTD into meaningful sections, divisions that help one to make sense of the overall shape of a DTD. We'll see all this in the next chapter.

◆§ Chapter 5

We'll Take the High Road...

Extending HTML, Even If You're Not Netscape, Microsoft or the World Wide Web Consortium

As a matter of fact, the *World Wide Web Consortium* (W3C) has established the HTML Editorial Review Board (ERB) as a forum for a small group of technical experts, representing a broad cross-section of the network publishing market, to carry on the formal specification of HTML. The ERB, chaired by Dan Connolly, includes active members from *Adobe, Apple*, HP, IBM, *Microsoft, Netscape, Novell, Pathfinder, SoftQuad, Spyglass, Sun*, and W3C itself. The group meets quarterly to develop, review and comment on proposals aimed at enhancing the HTML language and its capabilities. The group has worked on completing specifications for embedded objects, extending forms capabilities, and creating design capabilities with CSS1 cascading style sheets. The group developed the HTML 3.2 DTD, code named "Wilbur", to document *recommended practice* — what is widely used on the World Wide Web and supported by the member organizations — as of January 1996. The same group is expecting to go on to write the "Cougar" specification or the HTML 4.0 DTD and so on.

As a matter of opinion, the ERB is a virtual committee, a set of far-flung, world-travelling, telecommuting volunteers who are doing the hard job of creating formal specifications, made all the more complicated by the fact that time doesn't stand still. By the time that the specification for the recent HTML 3.2 DTD was written and more or less agreed upon, most major suppliers of HTML software — makers of browsers or editors, providers of online services — were well on their way to adding many major bits and pieces of functionality (that is: further element types and supported attribute values) beyond what the HTML 3.2 specification calls for.

Done right, this is a good thing. Public experiments are the core of progress for network publishing, and experimenting with additional markup (and its associated functionality) gives both developers and users a chance to gauge the value of proposed extensions.

Nothing is really quite this simple. Someone does an experiment which may or may not have broad appeal to communities of software vendors, creators and users. Nonetheless, with a pool of existing documents using the extension, the extension becomes a candidate for the next version of HTML. The opportunity is to have extensions, created by anyone, anywhere, with any sort of reasonable support, end up in common practice or in the next version of HTML. The risk is that the HTML specification could grow into a large, cumbersome free-for-all, with no discernible architecture to support it.

But, you might argue, the opposite would be worse! The Internet is the home of experimentation, exciting growth of capability in any number of simultaneous directions, and anything that one does to stifle such growth, would be not just a mistake, but a blow at the very principles that made the Internet into the vibrant virtual laboratory that it is.

Of course, extensions created by large corporations with clout are in a somewhat different category. *Microsoft* has published extensions to HTML which are the core of a full SGML representation of pages created for its multi-media browser. And in fairness, the world's largest software company has been rather circumspect in presenting its extensions as bona fide SGML applications to the Internet community for comment. *Netscape*, known for extending HTML and then telling the rest of us about it, wavers between being occasionally serious about SGML representation of its extensions and public diffidence.

Stop! You're Both Right.
So How Do We Make HTML Extensible?

The answer in this case is unusual: *Change the question.*

The real problem is *not* that various groups have extended HTML. Users of the Web have asked for more and more capability, and "extenders" are responding to market demand. Indeed, most of the responsible parties have been very good about publishing details about the nature of their extensions so that others can readily create documents that exercise them; indeed other software implementors can learn enough (or nearly enough) to implement the same capabilities themselves.

The problem is that mere words cannot do justice to describing when and how the extensions may be used. What's really needed is a clear, scientific description language; what's often called a *grammar*, that can unambiguously specify the use of the extension or extensions. As luck would have it, this is what full SGML provides.

The use of the term "extension" has really no meaning when you're thinking about full SGML. Any DTD can declare *any* set of element types and attributes and still formally conform to the requirements of SGML. It can begin (for example) with HTML and

- add new structures by declaring new element types
- add new controls or characteristics by declaring new attributes
- remove existing element types
- remove existing attributes and potential attribute value, and
- re-declare the content of existing element types.

The examples in this chapter will illustrate all of these mechanisms.

The Formalities. I Do Declare!

Careful readers will recollect that an SGML document includes both a document type definition and a document instance that conforms to it. To be more precise, a document instance begins with the set of declarations that defines the rules to which it adheres. A declaration, you will recall, is simply a kind of equation. The term on the "left" of the equation, the term being *declared*, is established as the equivalent of the parameters on the "right". For example:

```
<!ELEMENT body (chapter+)>
```

simply says that the element type BODY stands for a collection of one of more CHAPTER elements.

As we've seen previously, a document type declaration works much the same way. I could write the following declaration at the top of a document:

```
<!DOCTYPE book
[
<!ELEMENT body        (chapter+)>
<!ELEMENT chapter     (title, para*)>
<!ELEMENT (title | para) (#PCDATA)>
]>
```

This is a document type declaration that includes a declaration subset (between the square brackets). This is the moral, spiritual and technical equivalent of a statement equating BOOK with the declared element types that comprise it. Interestingly, this in turn is the equivalent of

```
<!DOCTYPE book SYSTEM "sample.dtd">
```

where a file is stored on the system as *sample.dtd* (also a declaration subset) contains the following set of declarations:

```
<!ELEMENT body     (chapter+)>
<!ELEMENT chapter  (title, para*)>
<!ELEMENT (title | para) (#PCDATA)>
```

We could go further. Both of those are the equivalent of:

```
<!DOCTYPE book SYSTEM "sample.dtd"
[
<!ELEMENT (title | para) (#PCDATA)>
]>
```

where the file stored on the system as *sample.dtd* contains the following pair of declarations:

```
<!ELEMENT body    (chapter+)>
<!ELEMENT chapter (title, para*)>
```

Notice the critical detail; the declaration subset embedded in the document type declaration in the SGML document entity that contains the document instance may augment or modify the declaration subset stored in the separate file. We could in fact have a DTD stored on the system as *extend.dtd* whose contents is as follows:

```
<!ELEMENT body    (chapter+)>
<!ELEMENT chapter (%text;)*>
```

The SGML document entity would begin like this:

```
<!DOCTYPE book SYSTEM "extend.dtd"
[
<!ENTITY % text    "title | para | note">
<!ELEMENT (%text;) (#PCDATA)>
]>
```

As you can guess, the effect of this mechanism is to allow you, *within the document entity,* to declare *or re-declare* element types, with or without using parameter entities.

This is better than useful — this is good clean fun. Early in this chapter you will see methods of declaring new element types and attributes within an HTML DTD. In the example following you will see that we can perform interesting transformations on that DTD without changing a single character in the file that contains it. All the changes can be made in the declaration subset before the document instance. Both of these methods have the same effect. *They extend* HTML *in a formal, standardized manner. Any* SGML *application will read the* DTD *and declaration subset and understand precisely the new markup that has been declared, and how it may be used.*

Not all the examples in this chapter use the declaration subset mechanism; some of the extensions are dramatic enough to require creating a new DTD. The subset mechanism will be discussed in the next example — and never again appear in this book! We'll continue to explore the creation and use of DTDs in the section entitled *Put a Little Hierarchy into Your Life* (p. 153).

❧ EXAMPLE 16

Striding off into the Subset

Goal of the Example:

The absolutely simplest case of extending HTML in a formal, standardized way is to announce, in the *prolog* to a document, what new markup you want to use. The example demonstrates practical uses of the idea, described in the previous section, that element type declarations in the declaration subset can override those in an external DTD.

Goal of the Application:

Our sample hypothetical Web documents are used to describe handling of hazardous waste materials. In documents such as these, it is critical that you be able to draw the reader's attention to information warning them of certain risks, or advising them of required procedures. The sample application allows us to declare available levels of warning in the declaration subset before the document instance — without touching the original DTD.

Is Influenced by/Builds on:

The example builds directly on the *htmsimpl.dtd* from the previous chapter. Of particular interest is that this method allows us to change the markup available to us on a document by document basis, if necessary!

Stored on the Accompanying Disk as:

Sample DTD: *htmsimpl.dtd*

Sample Instance: *subset1.sgm*

Step by Step:

Let's create a file called *subset1.sgm*. We really are going to move beyond HTML, even without physically altering the DTD. Include the document type declaration as you see it below. We'll modify it in a moment:

```
<!DOCTYPE html PUBLIC "Simplified HTML">
<HTML>
<BODY>
<H1>Attaching New Heads As Needed</H1>
<P>In this example, we declare a value for the parameter entity
for headings, that overrides the value declared in the DTD.</P>

<P>Here's that warning heading we're working to accommodate:</P>

<WARNHEAD>Urgent! Read this first!</WARNHEAD>

<P>Please do not flush when train is in station.
Close cover before striking. Mind your head.
Max headroom -- 48 points.</P>
</BODY>
</HTML>
```

Now the fun part starts. As you saw early in this chapter, a DTD actually consists of what we've been thinking of as the DTD (in a source file) *as well as* additional declarations in the declaration subset.

Example 16 — Striding off into the Subset

Change the opening line of *subset1.sgm* to the following:

```
<!DOCTYPE html PUBLIC "Simplified HTML" [
<!ENTITY % heading" "h1|h2|h3|h4|WARNHEAD">
]>
```

Everything between the square brackets is the declaration subset. All the lines in this example comprise the document type declaration.

Bonus:

Save the file. Fire up Panorama. Open *subset1.sgm*. The effect is *exactly the same* as if we had modified the %heading; declaration in the DTD itself.

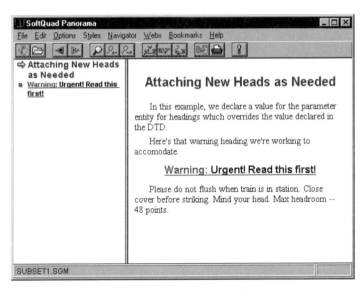

Figure 25. By a happy coincidence, WARNHEAD seems to have style characteristics associated with it already.

Normally when you invent a new element type you're also responsible for ensuring that it gets represented properly, either by creating a style sheet, or if you're a browser maker, perhaps building in the new display or functionality that's appropriate.

Going through Another Pretty Phrase

Goal of the Example and the Application:

One of the reasons for HTML's great resilience is that, for the most part, it defines element types that are publication-oriented. That is, it takes the approach that what Web users have in common is a desire to present their information using the traditional display components that have been with us for centuries — paragraphs, headings, lists, tables, cross-references and so on. Of course it also adds new and exciting *capabilities* to those, particularly in terms of live, dynamic cross-references. These components are thought of in the SGML community as being marked up text with *publication markup*.

But there is a second, vastly different (and many would say, vastly more interesting) approach to marking up information: *information content tagging*, the encoding of information so that it indicates what it is in terms of *the role it plays* in its environment, rather than how it looks or works on paper or on screen. Examples may make the distinction clearer:

Publication-structure Element Types	Information-content Element Types
Paragraph	Warning
Section	Abstract
Italic	Book Title
Bold	Part Number
List/List Items	Task/Procedures

For some people, the greatest contribution that full SGML brings is that it opens the Web up to information-content tagging. Suddenly you are free to call any piece of information by a name that need not compromise. Content can be marked up to indicate precisely what it is or does, instead of sharing a generalized name with information of a different sort. This exercise shows how to add meaningful content-oriented markup to the publication-structure markup now present in HTML.

Strictly speaking, a number of the element types in HTML, as it is today, do fall into the category of information-content tagging. They include, for instance, KBD (what you're to type on a keyboard), CODE (part or all of a computer program), SAMP, MENU, DIR and so forth. These element types are a legacy of the Web's origins in the world of computer engineering, and Dan Connolly's role as an author of HTML 2.0 while employed with HaL.

What Does Information-content Tagging Give You?

1. Bounded Searches

Searches that take into account the information structures represented by the markup. A reference to "sulfuric acid" may be more important to you in a "Warning" than in a simple "paragraph". You may be more interested in a reference to "safety procedures" in a "Chapter Title" in an aircraft operating manual than to find every reference in the whole manual. In the modern world of infoglut, we need *anything* that can help find *the right search hits* instead of the most hits.

On the sample disk, open *panodemo.sgm* in the *panodemo* folder. Search for "SGML". Notice how many hits you get by looking at the occurrence density display towards the right-hand edge of the screen. Now go back to your search command and search for "SGML IN <ST>" ("section titles"). The second search gives you only two hits, a much clearer picture of which sections of the document are most likely to be relevant. (And this is just a small document ...)

Example 17 — Going through Another Pretty Phrase

2. Meaningful Units of Retrieval

The traditionally non-databased realm of documents — as they move into databases (with the attendant benefits of management, workflow, check-in/check-out procedures, and so on) — deserves also to take advantage of meaningful units of retrieval.

Imagine that the sample file introduced in this section is actually part of a very long text describing hundreds of software products. They're stored in an SGML database and displayed across the Web in response to a query.

Let's say you ask your browser to find the product "Cheers". That is, locate "Cheers" when it appears in a PRODUCT element, or in a database field that holds the product name. Ideally, you would not have to know anything about the actual markup however. When it is found, you don't really want to retrieve just the line as typed into the example:

```
<PRODUCT>Cheers</PRODUCT> has been reduced
```

Instead, you would want the browser to show you the document context in which "Cheers" is found. You might ask for just the paragraph in which the entry appears, or every section where it is mentioned in a parts catalog. With SGML *tagging in the content, you have enough structure to build intelligence into your information.*

The implications of this are breathtaking: Parts of documents, stored in flat file systems or elaborate relational databases, can be served up in whatever containers make sense for the task at hand. A writer can get a paragraph or a press release for editing, a technician can call up a maintenance procedure, or an engineer can view all of the parts lists that mention a specific part by name. Everyone can access the information that they need — in a suitable context.

3. Formatting Distinctions

I've argued elsewhere many times that when you use a wordprocessor to makes something italic, you *lose* information. In our example, the markup tells us that the author knew that "Cheers" was a product name, or the name of a restaurant, or of a TV show. Arguably, the author succeeded in distinguishing the product name from other words in the text, but "Cheers" in an italic typeface offers no help to a computer that doesn't know who Ted Danson and Rhea Perlman are.

In plain vanilla HTML, distinctions are lost.

On a printed page, in one paragraph, I could have five phrases in italic that are quite distinct:

- a title (such as "*The* SGML *Handbook*", "*The Great Escape*", "*Don Giovanni*", "*The National News*" or "*New Prices from...*")
- a foreign expression (such as "*je ne sais quoi*" or "*arrivaderci*")
- a cross-reference (such as "in Chapter 5" or "see Part Number B9LMN8")
- some emphasized or emphatic text (such as "Priced to *leap* off the shelf..." or "**Good news** from ...")
- the name of a piece of software (such as "Cheers", "SoftQuad Panorama PRO", "Microsoft Internet Explorer" or "Netscape Navigator")

Figure 26. Distinctions are lost on the printed page.

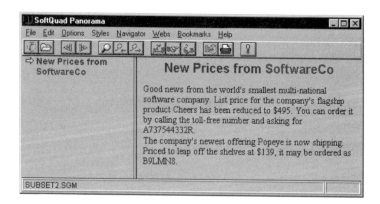

Example 17 — Going through Another Pretty Phrase

If I had more display capability, it might be appropriate to create unique markup for each of these, and to associate each element type with distinct formatting—and perhaps distinct actions. For example:

- Titles are perhaps bold italics, maybe in green.
- Foreign expressions can stay as regular text — perhaps linked to a Glossary.
- Cross-references can be, in the default style of the Web, underlined and blue.
- Emphasis could stay italic, or become bold, or purple (in a kid's book for instance).
- The name of the software could be bright red, slightly larger than the surrounding type, and dropped below the base line of the surrounding type.

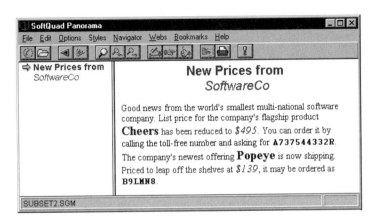

Figure 27. Semantic markup for distinguished information.

Is Influenced by/Builds on:

While this example builds directly on the *htmsimpl.dtd*, the concepts it presents were first popularized by the United States Air Force, through its SGML initiative entitled the "Content Data Model", part of the CALS work. This was the application that first raised the possibility that the documentation for an airplane might be made up of pieces which matched, one-to-one, the pieces of the plane.

Stored on the Accompanying Disk as:

Sample DTD: *htmsimpl.dtd*

Sample Instance: *subset2.sgm*

Step by Step:

In this example, we'll add information-content tagging for our manufacturing sales group to a set of element types that may appear (nearly) anywhere in HTML.

In the original DTD, *htmsimpl.dtd*, the TEXT parameter entity includes #PCDATA as well as B and I element types for highlighting of textual content as follows:

```
<!ENTITY % text        "#PCDATA | b | i">
```

We're simply going to re-declare it for our purposes. Accordingly, here is our new document type declaration:

```
<!DOCTYPE html PUBLIC "Simplified HTML" [
<!ENTITY % font        "b | i">
<!ENTITY % phrase      "partnum|price|mfgname|product">
<!ENTITY % text        "#PCDATA | %font; | %phrase">
<!ELEMENT (%font;)     (#PCDATA)>
<!ELEMENT (%phrase;)   (#PCDATA)>
]>
```

In this case we've been so daring as to throw away the element types that were previously allowed in %text;. We could, of course, as in WARNHEAD in the previous section, simply add our new element types to the existing set. In this example, however, we're replacing them entirely.

Example 17 — Going through Another Pretty Phrase

Counterexample

Notice that this technique works if the element type names declared as the replacement text in a parameter entity are used only by reference to it. You cannot redeclare COUNTEREXAMPLE, in the example below and get the effect you want by re-declaring it with brand new content in a DTD that includes, for instance, the following declarations:

```
<!ENTITY % counterexample "orderedlist|unorderedlist">
<!ELEMENT para        (#PCDATA|%counterexample;)*>
<!ELEMENT orderedlist (listhead?,(number,item)+)>
<!ELEMENT unordered   (listhead, item+)>
```

Strictly speaking however, this is completely legitimate provided you re-declare the parameter entity *and* declare contents for your new list types. There's no rule against declaring ordered list and unordered list and never using them. In your declaration subset you have to do something along the lines of:

```
<!ENTITY % counterexample "numlist|bullist|alphalist">
<!ELEMENT (%counterexample;) (item+)>
```

The Document Instance That Uses the New Element Types

Now create a new file, *subset2.sgm*. Clearly it needs to incorporate the new document type declaration:

```
<!DOCTYPE html PUBLIC  "Simplified HTML"[
<!ENTITY % font       "b | i">
<!ENTITY % phrase     "partnum|price|mfgname|product">
<!ENTITY % text       "#PCDATA | %font; | %phrase">
<!ELEMENT (%font;)        (#PCDATA)>
<!ELEMENT (%phrase;)  (#PCDATA)>
]>
<HTML>
<BODY>
<H1>New Prices from <MFGNAME>Software Co</MFGNAME></H1>
<P>Good news from the world's smallest multi-national software company.
List price for the company's flagship product <PRODUCT>Cheers</PRODUCT>
has been reduced to <PRICE>$495</PRICE>. You can order it by calling
the toll-free number and asking for <PARTNUM>A737544332R</PARTNUM>.</P>

<P>The company's newest offering <PRODUCT>Popeye</PRODUCT> is now
shipping. Priced to leap off the shelves at <PRICE>$139</PRICE>, it
may be ordered as <PARTNUM>B9LMN8</PARTNUM>.</P>
</BODY>
</HTML>
```

If you're typing this in, type both paragraphs as written. Doing so will increase the drama of the styles display later. Save the file.

Example 17 — Going through Another Pretty Phrase

Bonus:

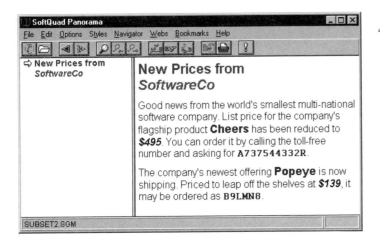

Figure 28. The "Vanilla" style sheet seems plain at first, but when you experience its subtle richness you may never go black again. The "Strawberry" style sheet, besides looking a bit seedy, is ripe with typographic presentation of semantics.

Check out *subset2.sgm*. Under the Styles menu, choose "Vanilla" and "Strawberry" styles and watch what happens. *Underneath, the* SGML *markup hasn't changed.*

But wait, there's no more...

There is no more! This is our last look at the subset. We now return to your regular scheduled program, working directly with DTDs. If you'd like to continue to explore making changes to DTDs from "outside", feel free to experiment with any of the sample DTDs. *Note that you can only re-declare parameter entities each time. You cannot re-declare any of the other declarations, although you can add new ones.*

We've seen that it is very simple to add lines to the declaration subset that override entity declarations in the DTD itself. *When would you ever want to modify the* DTD *when you can just perform overrides?* When the changes that you might make apply to all documents of a given type.

In this chapter, we will continue to modify the DTD in some very basic ways and then move to modifying the DTD in ways that you couldn't accomplish by redeclaring parameter entities or by declaring element types in the declaration subset.

Put a Little Hierarchy into Your Life

Goal of the Example:

After the previous chapter, you're used to uncovering parts of the HTML application, and using them outside of the context in which they were originally created — essentially just taking the parts that are most useful for the purpose at hand. Here we go further: we add element types to a heavily simplified subset of HTML in order to add capability that isn't normally there.

The example further demonstrates the use of containing elements — elements whose only purpose is to contain subelements. We've not previously made much fuss about a straightforward but important consideration. Perhaps you generally think of elements as holding data content — and vice versa. That is, if you want to identify some chunk of data as being *some type of object in particular*, then you wrap it with appropriate markup.

Element types that act as containers, however, appear at first glance to do the opposite. They may hold *nothing but* other elements. Their job is to group together elements at a certain part of a document's tree structure and allow them to be identified as one unit. The most common container structure (which we've seen already and have been taking for granted) is the list, which contains list items which may in turn contain either straight text or, for example, multiple paragraphs.

In this example, you'll see that the DIV element types (short for "division") are analogous to the hierarchical structures you'd find in a book: chapters, which contain sections, which contain subsections, and so on. Here a DIV element may contain either the normal textual content that you'd find in the BODY of an HTML document, or else one or more lower-level DIV elements.

Goal of the Application:

- To break a document up into logically nested components.
- To establish a straightforward method whereby, at any point in the document, an author may choose either

    - to insert paragraphs, anchors or text, or
    - to further divide the structure.

Is Influenced by/Builds on:

The specific naming convention — the idea of calling the containing elements DIVS — comes originally from Dave Raggett's 1994 draft specification for a future HTML, and divisions are now formally part of HTML 3.2. This example shows you one way to exploit their usefulness.

It would be an oversight not to mention that using containing elements in markup really builds on our intuitive sense of how documents work. Even though authors may use fewer keystrokes in marking up content if they *mark up* only the character data itself, rather than bothering with containers, in fact it is unnatural to ignore them. We all tend to think about collections of information, such as documents, in sections and subsections of some kind. Writers who organize their thoughts on paper or on computer screens invariably, and intuitively, imagine a structured outline of sentences, paragraphs, sections, titles, and parts of one type or another.

Stored on the Accompanying Disk as:

Sample DTD: *htmldiv.dtd*

Sample Instance: *htmldiv.sgm*

Example 18 — Put a Little Hierarchy into Your Life

Step by Step:

Early in the previous chapter, you were introduced to the notion of *containers*, when we divided the HTML DTD into HEAD and BODY. Now we go further and subdivide BODY into useful fragments. In effect, what we're doing is wrapping the H1, H2, H3, and H4 element types with the new DIV element types.

We pick up a large part of the DTD from the basic declarations we've been using:

```
<!ENTITY % heading "h1 | h2 | h3 | h4">
<!ENTITY % list    "ul | ol">
<!ENTITY % font    "b | i ">
<!ENTITY % phrase  "em | strong">
<!ENTITY % text    "#PCDATA | %font | %phrase;">
<!ENTITY % block   "a | p | %list;">
```

Note that, for the sake of simplicity, we're working only with four levels of heads although the actual HTML 2.0 DTD has six.

The critical new parameter entity is %block; which collects together the element types that serve, with the headings, as the basic contents of BODY.

```
<!ELEMENT html  (head, body)>
<!ELEMENT head  (title)>
<!ELEMENT title (#PCDATA)>
```

Nothing has really changed in the HEAD. It has become simpler again (without LINK) so as not distract us from the major point of the section, which is built on the declarations which follow here:

```
<!ELEMENT body (div+ |(%block;)+)>
<!ELEMENT div  ((h1|h2|h3|h4)?, (div+|(%block;)+))>
```

This is an interesting set of constructs. Each division begins with an optional heading, after which you have a choice:

- subdivide the division into lower level divisions, or
- insert any of the block elements.

Notice that headings can appear *only* at the beginning of a division.

This is a very strict DTD. Normally one might have wanted to loosen the rules up in order to allow %block; element types to appear before the first lower level division. That looser content model would look like this:

```
<!ELEMENT body (div+ |(%block;)+)>
<!ELEMENT div  ((h1|h2|h3|h4)?, (%block;)*, div*)>
```

Before we go any further, for comparison, we'll reprint the standard declaration for BODY:

```
<!ELEMENT body (%heading; | %block;)*>
```

Figure 29. *The tree view of this* DTD *illustrates the hierarchical structure introduced in this example. Documents created using this* DTD *may contain the usual mix of paragraphs, lists and anchors directly within a* BODY *element, but headings may only be used within a* DIV *element. Since a* DIV *element can contain nested* DIV *elements, documents can be structured like books — with chapters, sections and subsections.*

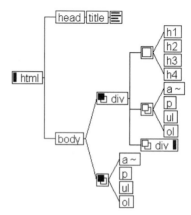

The big change in the new DTD is that %heading; is no longer allowed within BODY, at least directly. Instead, the headings now appear only at the beginning of division elements, rather than anywhere at all in the BODY.

Example 18 — Put a Little Hierarchy into Your Life

What we have gained is a structure that supports the following instance:

```
<BODY>
<DIV><H1>Example 18: Put a Little Hierarchy into Your Life</H1>
<DIV><H2>Goal of the Example:</H2>
<P>After the previous chapter, you're used to uncovering parts of
the HTML application, and using them outside of the context in
which they were originally created essentially just taking the
parts that are most useful for the purpose at hand. Here we go
further: we add element types to a heavily simplified subset of
HTML in order to add capability that isn't normally there.</P>

<DIV><H2>Goal of the Application:</H2>
<UL>
<LI>to break a document up into logically nested components</LI>
<LI>to establish a straightforward method whereby, at any point in
the document, an author may choose either to insert paragraphs,
anchors or text; or to further divide the structure.</LI></UL>
</DIV>

<DIV><H2>Is Influenced by/Builds on:</H2>
<P>The specific naming conventions -- the idea of calling the containing
elements DIVs -- comes originally from Dave Raggett's 1994 draft
specification for a future HTML, and divisions are now formally part
of HTML 3.2. This example shows you one way to exploit their usefulness.
</P>

<P>It would be an oversight to not mention that using containing
elements in markup really builds on our intuitive sense of how
documents work: Even though authors may use fewer keystrokes in
marking up content if they mark up only the content itself (rather
than containers), in fact it is unnatural to ignore them.</P>
</DIV></DIV></BODY>
```

There is one little detail that must be recognized in the example: everything between the start- and end-tags for each DIV is *contained* within that DIV. If there were no DIV markup, you might have to read the whole document to distinguish thematically connected content. The DIV elements are there precisely to make possible this logical grouping.

Meanwhile, in the Web World...

The DTD for HTML 2.0 supports several different interpretations of strictness in using markup, including a distinction between *recommended* and *deprecated* usage. (The DTD actually includes *duplicate sets of declarations* employing the SGML *marked section* construct which we'll discuss (p. 411) in *The SGML Primer*. Marked sections allow you to incorporate multiple versions of declarations in a DTD as well as multiple versions of content in a document instance.)

If we were to look at the declaration for %body.content; in the HTML 2.0 DTD (and being concerned only with the element types we're discussing here), we'd discover *two* slightly different content models from that of our example:

```
<!ENTITY % body.content "(%heading; | %block;)*">
```

HTML 2.0 recommends that the BODY element type consists of headings and block element types in any order. The *non-recommended* model for BODY adds %text; to that list. (I reprint its declaration as well.)

```
<!ENTITY % text          "#PCDATA | A | IMG | BR | %phrase; | %font;">
<!ENTITY % body.content "(%heading; | %text; | %block;)*">
```

The replacement text from %phrase; lists a number of element types that can appear within paragraphs, headings, and other block elements.

Example 18 — Put a Little Hierarchy into Your Life

The distinction between these two versions (or between the second one and the very formal use of DIV from our example) is quite dramatic: %heading; appears. Also, the declaration makes clear that headings, %text; (often simply called "percent text"), and the block elements, may appear in any number, in the BODY, in any order. This freedom has its advantages — the lack of restriction lets you interleave headings of any sort — pieces that you would expect to find only within paragraphs (such as B and I element types) and paragraphs themselves. In fact, including #PCDATA in %text; means you could, theoretically, create the following instance:

```
<H1>Heading</H1>
Text...
```

This is an example right out of the HTML 2.0 specification, accompanied by a note which indicates that the following version is preferred:

```
<H1>Heading</H1>
<P>Text...</P>
```

Why not simply allow the flexibility of the "deprecated" example? ("Deprecated" is an ISO expression for "discouraged".) Why am I being so old-fashioned as to think that straight text, bold and italic bits should happen only inside other elements, instead of standing alone? And if we go back to the *htmldiv.dtd,* why do I think there is a logical order for headings?

Advantages of Hierarchical Structure

Perhaps it's largely a question of personal taste, but beyond that (and recapping slightly), a hierarchically structured document has many advantages.

- Takes advantage of outliner software: It lets you manipulate whole fragments of a document, instead of highlighting a heading and scrolling until you find a sensible break point. In browsing software, this translates into navigational tools where a heading is not an isolated event, but is associated with the relevant piece of the document. Choose the heading and you choose the relevant section.
- Encourages a logically structured document, built on the principles that have worked for centuries: Chapters contain sections which contain sub-sections, and so on. We think, naturally, in such hierarchies and have for a long time. (Shakespeare's plays, for example, have acts, which contain scenes, which contain speeches, rather than a non-stop jumble of speeches broken only by occasional changes of location.)
- Supports the reusability of information in fragments by actually creating fragments. Without *containers*, all you really have in a document is a stream of text broken by arbitrarily named headings. With containers, if you want to copy, for instance, the section on "Supported Products" from your Web site, and use it on all appropriate pages, you need to pick up from the start of the DIV element right to its end-tag. Much simpler than having to scroll through gathering the relevant headings, images, tables, lists and paragraphs.
- Supports pointing to fragments: For example, imagine that you have a section of a Web document devoted to "The History of Markup". By associating attributes on that section with a keyword or cross-reference or index term, you are marking the entire section as being on that subject, not just the heading (which is how you would have to accomplish this in HTML 2.0 and other DTDs that don't use containing elements). Similarly, in a print publication, you would want an index entry to read (continuing this example) "markup, history of, pages 88–96". By associating the index entry with a < DIV > rather than an < H2 >, you can see that the index entry refers to the whole section.
- Allows, and perhaps encourages, the use of containing element boundaries to create more powerful search criteria.

Example 18 — Put a Little Hierarchy into Your Life

Bonus:

A sample navigator for this example (called *Table of Headings*) will appear on the Panorama Navigator menu when you load this file.

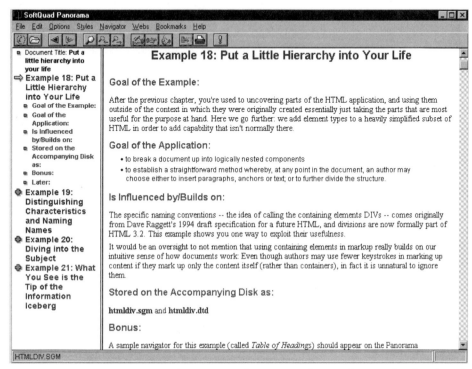

Figure 30. If you compare the navigator functionality introduced at the end of the previous chapter with that available in this example, you notice a not-very-subtle difference: The current sample navigator has "multiple levels". If you click on the plus sign in the outline view, it opens up to the containers below.

But wait, there's more...

As useful as the nested containers in the navigator are, they are only a small piece of the functionality containing elements bring. Later we'll see that searches based on containers allow us to be much more precise in finding information that we want. In any full-text search, there is a danger of being offered too many hits. By being able to say "Find 'landing gear' if it appears in a chapter title," you're able to avoid running into passing references to landing gear in footnotes and elsewhere, and just hone in on the critical data. Containing elements make such self-selection possible.

❧ CHAPTER 6

Leaving a Trail of Breadcrumbs

The World Wide Web, according to Tim Berners-Lee, includes the universe of networked information. That is quite a collection of information! (It isn't yet the *hyperdocument library system* that Douglas Engelbart envisioned decades ago.) What the Web currently lacks is a reliable catalog system and a standard way to provide information about information. There needs to be a way for a document creator to say what any document — or collection of documents — is about, who created it, when it was or should be published, and when it should be expired and withdrawn from publication. There needs to be a way for groups to work on a document and track who works on what, what changes are made, and for reviewers to be able to request changes.

For that information to to be useful to publishers and consumers, there must be a useful infrastructure to allow tools to manage it and locate it reliably. Certainly there are many proprietary document management tools and systems, but what the Web badly needs is standards-based tools for managing information — document control, link maintenance, revision history — and for search and retrieval of electronic information. The structures needed to facilitate these tasks can be readily expressed in SGML, and readily displayed in browsers.

SGML is suited to documents where the publisher wants to create appropriate markup for greater control over the display, for client-side processing, for a greater variety of link types, and for automatic generation of tables of figures or tables or contents. One can imagine browsing tools providing very specific functionality for specific families of markup. For example, a "card catalog" tool for library or museum holdings, or an "abstract service" tool for news and magazine articles.

In a future which includes an imponderable variety of file formats on the Web, it is crucial that a handful of extensible representations be widely available to support the actions that cross industry and applications boundaries. Some of these actions are:

- Resource discovery and retrieval
- Annotations and trails through other peoples' sites
- Document management, version control and revision history
- Effectivity control that provides alternate views of a single document
- Externalized links (essentially a database of links pointing into documents instead of the current model of embedded links)

The only information structuring language truly capable of supporting these horizontal requirements is SGML. My vision is that tools always recognize the boundaries of a given knowledge domain, that they continue to be optimized for work with formally standardized representations of information, not attempting to be all things to all people, but rather to provide the rendering for structured and accessible contents, and for structured and accessible information about contents — the so-called metadata.

Today SGML is making possible the use of the Web for very serious publication by people who understand the value of their information assets and who have, accordingly, chosen to store and manage that content in SGML. SGML can't solve all the Web's problems, but where extensible, unlimited textual markup will help, SGML is the answer.

As of this writing, a range of organizations, from the University of Michigan to the Text Encoding Initiative (a world-wide collaboration of humanist scholars) to *Intel Corporation* and the NASA/*Jet Propulsion Laboratories*, have put richly structured and complex documents on the Web. The U.S. *National Institute of Standards and Technology* (NIST) is collaborating with industry partners in a project to develop tools for creators of standards, particularly those people who are contributing to STEP (STandard for the Exchange of Product Data). A similar project is being undertaken in association with the News Industry Universal Text Format working group, a group of newspapers, wire services and other on-line providers for SGML representations of news industry metadata and articles.

This is only the beginning. At the time of this writing, small groups of experts working under the auspices of the IETF and the W3C are working on solutions to some of these problems. In the meantime, I hope that this chapter will help to expose the issues and offer some potential solutions.

Distinguishing Characteristics and Naming Names

Goal of the Example:

Systems of belief from time immemorial have established that you gain power from naming, from being able to call someone or something by his, or her, or its real name. As we saw in the previous example, you also gain control over information by recognizing and articulating what it is. This example demonstrates that capturing that knowledge in markup can be done with a tiny extension to a DTD.

This tiny metadata extension, propagated through the World Wide Web and supported by the simplest of bounded search tools would go a long way towards letting us find Web documents — the fancy term is "discover electronic resources" — that really are focussed on the specific topic we're seeking.

Goal of the Application:

- To offer information providers (authors, editors or publishers) a way to classify the subject or subjects of a document within the document itself, that is, to store a useful set of metadata inside the document, and to do so in a way which does not necessarily display inside a browser window.
- To offer support in the markup for the services readers need for useful searches of Web content searches based on categories such as "author", "publisher", or "date of publication", with which they are already familiar.

Is Influenced by/Builds on:

In March, 1995, Stuart Weibel of the Online Computer Library Center (OCLC), Joseph Hardin of the University of Illinois' National Center for Supercomputing Applications (NCSA), the birthplace of Mosaic, and I had the honor and pleasure of hosting 52 experts in electronic resource discovery at an Electronic Metadata Workshop (*http://www.oclc.org/research/Workshops/etc*). (Stu chaired the event.) One of the products of that working session was the information structure that I've transformed into the *metadata.dtd*. The current sample *keyword1.dtd*, is a gross simplification of that. As a true subset, however, it insists on creating documents that will conform to the parent DTD.

Stored on the Accompanying Disk as:

Sample DTD: *keyword1.dtd*

Sample Instance: *keyword1.sgm*

Example 19 — Distinguishing Characteristics and Naming Names

Step by Step:

If you're typing in the DTD, you'll notice that, like other samples, it's really a heavily simplified version of the previous HTML DTDs we've examined with a couple of new element type declarations. If you want to use this approach to storing and finding your documents, you can simply add the METADATA and SUBJECT element types to any DTD. Before we review how you'd do that, I would like to say that this sort of capability — the ability to narrow a search in a full-text database to contents that appear within a specific element — is available in middle- and high-end SGML database and browsing tools today, ranging from SoftQuad Explorer to OpenText PAT.

We're simply adding two new element types to what is allowed in the HEAD:

```
<!ELEMENT html     (head, body)>
<!ELEMENT head     (title, metadata?)>
<!ELEMENT title    (#PCDATA)>
<!ELEMENT metadata (subject)+>
<!ELEMENT subject  (#PCDATA)>
```

METADATA is the general catch-all element type that we use in the next two DTDs to hold all the information that is *about the information* that makes up the document instance. Although it will become much richer in its structure later, for now a META-DATA element can contain one or more SUBJECT elements. SUBJECT means the same as a *keyword*, but is slightly more ambiguous. That is, I chose to use the name *subject* because you might also imagine it is useful for formal terms used to classify the document, much like the "subject classification" cards at the good old library I grew up with. "Keyword", in that case, seemed more limited.

The DTD is darned simple. We're going to add subject elements to a document to help indexers classify it properly, and to help us find it later. The example is where the fun begins.

```
<HTML>
<HEAD><TITLE>Browsing Software Included with New SGML Book</TITLE>
<METADATA>
<SUBJECT>SGML on the Web: Small Steps Beyond HTML
<SUBJECT>computer software</SUBJECT>
<SUBJECT>SGML browsing software</SUBJECT>
<SUBJECT>SGML Internet interchange standard</SUBJECT>
<SUBJECT>HTML Internet interchange standard</SUBJECT>
</METADATA>
</HEAD>
<BODY>
<DIV><H1>"SGML on the World Wide Web" to Include Free Browser</H1>

<P>Before we begin, let me remind you that if you're looking at
this document in <I>SoftQuad Panorama</I>, be sure to check out
both style sheets. One will show you the file as if it were being
displayed in a traditional HTML browser, that is, with the contents
of the HEAD element invisible; and the other will reveal the metadata
so you can examine how the hierarchy works.</P>

<P>The most pleasurable aspect of this document is that its content
has to ensure that the metadata that was invented for it is accurate.
What I mean is: <B>Just because I tell you this document is about
a book which includes an SGML browser does that make it true?</B> If
not, of course, then the metadata may well serve the purposes of the
example if every way but the most important one.</P>

<P>I should certainly be showing you, by example, that metadata
is at its most valuable when it's accurate.</P>

<P>But in fact the metadata was chosen with a completely other
purpose in mind. I wanted to show you that one document could
quite sensibly require more than one <I>keyword</I> element, and that,
within the hierarchy of a structured keyword there might well be
a good reason to fork in the path, as the example does when it
insists that this book is about both HTML and SGML.</P>
</DIV></BODY></HTML>
```

Example 19 — Distinguishing Characteristics and Naming Names

Bonus:

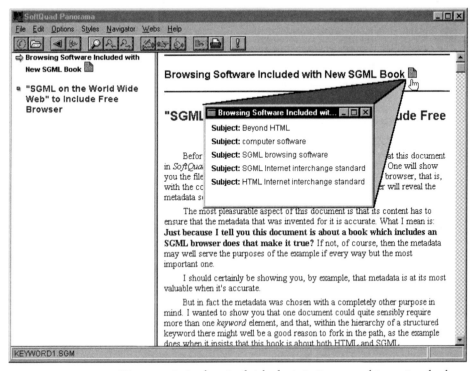

Figure 32. A simple pair of style sheets in Panorama lets us view the document as it would be seen in a Web browser that hides all the metadata behind an icon. When the icon is activated, with a mouse click, you are presented with a visible presentation of the subject classification elements.

◆§ EXAMPLE 20

Diving into the Subject

Goal of the Example:

Beyond the social goal (as we might call it) of creating techniques for finding electronic documents (on the Web or elsewhere), this section also recognizes and
describes one of the great SGML debates: *When do you use attributes to capture information and when do you use element types?*

The *keyword2.dtd* illustrates a useful trick — you can construct a DTD in such a
way that it may be used for documents which might not actually contain the contents they describe. That is, a document which conforms to this DTD could just act as
a "library card" for an external document which may not even be electronic. In fact,
the electronic metadata might refer to something that is not even a document — it
could be a painting or a Persian carpet. Later in this chapter, in Example 22 (*The
Combined Joys of Electronic Review and Machine Processing*) on page 191, the *htmlerd.dtd*
that appears is very similar in its potential usage, allowing you to store comments on
a document either directly within the document being reviewed, or in a separate file.

Step three of this example also introduces the "and connector" in element type
declarations, and demonstrates the use of the #FIXED keyword in an attribute definition list declaration.

Background:

SGML is a language, and like many languages, supports the idea that you can solve one problem in a variety of ways. As you will have noticed in the annotated version of the previous example's DTD, we could have provided a more useful version of the SUBJECT element type by giving it some hierarchical substructure as is typical of library classification schemes. A simple example makes clear why this turns out to be absolutely necessary. An article with

```
<METADATA>
<SUBJECT>crawl</SUBJECT>
</METADATA>
```

would be considerably more ambiguous (and bordering on useless as the result of a search) without a way of distinguishing:

- sports — swimming — crawl, from
- biology — locomotion — crawl — earthworm.

This may be a silly example, but nearly any subject keyword that you can think of is equally sensitive to the context in which it's found. The previous example's keywords really make sense only when considered as a group:

```
<METADATA>
<SUBJECT>SGML on the Web: Small Steps Beyond HTML
<SUBJECT>computer software</SUBJECT>
<SUBJECT>SGML browsing software</SUBJECT>
<SUBJECT>SGML Internet interchange standard</SUBJECT>
<SUBJECT>HTML Internet interchange standard</SUBJECT>
</METADATA>
```

Example 20 — Diving into the Subject

Goal of the Application:

While we're on the subject of document classification, let's think about *Yahoo!* and the enormity of the task that faces that hardy gang in Mountain View, California.

Founded at Stanford University in 1994 by Jerry Yang and David Filo — two Ph.D. candidates in Electrical Engineering — *Yahoo!* is now a commercial endeavor whose mission is to provide a straightforward library-like way into Net information. When you start a Yahoo search, you are shown a list of their highest-level classifications. Choosing one of the classifications will take you to another set of categories. Once you're at the second level, you may run into lower levels of categories, each more specific than the previous higher level, or you may come upon a Web anchor which will take you directly to a document on the subject.

The goal, then, of this sample application, is to create an application which will:

- make life easier for *Yahoo!* and similar cataloging services by building into a document the metadata needed to place the document accurately into the Yahoo classification structure
- make life easier for Yahoo! and similar services by letting a user create a "card catalog entry" that could just be emailed to the indexing service and which would contain just enough data to support an automated process for adding entries (including the address for the anchor, of course).

Is Influenced by/Builds on:

The current example extends *keyword1.dtd* by bringing forward the requirements of a real-world indexing service. This example was created with the cooperation of *Yahoo!*.

Stored on the Accompanying Disk as:

Sample DTD: *keyword2.dtd, keyword3.dtd*

Sample Instance: *keyword2.sgm, keyword3.sgm*

Step by Step:

The first step

The element declarations for the HEAD are very much as they were in the last example. The difference comes from the substructure created for SUBJECT:

```
<!ELEMENT html     (head, body)>
<!ELEMENT head     (title, metadata?)>
<!ELEMENT title    (#PCDATA)>

<!ELEMENT metadata (subject)+>
<!ELEMENT subject  (#PCDATA | classif)+>
<!ELEMENT classif  (#PCDATA | category)+>
<!ELEMENT category (#PCDATA | subcateg)+>
<!ELEMENT subcateg (#PCDATA | subcateg)+>
```

Obviously, in this example it has proven useful to gather together all the SUBJECT elements in one containing element. You may notice, if you examine other people's DTDs, constructs in which an element type is declared to contain nothing but one instance of another element type. This may have occurred because both names are used by the people creating the documents, and because it seemed, at a glance, to make sense. But watch out — there is rarely any good reason to have an element type that can contain, according to the DTD, only one other element.

Example 20 — Diving into the Subject

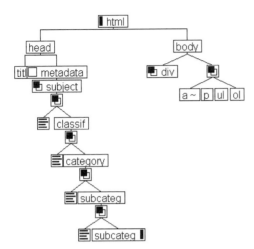

Figure 33. The tree view illustrates the repetitive content model of the SUBJECT *element type, offering perfectly logical choices at every level. The* SUBCATEG *element type is infinitely nestable, allowing an author or librarian to categorize and subcategorize to whatever level suits their needs.*

The repetitive content model offers you a perfectly logical set of choices at every level. Either insert the specific name for a classification, or a lower-level category, or both. "Both" is a sensible choice everywhere except at the bottom of the hierarchy, where it makes sense simply to give a keyword. Elsewhere, you'll notice that the sample says, for example, "This classificiation is called "computers" and it has a category within it called "software"." We could go on from there, "This classificiation/category is called "computers — software" and it has a category within it called "browsing"." We become more and more specific until we've pinpointed the particular subject of the article in question.

In this case, the article has several plausible hierarchical classifications. The first boils down to: "computers — software — browsing — SGML".

```
<HTML>
<HEAD>
<TITLE>Browsing Software Included with New SGML Book</TITLE>
<METADATA>
<SUBJECT>
<CLASSIF>computers
    <CATEGORY>software
        <SUBCATEG>browsing
            <SUBCATEG>SGML</SUBCATEG>
        </SUBCATEG>
    </CATEGORY>
</CLASSIF>
</SUBJECT>
```

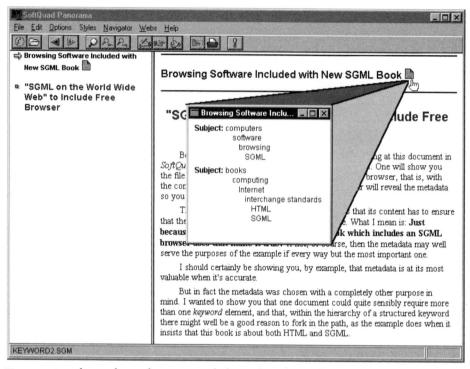

Figure 34. Open keyword2.sgm for a preview of what we have done so far. Be sure to check out both style sheets.

One style sheet will show you the file as if it were being displayed in a conforming Web browser, that is, with the contents of the HEAD element invisible. The other style sheet hides the metadata behind an icon which, when activated with a mouse click, will reveal the metadata so you can examine how the hierarchy works. Obviously this pop-up window is a handy place to stash subject classifications so that they aren't normally taking up valuable screen real estate.

Example 20 — Diving into the Subject

The second step

The second half of the example exploits the fact that in our element type declaration we allowed for any of the subelements of SUBJECT to be repeated. In this one sequence of markup, we've created two hierarchical classifications:

- books — computing — Internet — interchange standards — HTML, and
- books — computing — Internet — interchange standards — SGML.

```
<SUBJECT>
<CLASSIF>books
    <CATEGORY>computing
        <SUBCATEG>Internet
            <SUBCATEG>interchange standards
                <SUBCATEG>HTML</SUBCATEG>
                <SUBCATEG>SGML</SUBCATEG>
            </SUBCATEG>
        </SUBCATEG>
    </CATEGORY>
</CLASSIF>
</SUBJECT>
</METADATA></HEAD>
```

Note   You may have heard about being able to leave off end-tags (and even start-tags) in SGML and HTML. We'll discuss this in some depth later, but let's note in passing here that if I had left the end-tags off of SUBCATEG, we would not have known whether the topic "SGML" was nested *within* "HTML" or if they were both at the same hierarchical level. The unambiguous use of the end-tags eliminated any confusion.

On other occasions, of course, where end-tags and start-tags can be unambiguously inferred from the context, it is very useful — if fact it can make instances much clearer — to omit them whenever possible.

The third step: a mite more meta

Let's create one more richly extended version of this sample, which we'll call *keyword3.dtd*. We extend the richness of element types and attributes in this one, and also, happily, it will show you why it made sense to insist on having an element type called METADATA in this example, even if all it contained was a set of elements all with the same element type name, in this case SUBJECT.

Let's extend that now, adding another containing element to hold a unique identifier for the document, associate it with a publisher and specify its edition.

```
<!ELEMENT metadata (unique, subject)+>
```

The UNIQUE element type represents the notion that if you've got a way to express a useful structure that works, there's no reason to invent another. There's no rule that says you can't combine the general structure of an HTML document with the electronic review capability from CALS and the unique identifier structure from the OCLC metadata work. In fact, that's precisely what we've done here.

Note   Our "unique identifier" element should not be confused with SGML's "unique identifier" (ID) attribute.

Ordering one of each

In a now famous cinematic scene, Jack Nicholson deals head on with a system that won't let him order the items that he wants for his breakfast, even though the same ingredients are being served for lunch in other combinations. Here we'll see that SGML provides a convenient way to say "I want one of each of those, and I don't care when (in which order) I get them."

Examine the UNIQUE declaration. You've led a sheltered life, dealing only with commas (the sequence connector) and vertical bars (the or connector). Here you meet the ampersand, the "and" connector whose formal meaning is "in any order":

```
<!ELEMENT unique (identifier,(edition? & publisher? & date?))>
<!ELEMENT (edition? & publisher? & date?) (#PCDATA)>
```

In plain talk, the "and group" reads: Optionally tell us the EDITION of the work, and optionally the name of the PUBLISHER, and optionally the DATE, in any order.

Example 20 — Diving into the Subject

What kind of scheme are you cooking up?

The scheme attribute value tells us the domain in which the contents of an IDENTIF-IER element is unique (or allegedly unique, or nearly unique perhaps — there's no guarantee that a URL, for instance, will be unique). The other attribute is a simple way out if you need to use an identification scheme not represented in the list.

```
<!ATTLIST identifier scheme (url|urn|isbn|issn
                            |sici|messageID|FPI|other) "URL"
                     other  CDATA #IMPLIED>
```

If you choose "other" as the value of your scheme attribute, the idea is that you're are then supposed to fill in the name of your scheme as the value of the other attribute. The other attribute value should be empty if you choose one of the listed schemes.

```
<!DOCTYPE HTML PUBLIC "Structured Keyword and Metadata">
<HTML>
<HEAD>
<TITLE>Browsing Software Included with New SGML Book</TITLE>

<METADATA>
<UNIQUE>
<IDENTIFIER SCHEME=URL>http://www.sq.com/papers/beyond-html.html</IDENTIFIER>
<EDITION>First Release</EDITION>
<PUBLISHER>Prentice Hall</PUBLISHER>
<DATE>September 1, 1996</DATE>
</UNIQUE>

<SUBJECT>
<CLASSIF>computers
    <CATEGORY>software
        <SUBCATEG>browsing
            <SUBCATEG>SGML</SUBCATEG>
        </SUBCATEG>
    </CATEGORY>
</CLASSIF></SUBJECT>
```

```
<SUBJECT>
<CLASSIF>books
    <CATEGORY>computing
        <SUBCATEG>Internet
            <SUBCATEG>interchange standards
                <SUBCATEG>HTML</SUBCATEG>
                <SUBCATEG>SGML</SUBCATEG>
            </SUBCATEG>
        </SUBCATEG>
    </CATEGORY>
</CLASSIF></SUBJECT></METADATA></HEAD>

<BODY>
<DIV><H1>"SGML on the World Wide Web" to Include Free Browser</H1>

<P>Before we begin, let me remind you that if you're looking at
this document in <I>SoftQuad Panorama</I>, be sure to check out
both style sheets. One will show you the file as if it were being
displayed in a traditional HTML browser, that is, with the contents
of the HEAD element invisible; and the other will reveal the metadata
so you can examine how the hierarchy works.</P>

<P>The most pleasurable aspect of this document is that its content
has to ensure that the metadata that was invented for it is accurate.
What I mean is: <B>Just because I tell you this document is about
a book which includes an SGML browser does that make it true?</B> If
not, of course, then the metadata may well serve the purposes of the
example if every way but the most important one.</P>

<P>I should certainly be showing you, by example, that metadata
is at its most valuable when it's accurate.</P>

<P>But in fact the metadata was chosen with a completely other
purpose in mind. I wanted to show you that one document could
quite sensibly require more than one <I>keyword</I> element, and that,
within the hierarchy of a structured keyword there might well be
a good reason to fork in the path, as the example does when it
insists that this book is about both HTML and SGML.</P>
</DIV></BODY></HTML>
```

Example 20 — Diving into the Subject

Bonus:

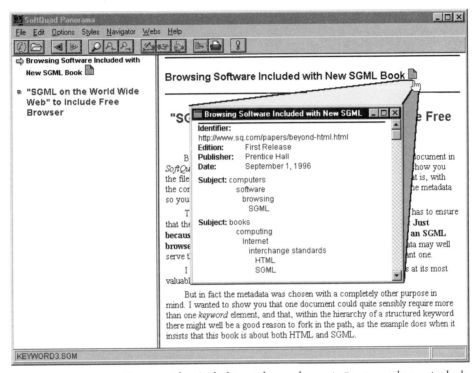

Figure 35. *If you're looking at keyword3.sgm in Panorama, be sure to check out both style sheets.*

One style sheet will show you the file as if it were being displayed in a conforming Web browser, that is, with the contents of the HEAD element invisible. The other style sheet hides the metadata behind an icon which, when activated with a mouse click, will reveal the metadata so you can examine how the hierarchy works.

But wait, there's more...

The last few examples were concerned with recording subject indexes and revision information, in the next example we'll include metadata to record a document's history and expiration. And we'll do it in an unusual way, just to raise a quandary.

◆ EXAMPLE 21

What You See is the Tip of the Information Iceberg

Goal of the Example:

The *history.dtd* introduces a simple case of attribute values describing the steps involved with the creation of a document. One goal of the example, then, is to further explore the range of capabilities of attributes, including document-level attributes such as those in this application.

A second (and equally important) goal is to introduce the idea of document history, a subject which, if pushed further, would take us to collaborative authoring, revision control, workflow management, and directly to document management.

Goal of the Application:

For documents of value, what you see on the screen or on paper is often just part of what could be defined as the *whole document*. In this sense, the whole document includes all its associated data — who created it, when, in response to what; when it was published or posted, with whose approval, and where; when it should be updated or removed; which version you're looking at, and whether it is the latest version, or has been supplanted by another, and if so, where that document lives.

The goal of this application is to begin to capture some of the data in a way that can be useful to any monitoring system, whether automated or human. You'll see from the sample file that even the simplest of software programs, a small agent that would ransack your Web site looking for stale-dated documents, would be very valuable indeed.

Is Influenced by/Builds on:

The *history.dtd* is built directly on the HTML 2.0 mechanisms we've previously explored.

Stored on the Accompanying Disk as:

Sample DTD: *history.dtd*

Sample Instance: *history.sgm*

Step by Step:

When we created attributes for the METADATA element type, there was an implication that the attribute values would apply to the entire document. If we gave a SUBJECT element the content "Pope John Paul II", we were, in effect, saying that the *entire* document was about the pope. All the elements allowed in an HTML HEAD element are similarly high-level, all covering or referring to, or influencing the whole document.

So, strictly speaking, we could have chosen any number of ways to capture the historic details of the document that this application records:

- Who wrote or otherwise originated this document?
- If necessary, who authorized its being posted to the Web?
- When was it posted?
- When will it expire? Or, put another way, when it will no longer be relevant? Or even more strongly: By what date will it be an embarrassment to have this page still up on our Web site?
- And, just for the record, what version is it anyway?

We might have created a set of attributes for the existing META element type — a plausible place for this sort of content. We might have declared a brand new element type called HISTORY, and then created five subordinate element types for it, called CREATOR, APPROVAL, POSTDATE, REMOVEBY, and VERSION.

Example 21 — What You See is the Tip of the Information Iceberg

Instead, I chose to add five new attributes to the highest-level element type, the document element type, HTML itself.

```
<!ELEMENT html (head, body)>
<!ATTLIST html creator  CDATA #REQUIRED
               approval CDATA #IMPLIED
               postdate CDATA #IMPLIED
               removeby CDATA #REQUIRED
               version  CDATA #IMPLIED>
```

This is an odd approach, since the HTML element has no other attributes. Indeed, the HTML specification documents make it clear that a conforming HTML document need not even include the <HTML> and </HTML> tags. Why create attributes for those now? I did this for several reasons.

A *legacy technology reason*: All, or nearly all, of the deployed Web browsers recognize attributes as something to not be displayed. While I have written earlier about how browsers *should not display any contents of a* HEAD *element*, they currently do. We'll have to live with that effect for the metadata we've looked at earlier, if necessary. There is, perhaps, not that much harm in seeing the subject keywords for a document strung across the top of the first page, and, in fact, this is where improvements to browser capabilities come from. If enough people ask the implementors to hide the HEAD element type's contents, they might. In summary, then, if we had put the historical information into an element type instead of into attributes, documents that use this facility might produce unexpected and unwanted results in the current batch of browsers.

A *simplicity of technology reason*: The historical information is in a different category from the metadata information. It is private, a part of the managerial record of the document over time. You're likely not to really care if someone reads it and, yes, it should (or could) be stored with the document, in part because you may later want to build small pieces of technology to exploit that new information — perhaps a daemon that alerts the creator three days before the removeby date that the document is about to expire. For this to happen very smoothly, it is handy for the required input to this process to be available in a completely predictable way. If there were a separate element type containing the historic record, for consistency with other uses of the HEAD element type, we would have to allow it to occur anywhere in HEAD. Our daemon would have to find it. Instead, with the attributes attached to the top-level HTML element type, the daemon knows right where to look.

If the attributes exist, they'll be right there; the software need look no further. More importantly, if they don't exist, the software will know that very quickly too.

"If they don't exist" is a funny supposition, given that if we look to the DTD we see that two of the attributes have the keyword #REQUIRED. This means just what you think it means: For a document built with this DTD to be valid, it *must* contain values for the two attributes which our daemon needs to do its work.

```
<HTML CREATOR="MURRAY MALONEY"
      APPROVAL="YURI RUBINSKY"
      POSTDATE="SEPTEMBER 1, 1996"
      REMOVEBY="LEAVE IN CIRCULATION"
      VERSION="FINAL">
```

"If they don't exist", in fact, is a nod of the head to reality. Yes, we've built an application that *requires* creator and removeby, and, in our fictional daemonic scenario, you have a piece of software that checks all the documents on your Web site every day at midnight for this information. But the hard cold truth is that not everyone who creates documents in your organization uses this DTD. The people who do use it don't always check that they've created valid documents; and, finally, there are documents that we already have up on the Web which predate our decision to invent these attributes.

Raising a quandary

This brings us to one of the basic quandaries of DTD creation: *Should a DTD provide guidance or reflect current realities?*

- In the current case, for instance, we could have given the keyword #IMPLIED to creator and removeby, making them optional. The advantage would have been that *all our documents* (given that they use good HTML elsewhere) could have been declared valid. People who wanted to add the new attributes could have done so, and the new approach would have been supported by the new DTD. This is the "legacy-embracing" approach, whose underlying principle could be summed up as: "Better to have the greatest number of conforming documents so you can work with them later using SGML-conforming systems. Build a loose DTD."

Example 21 — What You See is the Tip of the Information Iceberg

- The contrary approach, as embodied in this section's *history.dtd*, however, could be stated as: "Let's encourage the next generation of documents to conform. The way we accomplish this is by creating DTDs that *require* good behavior."

```
<!ELEMENT html (head, body)>
<!ATTLIST html creator  CDATA #REQUIRED
               approval CDATA #IMPLIED
               postdate CDATA #IMPLIED
               removeby CDATA #REQUIRED
               version  CDATA #IMPLIED>
```

- In a previous section I mentioned that there are switches in the HTML 2.0 DTD to switch between "Recommended" and "Deprecated" modes. This is a third approach, one that says: "Build into one DTD the mechanisms to check that someone if doing the right thing, but give them a chance to turn those mechanisms off too."

Although I think it made sense in the case of HTML, there are two potential problems with using this approach for other applications: You give people the opportunity to create new documents that don't take into account the recommended procedures, and you make a far more complex DTD, full of duplication, where the recommended procedure and the deprecated procedure must both appear — and rife with the possibility of subtle errors caused by the interplay of the switching mechanism.

Bonus:

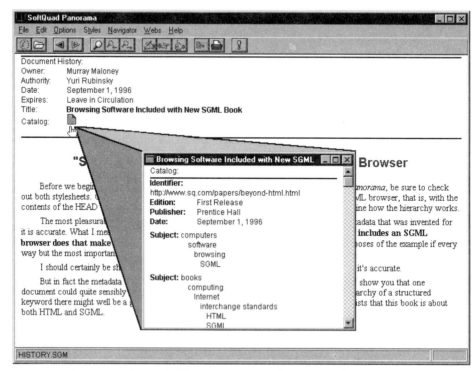

Figure 36. When viewing the sample file in Panorama, you'll notice that the style sheet mimics a Web browser view; the history vanishes. Now, switch to the "Meta Data" style sheet to reveal the document history information. The now familiar icon, concealing the document's subject keywords and identity, can be activated with a simple click of the mouse.

The Combined Joys of Electronic Review and Machine Processing

Note Please be aware that this is the longest and most complex example in this book. The subject of electronic review, and the issues surrounding it, is difficult enough to understand without the added complexity of trying to do something useful about it. Nonetheless if you choose to proceed, intrepid explorer that you are, don't be surprised if you have to review this example, and the two that follow, several times.

Goal of the Example:

Let's call the capability described in this section "ERD", a simple acronym standing for "the Electronic Review of Documents". Several years ago, Melinda Stetina of *Unisys* (now Melinda Barnhardt) proposed the creation of a small set of SGML element type and attribute definition list declarations that could be used with any of the dozens of DTDs being created for the US *Department of Defense* under the CALS Initiative. A subcommittee of the CALS *Electronic Publishing Committee* (in turn part of the Standards Working Group) went off and created the declaration set and accompanying procedures that form the inspiration (and contribute the declarations) for the application created for this book.

I had the pleasure, in the early days, of working with the committee, and have had a soft spot in my heart for this declaration set ever since. It's clean, clear, succinct, and has a lot of power. Well implemented in software, it can dramatically increase the productivity of any group of people who collectively contribute to the creation of an electronic document.

While designed originally to work with very large documents, the ERD set could also help with electronic review of the smaller documents that people put up on a Web site. Accordingly, I've merged the CALS ERD set with the HTMLDIV application. Simultaneously, as an example for the book, the application should serve:

- To demonstrate the value of reusable, modular DTD subsets, a selection of declarations that may be introduced into any DTD where the capability is applicable. In fact, if you use the *htmlerd.dtd*, it is likely to work in SGML software that already knows about the CALS Electronic Review DTD subset.
- To introduce the idea that one DTD may be used in two dramatically different ways. In the current example, HTML remains the document element type, but within the HTML element, two conforming document instances might have *no* element types in common.
- To introduce *inclusions* (also called *inclusion exceptions*), which are element types declared in the DTD outside the confines of a specific model group. Includable elements can occur *anywhere* within the content of the element type in whose declaration the inclusion is declared, including the content of nested subelements.
- To introduce *exclusions*, (also called *exclusion exceptions*) which are element types declared in the DTD specifically *not* eligible to occur at any level of the content of an element type in which they might otherwise have been permitted.
- To continue to distinguish between the free-form and potentially hierarchical information that should be marked up as the content of element types and the more "data-like" information — in this case, machine-processable — that should be represented by attributes.

Goal of the Application:

In a working environment in which Web documents are reviewed by several people before being posted, it makes sense for the reviewers to do so electronically. We know for certain, after all, that electronic versions of the documents exist, and we can be fairly sure that, in an environment in which collaborative creation of Web documents is a normal activity, people will have electronic mail capability. Now all we need is the software to take advantage of the structures we are about to create.

A very simple goal lies at the core of this sample application: to provide the required SGML element types for the review of SGML text documents electronically using SGML for the comments. The capability supported by these elements enables reviewers located in diverse environments to make and exchange comments on multiple copies of a document file over a network. The comments may then be sorted, processed, and incorporated into the document by the "owner" system.

The previous paragraph, more or less, is lifted directly from a United States Department of Defense specification for the delivery of electronic information entitled MIL-M-28001B. Some of you, denizens of the Internet that you are, may not be familiar with US military specifications, so, with permission, I've reprinted the pages from *Appendix C* of that document that are relevant to the goal of this section.

Is Influenced by/Builds on:

The application brings together the HTMLDIV application and the strange and somewhat foreign world (for most people) of CALS. It does hope also to surprise people who assume that anything created by a committee somehow connected with the military must be incomprehensible. With just a few optional attributes left out, the ERD fragment here is directly copied from the CALS version. (A second small change involves the removal of the minimization parameters. You've not yet met them in this book, but will in Chapter 7 (*Fresh DTDs*) on page 227.)

Stored on the Accompanying Disk as:

Sample DTD: *htmlerd.dtd*

Sample Instance: *htmlerd1.sgm, htmlerd2.sgm*

Step by Step:

The annotated DTD and the original CALS documentation both appear over the next few pages. I don't want to duplicate the explanations from the CALS specification, but would like to draw your attention to certain key points. The critical new line in the DTD — and the one that explains the philosophy of the application — is the declaration of the document element type, which is still HTML:

```
<!ELEMENT html ((head, body)|(mrinfo, modreq*))>
```

For the first time, we are being asked to believe that an HTML document might consist of something *other than* HEAD and BODY. In fact, we're being told that an HTML document now consists of *either:*

- the traditional HEAD followed by BODY, or
- a required MRINFO element (for "Modification Request Information") followed by any number of MODREQ elements (each being a modification request).

Let's Look at the Second Case First

Choosing to create a document instance pursuing the second choice (MRINFO, etc) means we can now create a perfectly legitimate HTML document which consists of nothing but the comments we choose to make about a separate, subject document. In fact, if several of us are commenting on one document, we can each create a separate file of our comments which might later be merged together into one document.

With the proper attributes, those files could be merged and sorted into any of:

- order of appearance of a specific phrase or element
- order of priority (assuming an attribute that stores the priority of each comment)
- order by reviewer name or date of review
- order based upon which comments have been resolved already
- indeed, *any order at all* given attributes that store the information which we'll use to perform the sort.

In practical terms, then, we could have the following document instance:

```
<HTML>
<MRINFO>
<IDENTIFIER TYPE="URL">
http://www.example.edu/sample.sgml
</IDENTIFIER>
<MODREQ>
and here the first actual modification request would appear...
</MODREQ>
<MODREQ>
the second modification request would appear here ...
</MODREQ>
<MODREQ>
and so forth...
</MODREQ>
```

It would be a completely fair question to ask why one wouldn't create just a tiny DTD with the element types needed for the collection of MODREQ elements, and not merge them in with the HTMLDIV application.

Reasonable idea, but it would not give us either of two capabilities that arise only out of the integration:

- the ability to intertwine comments with the original document instance, or
- the ability to include entire portions of the subject document — or a rewritten, suggested version of the subject document — *complete with markup* within a MODREQ. (I'll return to this when we discuss the magic powers of the MRCHGTXT element type, below.)

Meanwhile, Back to the Other, Intertwining, Case

The top-level declaration, you recall, gave you a very large choice of how to begin:

```
<!ELEMENT html ((head, body)|(mrinfo, modreq*))>
```

Instead of creating a document instance consisting only of MRINFO and MODREQ elements, we could create what looks at first glance like normal HTML:

```
<HTML><HEAD><TITLE>Electronic Review of Documents</TITLE></HEAD>
```

Before we go any further, we need to consult the DTD to see what's allowed in BODY:

```
<!ELEMENT body (div+ |(%block;)+) +(modreq)>
```

This is, in fact, the good old declaration from HTMLDIV, back again. BODY consists either of a series of DIV elements *or* anything declared as one of the %block; element types. Something new appears at the end of the declaration. This is the inclusion, which indicates that occurrences of the MODREQ element may appear *anywhere* within the tree structure that makes up the content model for BODY.

The implication is quite impressive — you can simply place a MODREQ element anywhere you want within the body of your document. This action is much like inserting an SGML comment in the document — SGML comments may occur anywhere, and don't affect the validity of the instance — but is much more powerful. The MODREQ element types:

- can be heavily structured, and the markup within (particularly in attributes) can be used for the automated processing that is a large part of the goal of this application
- can be tracked, managed and printed if necessary, just as any other portions of the instance can be
- can be nested (as I explain below): a MODREQ can be used by a second reviewer to comment on the comments of a first reviewer.

In our example, then, let's add a MODREQ. We've said they're only allowed in the BODY (although I admit that there may well be times when you want to comment on the contents of a HEAD element). This is consistent with existing philosophy in HTML that says that a different set of element types may appear within HEAD than appears in BODY — that is, in a document with almost no markup, you should still be able to tell whether you're in the BODY or the HEAD. Back to the example, then:

```
<HTML>
<HEAD><TITLE>This Document Needs to Be Edited!</TITLE></HEAD>
<BODY>
    <MODREQ>
    The modification request would appear here and because it appears
    right away within BODY, we assume it is a comment on the entire
    contents of the BODY element. ...
    </MODREQ>
<H1>The Document Will Be Edited Soon</H1>
<P>HMTL is the markup language of the World Wide Web, created originally
for documents created largely by computer specialists and physicists.
    <MODREQ>
    You can imagine a comment such as: The first paragraph of the document
    contains an egregious error and should be cleaned up before publication.
    But if I saw this, I might want to know who wrote it, what was being
    proposed instead, and so forth. The answers to those questions appear
    in the subelements of MODREQ.
    </MODREQ>
Notice that we're still inside the paragraph. Our
second comment refers only to this paragraph.</P>
```

Let's examine the sub-structure within an individual modification request.

From Here on, the Explanation Applies to Both the Separate File and the Intertwining MODREQ Methods

For ERD to work, the following declarations are merged into the HTMLDIV application:

```
<!ELEMENT modreq (mrinfo?, mrmod, mrrespns?)>
```

Straightforward enough. A modification request begins with optional MRINFO, followed by a required MRMOD, which is the body of the modification itself. MRMOD is followed by an optional *modification request response*, a reply from someone else in the workflow explaining the "disposition" of the comment, that is, what happened to it.

Figure 37. The tree view illustrates the full richness the DTD.

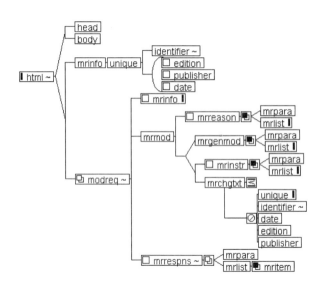

Notice that MRINFO is optional here, even though it was *required* in the "separate file" approach to commenting examined above. There's a very straightforward explanation — MRINFO is where we store the unique identification of the subject document we're reviewing. In the intertwining, intermingling approach to commenting, we're already in the subject document. (When your comments are in a separate document, yes, absolutely, you have to indicate within that document which subject document you're referring to.)

The next question turns out to be: So why, in the intermingled method, do you need one at all? If you and a group of colleagues were reviewing this document, it would be perfectly reasonable for each of you to do so by inserting comments directly into the text. It would be boring to continuously have to put in all the identification information and none of you would bother. But, at some point, the comments would be gathered for action by the writer or editor of the original document. That person doesn't want to receive duplicate copies of that original, only the comments. A small software application would race through the comment-embedded versions, simultaneously gathering modification requests and automatically inserting any data that was insertable. (Such as your name, for example, the date, the unique identifiers of the elements in which the MODREQs were embedded. *Computers and software are supposed to make your life easier, not harder.* This last statement may come as a bit of a surprise...)

The Attributes of the MODREQ Element Type

Much of the data involved with a modification request is carried in attributes of the MODREQ element type:

```
<!ATTLIST modreq id ID             #REQUIRED
             xref      NAME         #IMPLIED
             refpos    (prexref|postxref|xref) xref
             by        CDATA        #REQUIRED
             date      CDATA        #REQUIRED
             priority  (1|2|3|4|5)  #IMPLIED
             category  NUMBER       #IMPLIED
             topic     CDATA        #IMPLIED>
```

This is an extensive list. Luckily it all makes sense:

id   The unique identifier of the modification request itself, not the text upon which you're commenting. This lets someone create a MODREQ pointing to yours, or indeed, lets any element with an IDREF attribute refer to it.

xref   If you're storing the modification requests in a separate file, then you need to have a way of pointing to the elements upon which you're commenting. The xref attribute is where you place the unique identifier of the subject element. We learned earlier that it is normal procedure to use the keyword IDREF in an attribute definition list declaration for those attributes that refer to element types with an ID. Here, suddenly, that's not occurring. The explanation — ID and IDREF only work together if they're *in the same document*. That is, you cannot have an IDREF in a document without a matching ID. If you place all your modification requests in a separate document, and were using the IDREF attribute value type, your SGML parser would report errors. Instead, here, we declare the xref attribute with a declared value of NAME (*name*) which, by no coincidence, has the same spelling rules as an ID. That is, it must begin with an alphabetic character, which may be followed by letters, numbers, periods, or hyphens.

refpos "Position of the reference" tells us more precisely where the modification request is pointing. In particular, if the MODREQ includes new content which you would like to have included in the subject document, this attribute tells the recipient (either human or computer) whether the new material comes before, after, or on top of the named xref.

Notice, by the way, that the refpos attribute has a default value of "xref", meaning that the intent is to replace the named element.

by Who made this request?

date When was it made?

priority How important is it? Naturally, on a scale of one to five, you need to indicate to the reviewers which end of the range means that the comment has the highest priority, and which has the lowest. For our purposes, let's assume that five means "top priority".

category

Interestingly, the category attribute is expected to be a number. This has a charming kind of defense department feel to it. Obviously you need documentation to tell you what the categories are, and which numbers they're associated with. For our purposes here, let's assume the following: (these are not the CALS categories)

1. *Technical.* This is more than a suggestion. Here the reviewer is essentially saying "What you've written here simply doesn't work."
2. *Fundamental.* This is related to editorial changes, but is more in the "I insist" category. Spelling mistakes would fall into this group, as would errors of grammar.
3. *Editorial.* This would be a suggestion for improvements to the wording.
4. *Structural.* The reviewer has suggestions for changes to the structure or organization. Reordering items in a list or rearranging the structure of a paragraph, for example.
5. To be truthful, I can't think of another category, but you might. I've left it in the declaration. Document it for your own purposes and use it with enthusiasm.

topic

This is an open-ended attribute, declared as CDATA, which means it can be a longish verbal description, or a concise keyword or two. In the best of all worlds, you might have a fixed list of topics upon which people comment. If you did so, you could then sort the comments into order by topic.

The MRINFO Element Type

Inside the MODREQ, the first allowed element is MRINFO:

```
<!ELEMENT mrinfo (unique)>
```

Recall that many pages ago I mentioned that no element type should normally be declared as containing nothing but a single, required element. And yet, here one is. This is *not* a strictly normal condition, and not to be encouraged. You'll see below that it has a small sub-structure intended to uniquely identify the document. We need the same functionality here so we know which document we're pointing at.

At the same time, for consistency with existing software that handles ERD, I've preserved all of the element types and attribute names, throwing away a few attributes that seemed less relevant now that we're no longer in the army. What we're really seeing here is a way of saying, in full SGML, "This ERD and CALS-conforming element type MRINFO really is exactly the same as the Metadata Initiative element type called UNIQUE." If you have software that handles ERD, its control over the process will end with MRINFO. If you have software that knows about Web metadata, its control over the data begins at the top of the small hierarchy of elements snuggled inside UNIQUE. (We'll get to those element types in a few moments.)

The MRMOD Element Type

```
<!ELEMENT mrmod (mrreason?, (mrgenmod|(mrinstr?, mrchgtxt)))>

<!ELEMENT (mrreason|mrinstr|mrgenmod)        (mrpara|mrlist)+>
```

A very straightforward structure inside the actual modification request itself:

- An optional MRREASON — you may explain why you think the change needs to be made. It's optional because you may have either the authority, clout or bank account to simply insist on the change without giving a reason.
- A choice between proposing a "general modification", something that applies to the whole container in which you've placed the MODREQ, or
- An optional set of instructions, the MRINSTR, followed by
- A request to change the text, using the MRCHGTXT element type.

MRREASON, MRGENMOD and MRINSTR all contain nothing but paragraphs and lists. They've been given names that one hopes will be unique and not used anywhere else in an application so that they can have a very simple content model unaffected by the treatment elsewhere in the DTD of paragraphs and lists.

The particular strength of MRGENMOD reflects the context-sensitive strength of the entire MODREQ element type (as we saw in the first examples). MRGENMOD *counts on its context*. Put one on a list with the contents "Needs work!" and it says that there's a problem with the list. Put the same element with the same content at the beginning of the BODY and it tells you the whole document has problems.

At the beginning of the section, I mentioned "magic powers". The magic happens inside the MRCHGTXT element type:

```
<!ELEMENT mrchgtxt ANY>
```

The declaration for "Modification Request Change Text" (MRCHGTXT for short) really is doing just what you think. *Any* element type from the DTD is allowed in the content of this element type. Think about its role in the DTD, allowing the reviewer of a document to suggest replacement content for elements in the source document. What could be more necessary that to have a mechanism to include entire elements and their subelements (if needed) in recommending new content? The SGML ANY keyword is perfectly suited for this purpose.

There's a little more to this declaration; I was highlighting the pieces of the puzzle one at a time. The following is the full declaration for MRCHGTXT, introducing the idea of exclusions, element types that are expressly forbidden from appearing in the content of the element type in which they are declared:

```
<!ELEMENT mrchgtxt ANY -(unique|identifier|date|edition|publisher)>
```

Exclusions are the opposite of the inclusion capability that we met when discussing where MODREQ element types are allowed within our new variation of an HTML document. The declaration for MRCHGTXT indicates that, overriding the ANY keyword, *none* of the element types may appear within MRCHGTXT that have been declared only to uniquely identify the document on which we're commenting. Notice that we haven't excluded any of the element types that comprise the modification request. This allows us to comment on other people's comments — they can be nested inside each other.

The MRRESPNS Element Type

```
<!ELEMENT mrrespns (mrpara|mrlist)*>

<!ATTLIST mrrespns disposn  NUMBER  #IMPLIED
                   status   NUMBER  #IMPLIED>
```

MRRESPNS is where the follow-up takes place. Optionally, someone can describe (using normal text in paragraphs and lists) what he or she thinks of the modification request, or how it was absorbed or ignored. Further, using the attributes and a formal numeric procedure (numbers from one to five, for example), the MRRESPNS can carry information about its status (what's been done as a result of the comment) or disposition (what has happened to the comment itself). This number business is a bit CALS-ish really, and in your own environment you could replace that with an attribute definition list declaration such as:

```
<!ATTLIST mrrespns disposn (agree|disagree|preserve|ignore) #IMPLIED
                   status (fixed|altered|unchangd)         #IMPLIED>
```

Strikingly apparent here is the role of the software itself (and your pages of instructions) in making the application work. What does it mean to have to indicate a number to stand for the "disposition"? In my second example, what is the difference between "fixed" and "altered"? (I figured that "fixed" means "I did what was asked for in this modification request" while "altered" means "I changed it, but not exactly how you asked". For either pair of attributes to make sense to your users, the documentation needs to make clear the *semantics* of the names and values.

Finally, we close off the ERD fragment by declaring contents for the paragraphs and lists:

```
<!ELEMENT (mrpara|mritem) (#PCDATA)>

<!ELEMENT mrlist        (mritem+)>
```

So, here is a portion of a sample document that exercises some of the element types that we have just explored:

```
<!DOCTYPE HTML PUBLIC "HTML with Electronic Review">
<HTML>
<HEAD><TITLE>Electronic Review of Documents</TITLE></HEAD>
<BODY>
<DIV><H1>An Editorial about SGML and the Information Highway</H1>
<P>We have an brand new chance to make an infrastructure that we can
all get access to, and to set up a set of ground rules that will allow
all seekers after information or entertainment to pick how they want
to display the information they come across, and to sign up for any
or all the services which will be available without being limited or
constrained by the whims (and stiff billing practices) of just one
cable service company, or just one phone company, or just one
arbitrary conglomerate.</P>

<MODREQ ID="NEW.OPPORTUNITY" BY="SAM" DATE="SEPTEMBER 4, 1996">
<MRMOD>
<MRREASON>
<MRPARA>
The original language is a little too casual, and I think that criticism
of the cable industry is an unnecessary digression. I suggest:
</MRPARA>
</MRREASON>
<MRCHGTXT>
We have an unprecedented opportunity to build an accessible
infrastructure, and to establish a set of ground rules that
will allow all seekers after information or entertainment to
choose the display device of their choice, to sign up for any
or all the services that will be available without being
constrained by the whims (and billing practices) of just one
cable company, or just one phone company, or just one arbitrary
conglomerate.
</MRCHGTXT>
<MRRESPNS DISPOSN="AGREE" STATUS="ALTERED">
<MRPARA>
I'd like to use 'subscribe' rather than 'sign up for'.
</MRPARA>
</MRRESPNS>
</MODREQ>
```

Tying It All Together

We're not done yet. (Interesting how much longer the explanation is when we implement examples lifted directly from the outside world instead of examples invented just to explain specific ideas!)

We're going to re-use some metadata that you may recall from Example 20 (*Diving into the Subject*) on page 173. Our current application can certainly take advantage of a UNIQUE identifier element type.

```
<!ELEMENT unique (identifier,(edition? & publisher? & date?))>
```

The edition, publisher and date information supplements the IDENTIFIER element type in order to help ensure that all of the reviewers of the source document are talking about the very same version of it.

If it ain't broke, fix it

As we saw earlier, we can select the scheme from a list:

```
<!ATTLIST identifier scheme (url|urn|isbn|issn|sici
                            |messageID|FPI|other) "URL"
               other  CDATA #IMPLIED>
```

This is overkill for our purposes if we know we're only working with documents either already up or about to go up on our Web site. Instead, using the #FIXED keyword, we can limit the scheme right in the DTD itself, and *never* have to fill it out:

```
<!ATTLIST identifier scheme NAME #FIXED "URL">
```

The keyword #FIXED means precisely what you'd imagine. The value of the attribute is *fixed* in the declaration, and cannot be changed. In this context, what it means is that *all* IDENTIFIER elements effectively are written like this:

```
<IDENTIFIER SCHEME="URL">
```

You never have to actually include the attribute. The SGML parser infers it for you. Later programs that count on knowing the attribute value will be able to find it.

A *Final Word about* IDs

The ID attribute declarations in the DTD make possible the use of the "separate file" approach that we discussed at the beginning of the section. Here we establish that all the major containing elements are given an ID attribute affording us a place to assign unique identifiers for each:

```
<!ATTLIST (div|p|%list;|li)
           ID    ID  #IMPLIED>
```

These identifiers, as we saw in the discussion of MODREQ, are referenced in that element type's xref attribute. Unless you're using the intertwined comments approach, every instance of an element that is referenced must have an id.

Anti-Bonus:

No free ERD software (that I know of) exists. Accordingly, while you can experiment with the display of a commented document examining the style sheets available in Panorama, to create new sample instances, you'll have to work from scratch or edit *htmlerd1.sgm* (in which the review comments are embedded in the subject file) and *htmlerd2.sgm* (in which responses have been added to the subject file).

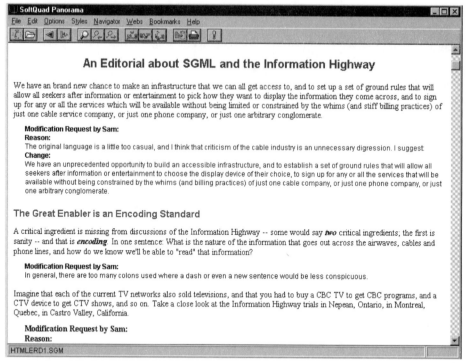

Figure 38. In htmlerd1.sgm, you can see a number of modification requests.
Some include a reason and a suggested change.

But wait, there's more...

Fixed attribute values are an SGML construct that was fairly obscure until Dr. Charles F. Goldfarb invented the architectural form, a construct used in the ISO HyTime standard, which will be very briefly discussed in Chapter 8 (*You Can Get There From Here*) on page 263.

The final two examples in this chapter are, in effect, the continuation of the story after the review process. They record the changes that would be made to a source document over time, as it goes through a revision cycle.

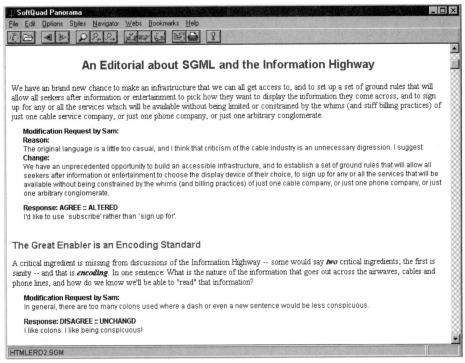

Figure 39. In htmlerd2.sgm, you can see responses to the modification requests.

- Imagine yourself using *htmldiv.dtd* to create a document that is up on the Web. But it's now time to update it, so you email a copy to the people who are to review it...
- They use *htmlerd.dtd* to record their comments and suggestions. You fold the comments together, following the good advice, ignoring the bad, and make the changes...
- You use *rev-simp.dtd*, (see the next example) to highlight the changes from the previously posted version.

While I Wasn't Watching, What Changed?

Goal of the Example:

The *rev-simp.dtd* takes the idea of using attributes to track historical information (which we saw several examples ago in *history.dtd*) and applies it to small parts of a document.

The example also serves as a reminder of how useful containing elements are. The revision control attributes apply to the entire contents of the element to which they are attached.

The goals of the example, then, are:

- To further explore the use of attributes to carry crucial information and to capture the history of a document
- To further exploit containing elements.

Goal of the Application:

- To store, in any document instance, sufficient instructions to recreate both a previous version and a new version of that document, incorporating information regarding what has been added to, deleted from or moved within the earlier version.
- To store, if necessary, duplicate copies of certain elements, where a new one replaces a previous version or where an element has been moved to a new location.

The application presumes a process (either manual or automated) during which the revision control information is purged from the document instance, and a clean, current copy is created for formal release. When the time comes to produce a new version, the attributes are used again.

Is Influenced by/Builds on:

The revision control attribute in this DTD is associated both with existing HTML 2.0 element types and with the DIV element types resurrected from the *htmldiv.dtd* example.

Stored on the Accompanying Disk as:

Sample DTD: *rev-simp.dtd*

Sample Instance: *rev-simp.sgm*

Step by Step:

As with the *history.dtd*, we could have handled the requirements for the current application in various ways:

- by adding attributes to existing element types
- by creating new element types, or
- by using new attributes on new element types.

Let's examine each possibility.

Adding Attributes to Existing Element Types

New attributes on existing element types make the presumption that the elements described by the markup — the paragraphs, headings, etc. — happen to be plausible units for revision control. Let's say you want to add three words to the middle of a

Example 23 — While I Wasn't Watching, What Changed?

sentence. If there is no element type created specifically to allow such an insertion, then this approach presumes that the existing element types are close enough; that is, you'd be prepared to indicate that a whole paragraph has changed, and not worry about the "finer granularity" of the actual change.

Creating new element types

Creating new element types has the advantage of letting you create content models that will support the granularity you desire, but has disadvantages too. You could end up with quite an effective short list of new element types:

- INSERT: would allow you to surround any new content with <INSERT> and </INSERT>. The difficulty is that the content model for the INSERT element type would have to include every element type that could possibly end up being inserted, and you would lose the usefulness of validation inside an element with such a model.
- DELETE: suffers from the same problem. You would want to be able to surround any content that needs to be deleted with <DELETE> and </DELETE>. (I trust the reason for this is clear: you can no longer simply delete content from the document instance because you want a record of the changes. Another way of looking at the problem is that you want to be able to generate either version of the document, using the markup.)
- MOVEFROM: might be excessive. If a unit of content is to move from one place to another, it may be sufficient to simply mark the original location with a DELETE element. There is a school of thought that says in the case of very important documents you really do want to be able to recreate all the steps in the editing process for full revision control. Capturing just the results of the process (DELETE and INSERT would accomplish this) isn't good enough. Also, the two parts of the move could be so far away in a document that you might never notice them unless they have a specialized element type of their very own.
- MOVETO is the other half of the pair, roughly equivalent to the INSERT element type. If you wanted to pursue the paired-element approach, you would be likely to link the MOVEFROM and MOVETO element types together using ID and IDREF attributes.

Inventing new attributes for new element types

Inventing new attributes for new element types suffers from the same problems as the previous approach, the invention of new element types without attributes. As always there are many ways to address the requirement:

For example, a separate pair of START-REV and END-REV element types could have been created with appropriate attributes on START-REV to carry the revision control information and with ID and IDREF attributes to link them together. They would have been declared as EMPTY element types since revisions can span any other element boundaries. The way to employ this would simply be to indicate the beginning of a change with the START-REV start-tag (remembering that EMPTY elements have no end-tags) and the attributes it needs Here's an example:

```
<P>Inventing new attributes <START-REV ID="REV1" ACTION="DELETE">
and other markup can be fun. The empty element approach
lets us start a change in one paragraph, and not care
where it all ends.</P>
<P>By the time we get to the next paragraph, we have to
remember we're still deleting, at least up to where we
get to the idea of creating markup<END-REV IDREF="REV1">
for new element types suffers from the same problems as
the previous approach.</P>
```

Text in bold face are the words that are to be deleted (along with the markup).

This approach is sound, and has been employed in several of the major public SGML applications. It has some difficulties, from the point of view of our purposes:

- You cannot validate the markup. An SGML parser is obliging much of the time, helping you determine whether your contents will safely and happily pass through your production system, or to your display software. But in the present case, the parser cannot tell you, for example, whether each START-REV has a matching END-REV. The best it can do is to let you know if you have an IDREF on your END-REV which points to a non-existent START-REV ID.
- The example illustrates why you *would* want to use this approach — that is, the deleted part includes the end- and start-tags of a paragraph, crossing element boundaries — but I contend that this is not a particularly common occurrence. The example file, *rev-simp.sgm*, shows the more natural tendency of changes to occur within useful logical boundaries.

Example 23 — While I Wasn't Watching, What Changed?

And Today's Winner Is:

To build this application, all we've done is add declare one new attribute for each of the most useful containing elements:

```
<!ATTLIST (div|p|%list;|li)
            ID    ID              #IMPLIED
            role (insert | delete) #IMPLIED>
```

What do I mean by "most useful containing elements" in the previous paragraph? Why am I being rude to HEAD, BODY, A, and so forth? It's all intuition, in fact. You have to examine your DTD, and consider the way you and your colleagues work. What is the most useful size of document part that you want to track for its changes? What is a sensibly large unit? Bigger than B or I, I'd say, but smaller than the large head and body divisions. It's up to you. You can attach revision control attributes (in either this application or the next one) to any element types you choose.

Two small parts of the sample file, *rev-simp.sgm*, follow. The first shows the use of the attribute to indicate that any entire DIV element has been removed from the document; the second illustrates a new paragraph that has appeared in this version of the document:

```
<DIV ROLE="DELETE">
<H1>The Formalities</H1>
<P>Careful readers will recollect that an SGML document includes
both a Document Type Definition and a Document Instance that conforms
to it.</P>
<P> [...] </P>
</DIV>
```

```
<P ROLE="INSERT">
The same sample file, renamed to indicate a relationship with the new
<I>revision.dtd</I>, has been updated to reflect certain changes. One
division has been marked for deletion. (Notice that I don't say
<I>deleted</I>; that's now a separate step.) This paragraph has been
added in. The attributes are set accordingly.</P>
```

Bonus:

Choose from the Panorama styles menu to view the document with and without the revisions visible. All three versions, before the changes, with the changes in progress, and after the changes have been integrated, may be displayed.

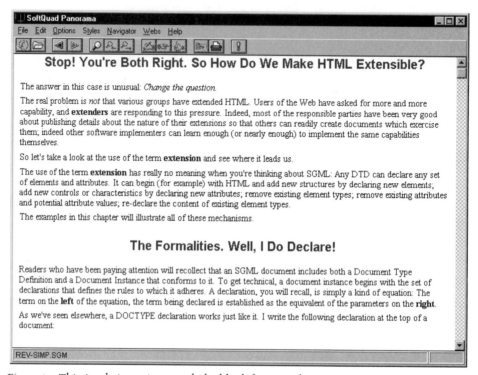

Figure 40. This is what rev-simp.sgm looks like before any changes are started.

Example 23 — While I Wasn't Watching, What Changed?

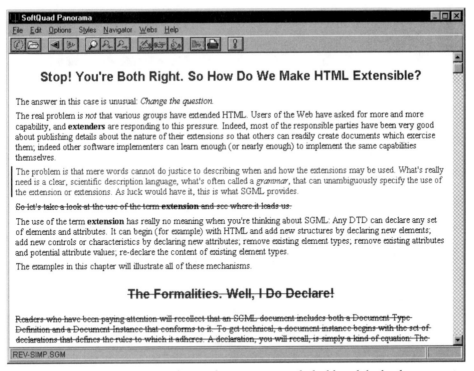

Figure 41. This is what rev-simp.sgm looks like while the changes are in progress

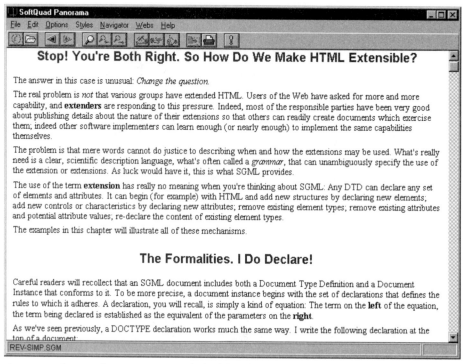

Figure 42. This is what rev-simp.sgm looks like after the changes are integrated

But wait, there's more...

In the next section, we build on the simple structures of *rev-simp.dtd* to produce an "industrial strength" application. All it takes is a few more attributes.

Have We Outgrown Looseleaf Binders Yet?

Goal of the Example:

The *rev-ata.dtd* takes the idea of using attributes to track historical information (which we saw in its preliminary form in *rev-simp.dtd*) and applies it to a production environment in which revised parts of a document must later be merged with a previous version. A typical situation with such a requirement would be one in which a very large set of documentation is received on an infrequent basis, but updates appear relatively frequently. The idea is that software would take the second document, and following instructions embedded in that document's attributes, would merge it with the original (using unique IDS in the source document), thereby producing the updated version of a very large documentation suite.

As with the *history.dtd*, we could have handled these in various ways. I chose to turn for inspiration to the SGML application development work of the aerospace industry, whose use of SGML for maintenance manuals and procedures ranks among the world's most critical applications. If the wrong version of a repair procedure is used in the course of an airplane's maintenance operations, lives could be at risk.

The goals of the example, then, are:

- To explore the use of attributes to merge information from two documents, or, more precisely, to allow us to merge two documents
- To draw attention, in a quiet way, to the fact that much of what we all learn about DTDs comes from the collective pool of wisdom being gained around the world by thousands of individuals in dozens of industry sectors about the creation of SGML applications. In the case of the revision control attributes, they are a slightly modified version of the attributes applied to revisions in an industry that lives and breathes control over its documents: the aerospace industry.

Goal of the Application

To build an application that will support the creation of a separate file of changes to a document which could be merged, when appropriate, with a previous version to build a new revision.

Is Influenced by/Builds on:

Two SGML applications that never expected to be introduced meet in this simple example. We bring a little piece of the *Air Transport Association/Aerospace Industries Association* SGML committee's work to bear on the task at hand, and weave into our HTML four attributes lifted (with modification) from the ATA Spec 2100 (as we call it in casual conversation).

As with the last example, the revision control attributes in this DTD are associated both with existing HTML 2.0 element types and with the DIV element types resurrected from the *htmldiv.dtd* example.

Insofar as this example also explores the idea of external processes adding to or subtracting from a document via a separate file, this example also builds upon the philosophy behind the *htmlerd.dtd*. It has a similar delicate insouciance about it (as a wine-taster might say).

Example 24 — Have We Outgrown Looseleaf Binders Yet?

Stored on the Accompanying Disk as:

Sample DTD: *rev-ata.dtd*

Sample Instance: *rev-ata.sgm*

Step by Step:

No beating around the bush. *This chapter has gone on long enough.* Here is the new attribute definition list declaration for the major containing elements:

```
<!ATTLIST (div|p|%list;|li)
          id       ID             #IMPLIED
          changed  (new|replaces|deletes|unchangd) #IMPLIED
          attach   IDREF          #IMPLIED
          position (before|after) #IMPLIED>
```

The *rev-simp.dtd* gave us a very simple way of tracking whether content was inserted or deleted, but didn't solve the far more interesting problem: How can we avoid bloating the subject document with volumes of changes? We can imagine an information distribution scenario in which this matters a great deal. An aerospace manufacturer might send out, once a year, a CD-ROM with masses of technical information on it. But changes occur to small portions of that information on an on-going basis. An airline (the recipient of the CD-ROM) could dial into a password-protected computer and simply download the changes to the content. (The ATA provides these changes in units it calls "anchors" — not to be confused with the anchors of hyperlinks.) The SGML browser that the airline uses to read the technical information would load the downloaded file into its memory and then replace, insert or delete the subject contents according to instructions in the attributes.

Accordingly, we need the functionality of the *Simplified Revision* application combined with a mechanism for ensuring that we can point to the original elements and pass instructions to the browser. The ATA attributes above do that. Let's examine each in turn:

id   As with the MODREQ element type, we need to be able to refer to *any element* in the source document. You're not likely to want to create unique identifiers for each element, but software exists to perform this simple function, guaranteeing their uniqueness.

changed   A simple yes/no question with embellishments. Has this element changed? How? In the subject document, none of these attributes will be specified, naturally, because it's only later that we change them. In a file consisting of changes, all of them will need to indicate the nature of the change. The set of choices is:

> *new*   The entire new element (including its markup) is either inserted before or after the element that is identified by the attach attribute
>
> *replaces*   The entire new element (including its markup) replaces the entire subject element (including its markup) which is identified by the attach attribute
>
> *deletes*   The new element causes the system to remove the subject element (including its markup) identified by the attach attribute
>
> *unchangd*   The element is provided for information only, or because it is part of a larger unit of revised information. Another compelling reason to have this availability is that someone may ask to have original subject information re-sent to them.

Example 24 — Have We Outgrown Looseleaf Binders Yet?

attach   To what element in the subject document is the change-bearing version attached? The new element (or revised element or instructions to delete), through this attribute, points at the unique ID value of the effected element.

position   The position attribute tells us (and/or our software) what is to be done. The set of choices is straightforward. In combination with a changed attribute of "new", the effect of the new element is to be inserted:

> *before*   the element identified by the attach attribute
>
> *after*   the element identified by the attach attribute.

We have an interesting choice with regards to the attach attribute. Assuming we leave it just as it has been declared in the example above, notice that when we have a document that consists of nothing but changes to the subject document, that file will *not* be valid SGML. It will contain element types with IDREF attribute values which don't point at ID values in the same document. Once they're merged, however, that problem will go away. In fact, validation at that point may indicate markup errors if you receive a parser message telling you that an IDREF has not matching ID.

On the other hand, as we did in the MODREQ element type previously, if we give attach the declared value of either NMTOKEN or CDATA, then the document listing the changes will parse both standalone and once merged into the source text, but we do lose the ability to ensure that there is a validatable relationship between the attach values and the id value of each element.

Bonus and Anti-Bonus:

There is no software on the disk accompanying this book that will automatically merge a subject document with a collection of changed elements, cleverly replacing, inserting and deleting. Sorry. But you can get the same effect by examining the different presentations of the document that I've included on the disk.

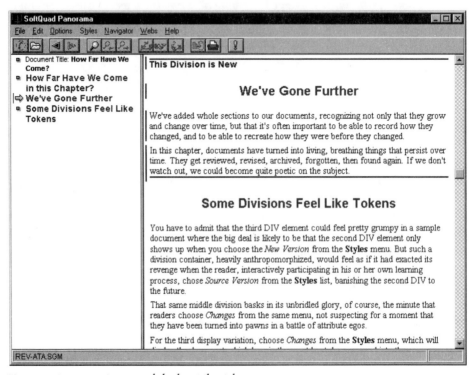

Figure 43. Open rev-ata.sgm and check out the styles.

But wait, there's more...

This concludes the major HTML-centric portion of the book. We'll catch up with HTML again (and further extend it!) after a brief visit to other applications.

✎ PART III

Stepping Beyond

❧ CHAPTER 7

Fresh DTDS

I know what you're thinking. You're saying to yourself, "He's toying with us. He's adding little bits and pieces of new capability to HTML just to be tantalizing. When is he going to show us fresh, new DTDS, built from scratch for *some specific purpose*, without this legacy of HTML-ness stifling them like an old-fashioned vest that, strictly speaking, is just a little too tight around the waist?"

This is that moment. The applications in this chapter, designed for a handful of particular purposes, will work only with full SGML software. The previous examples, though they contained special functionality beyond HTML, nonetheless could be displayed (with varying degrees of usefulness) with standard, off-the-shelf Web browsers. Not this new crowd.

In practical terms, this means:

- Documents created with the markup declared in these applications *must* begin with a document type declaration associating them with their DTD. There is no longer a cheap fallback of opening the instance in an HTML browser knowing that *something* will work.
- By extension, you need to have (or create) style sheets for each DTD. The CD-ROM that accompanies this book includes styles for each sample DTD.

If you've already been enjoying style sheets for the HTML-based examples, and have been consistently using a document type declaration, then nothing changes. You *have* been working with full SGML throughout the book. Don't let the knowledge that you recognized some element types as having HTML names get in the way of that fact.

In this section, you will see that the names of element types can be whatever makes the most sense — for you, for your colleagues, for your publishing or database system, or for the industry in which you work. Accordingly, element type names should be thought of as a source of comfort, or even luxury. *Remember that you create these names.* A DTD, therefore, is a mechanism for bridging two worlds:

- Subject matter experts (engineers, financial analysts, technical writers, testers of pharmaceutical products, whoever) can provide the actual element type names and the names of the attributes and their potential values. In this way, the DTD reflects the real language of the domain, offering terms that have meaning to practitioners in the field.
- Document analysts or production system or database experts provide the structures, designing the receptacles (so to speak) into which data gets placed. Those structures must reflect the technical requirements of the system; to a great extent the naming conventions can reflect the sociological requirements of the people involved.

For example, it is likely to be appropriate in an aerospace setting to have engineers provide the legend associated with an illustration. A DTD created for their use might give them a choice of listing "risks", "stresses" or "limits". For the engineers, choosing one of these terms from a pick list or a toolbar would be completely intuitive (and also reflect how this information should be stored in a parts database).

Figure 44. A picklist offers a set of possible entries for an aerospace engineer to annotate the legend of an illustration. A context-sensitive SGML editor knows which element types are usable at any point in a document.

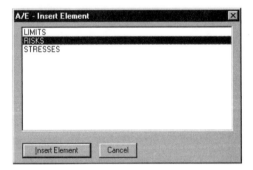

The document instance such engineers create, however, might be sent to a technical writer whose sense of meaningful structures more closely approximates the look of the final pages or display. As the document opens in the writer's environment, the markup (and portions of the content, if necessary) could be transformed to match the requirements of the authoring or editing step.

The engineer creates a document much like this:

```
<LEGEND PART="A737544332R">
<LIMIT COMPNT="1">16.4 psi
<LIMIT COMPNT="2">228 psi
<LIMIT COMPNT="3">24.66 psi
```

The technical writer sees the same document, after its automatic transformation, as:

```
<LIST>
<HEAD>
Legend for list of limits for components
of Part A737544332R</HEAD>
<ITEM>1. 16.4 psi
<ITEM>2. 228 psi
<ITEM>3. 24.66 psi
```

Are these the same? Is the actual information content identical for both these examples? Perhaps to a trained human reader they are, but, interestingly, I think one could argue that the first one, the engineer's version, would be more useful to a computer, particularly to software that was performing stress tests or other automated procedures. This is a digression, and not the subject of the current or any other chapter in this book.

Note   The examples do bring us neatly to Rubinsky's Second Law: *One of the things computers do well is transform consistent input to useful forms of consistent output. Let them. Indeed, encourage this behavior.*

Which means that we can take advantage of a freedom to create full SGML applications whose markup grows entirely out of the subject matter and our uses of it. As HTML proves, SGML applications don't have to be complicated or long-winded to be useful — and popular.

The examples in this chapter have been created or chosen specifically because they illustrate how far you can go using SGML in the creation of documents that make sense in daily life: press releases, agendas and minutes for meetings, collections of slides.

And of course, there are still a few SGML constructs and capabilities to be introduced.

🐦§ Example 25

Stop the Presses!

Goal of the Example:

If you've been keying in the examples given throughout the book so far, congratulations. You probably have learned the material better that way than the rest of us, and you have also come face to face with one of the original requirements for full SGML: Shortcuts. Why, you may have been wondering to yourself, do I have to type in all the start- and end-tags when often it was pretty clear that any computer worth its chips would have been able to determine what the markup should be? This section introduces the notion of markup minimization.

Goal of the Application:

- To create the markup needed to support press releases that are published with two different formats
- To create an application that can be keyed in by people unfamiliar with full SGML using the minimum amount of markup.

Stored on the Accompanying Disk as:

Sample DTD: *pressrel.dtd*

Sample Instance: *pressrel.sgm* (which includes all the markup), *pressmin.sgm* (which omits as many tags as possible), *presspan.sgm* (which is built specifically for use with Panorama — see the note in "Bonus", below).

Step by Step:

SGML's optional markup minimization features allow markup in the document instance to be significantly reduced by a variety of techniques including shortening or omitting tags when the parser can infer them from the content model of the current open element.

In a DTD, two extra characters, entered between the name and the content of the element type declaration, define whether or not a tag can be omitted. The first character represents the start-tag; the second character represents the end-tag.

Thus far, in this book, element type declarations have been of the form:

```
<!ELEMENT pressrel (front, body, contact)>
```

Let us assume that we wish to indicate that the PRESSREL element type may not have to have, in a document, its end-tag explicitly typed in. To make this clear, in the same declaration, including the omitted tag minimization parameter, we would type:

```
<!ELEMENT pressrel - o (front, body, contact)>
```

The minimization symbols are:

- O (the letter, not the number zero) to indicate that the tag *may be* omitted under certain clearly defined circumstances. It is possible for the start-tag to be omissible on some but not all occurrences of a particular element type.
- - (a hyphen) to indicate that the tag is required.

Example 25 — Stop the Presses!

The DTD for press releases has been designed to take into account that people writing such documents may not be SGML experts. The DTD indicates a number of places where start- or end-tags may be omitted. Let's examine it line by line:

```
<!ELEMENT pressrel - o (front, body, contact)>
```

Here, it is always possible to omit the end-tag of the document element. When there's no more document entity, the parser closes any remaining open elements.

```
<!ELEMENT front o o (head, subhead?, date, relnote?)>
```

Our press release begins with a *required* FRONT element. Accordingly, it will always be possible to omit the start-tag. When the parser gets to the end of the <PRESSREL> start-tag, it will expect <FRONT>. Failing to find one, it will check the DTD to see what's required, and imply the missing piece of markup.

```
<!ELEMENT body o o (slug?, (%paratyp; | %lists;)*)>
```

BODY acts similarly. Our parser reaches the end of either the DATE or RELNOTE element types, expects the end of the FRONT element, and finding none, implies one. According to the DTD, only one thing is now allowed, <BODY>, the start-tag for the body element. Not finding it next, the parser implies one.

```
<!ELEMENT (%paratyp;| relnote) - o (#PCDATA | %paracon;)*>
```

All of the "paragraph-like element types", PARA, BQ, NOTE, RELNOTE, and so forth are peers, at the same level within the hierarchy. It is simple, therefore, for a parser to know to close off any of such element types whenever it runs into a peer element (also called a "sibling").

```
<!ELEMENT slug - o (date, place)>
```

SLUG has an omissible end-tag since it may contain none of the element types that may follow it. A parser knows, therefore, if it sees a PARA or a BQ, (after DATE and PLACE, then it's time to close SLUG and move on to the rest of the BODY.

```
<!ELEMENT (%lists;) - - (lhead?, litem)+>
<!ELEMENT litem    - O (#PCDATA | (para | %lists;)*)>
```

I've insisted on having both start- and end-tags for lists since lists may be nested inside of list items. If you allow omissibility in this case, you may always be confused as to whether a specific list item is contained in a parent list or a child (or nested) list.

```
<LIST1>
<LITEM>We're in the first item in the top-level list.
  <LIST2>
  <LITEM>This is the first item in the nested list.
  <LITEM>This is the second item in the nested list.</LITEM>
  <LITEM>Under the circumstances, this could be the start of
  a third list item within the LIST2 element or, back out
  in the hierarchy, this could be the second item in the top-level list.
```

In the list example, we can track it all smoothly as far as the start-tags go — we're counting on there being no omitted start-tags — but once we get to missing list end-tags, we still have the potential for confusion.

```
<!ELEMENT (date | name) o o (#PCDATA)>
```

DATE and NAME can have minimized start-tags for exactly the same reason — both are required elements within their parents. The omissible end-tags are the result of the lack of ambiguity in the elements that follow them. Naturally, you cannot omit the end-tag of one element type and also omit the start-tag of the next one.

```
<!ELEMENT place    - o  (#PCDATA)>
<!ELEMENT contact - o  (name, affil?, phone?)>
<!ELEMENT (affil | phone) - o (#PCDATA)>
```

Usually a large number of element types may have omissible end-tags, simply because the element types that may follow them are not allowed within them. The start-tag of a peer element will close off the previous element. We'll see examples of this in the document instances coming up very soon.

Example 25 — Stop the Presses!

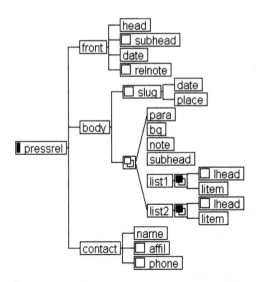

Figure 46. The tree view illustrates the Press Release DTD.

```
<!ELEMENT (%paracon;) - o (#PCDATA)>
```

The only circumstance under which you can omit the end-tag of one of the "paragraph content" style of element types is when the quote, or emphasized phrase, or whatever it is, ends at the end of the parent element. When you hit the end of the paragraph, for instance, all still open subelements must be closed off. The important point here is that even though the tag is omissible, it can be omitted only in unambiguous circumstances. If it were omitted in the middle of the paragraph, for example, the rest of the paragraph would be treated as part of the "paragraph content" element. For that reason, it is usually best not to make such tags omissible.

```
<!ELEMENT head o o (#PCDATA | %paracon;)*>
<!ELEMENT lhead - o (#PCDATA | %paracon;)*>
```

HEAD is the required first element within FRONT. Leaving its start-tag off would be completely acceptable. The LHEAD end-tag can be omitted because the only other element type that is allowed in the lists is LITEM, and it will always have its start-tag.

Whatever you minimize

Let's see this all in practice. The first example is a minimized instance of the PRESSREL application:

```
<PRESSREL>New Book Proposes Tag Power for the Internet
<SUBHEAD>
<EMPH1>SGML on the Web: Small Steps Beyond HTML</EMPH1>
Advocates Extending World Wide Web Markup
</SUBHEAD>
<DATE>2 August 1997
<RELNOTE>for immediate release
<SLUG>3 August 1997
<PLACE>Toronto
<PARA><Q>If the World Wide Web doesn't grow to fully fulfill
the requirements of a discerning public and a fiercely competitive
environment for information providers, it will fade away fast,</Q>
said Yuri Rubinsky and Murray Maloney, authors of a new text
published by Prentice-Hall, a division of some very large
publishing operation.
<PARA>Delayed indefinitely by the the authors' insistence on
being current with the latest changes to the Web,
<EMPH1>SGML on the Web: Small Steps Beyond HTML</EMPH1>
was finally released against their wishes.
<PARA><Q>What can we say?</Q> they said,
<Q>These days any reference work is out of date
the minute it comes off the presses.</Q>
<CONTACT>George Meteskey
<AFFIL>Dept of Information
<PHONE>416 555-1212
```

The parser expands

An SGML parser will take the minimal markup that it sees, and expand it. Here is the same document after parsing:

```
<PRESSREL><FRONT>
<HEAD>New Book Proposes Tag Power for the Internet</HEAD>
```

Example 25 — Stop the Presses!

The parser implied the start-tags for FRONT and HEAD, as well as the HEAD end-tag.

```
<SUBHEAD>
<EMPH1>SGML on the Web: Small Steps Beyond HTML</EMPH1>
Advocates Extending World Wide Web Markup
</SUBHEAD>
<DATE>2 August 1997</DATE>
<RELNOTE>for immediate release</RELNOTE></FRONT>
```

The parser sees the RELNOTE start-tag and implies the end-tag for DATE. Then, far more dramatically, it sees the SLUG start-tag, and closes off RELNOTE and FRONT, and opens BODY.

```
<BODY><SLUG>
<DATE>3 August 1997</DATE>
<PLACE>Toronto</PLACE></SLUG>
```

The appearance of *data* rather than markup within SLUG lets the parser know something is missing. It implies the start-tag for DATE, and then the start-tag for PLACE tells it an end-tag is needed for DATE too.

Then `<PARA>` closes both PLACE and SLUG. We are just racing along here!

```
<PARA><Q>If the World Wide Web doesn't grow to fully fulfill
the requirements of a discerning public and a fiercely competitive
environment for information providers, it will fade away fast,</Q>
said Yuri Rubinsky and Murray Maloney, authors of a new text
published by Prentice-Hall, a division of some very large
publishing operation.</PARA>
```

All the PARA elements are closed off by the next paragraph's start-tag.

```
<PARA>Delayed indefinitely by the the authors' insistence on
being current with the latest changes to the Web,
<EMPH1>SGML on the Web: Small Steps Beyond HTML</EMPH1>
was finally released against their wishes.
</PARA>
<PARA><Q>What can we say?</Q> they said,
<Q>These days any reference work is out of date
the minute it comes off the presses.</Q></PARA>
</BODY>
```

The `<CONTACT>` start-tag closes both PARA and BODY. Strictly speaking, we could have had it close off the quotation as well, but I'm old-fashioned when it comes to the %paracon; elements, and believe it really is good practice to close off elements embedded in paragraphs or similar structures. You can imagine, for instance, wanting to add a sentence to the paragraph and losing all track of the fact that the quotation end-tag is implied.

CONTACT has a required NAME element, whose start-tag the parser inserts as soon as it sees the data. <AFFIL> implies the </NAME>. <PHONE> implies the </AFFIL>.

```
<CONTACT>
<NAME>George Meteskey</NAME>
<AFFIL>Dept of Information</AFFIL>
<PHONE>416 555-1212</PHONE>
</CONTACT>
</PRESSREL>
```

And, finally, the end of the document forces the parser to close all remaining open elements. All this in the twinkle of an eye.

Minimally enthused about all this

I confess it's a bit difficult for me to wax too enthusiastic about all the commotion I've just described. Most people in production environments don't actually type SGML markup. The ISO committee that created the standard was conscientious and methodical in imagining techniques to ease the burden on people creating SGML documents, but by now, a decade later, a great variety of software exists to insert markup for you, from scrolling picklists and from toolbars. You should never have to pause in the creative rush of composition to ask yourself whether you are able to omit some markup because it's contextually required and the resultant document instance is unambiguous.

The effects of skillful markup minimization are, nonetheless, dramatic, and this book would have been incomplete without some mention of it.

Example 25 — Stop the Presses!

Bonus:

If you have any SGML parsing tools (or editors with a built-in parser), you may enjoy looking at *pressmin.sgm*, seeing how little markup it includes, and then examining the output of the parser. The output should match *pressrel.sgm*, whose markup is the fully-expanded equivalent of that in the first file.

```
<!DOCTYPE PRESREL PUBLIC "Press Release">

<PRESSREL>New Book Proposes Tag Power for the Internet
<SUBHEAD><EMPH1>SGML on the Web: Small Steps Beyond HTML</EMPH1>
Advocates Extending World Wide Web Markup
</SUBHEAD>
<DATE>
<RELNOTE>
<SLUG>
<PLACE>
<PARA><Q>If the World Wide Web doesn't grow  to fully fulfill
the requirements of a discerning public and a fiercely competitive
environment for information providers, it will fade away fast,</Q>
said Yuri Rubinsky and Murray Maloney, authors of a new text
published by Prentice-Hall, a division of some very large
publishing operation.
<P>Delayed indefinitely by the the authors' insistence on
being current with the latest changes to the Web,
<EMPH1>SGML on the Web: Small Steps Beyond HTML</EMPH1>
was finally released against their wishes.
<P><Q>What can we say?</Q> they said,
<Q>These days any reference work is out of date
the minute it comes off the presses.</Q>
<NAME>George Meteskey
<AFFIL>Dept of Information
<PHONE>416 555-1212
```

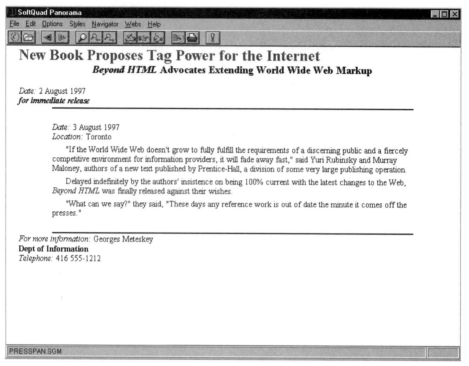

Figure 47. *Open presspan.sgm with Panorama to see how this simple struc-ture translates into an effective page design.*

There is a third version of the same file, *presspan.sgm*, that is less heavily minimized. This version has been prepared particularly for use with Panorama. The browser's parser represents a trade-off between two heavily competing points of view and capabilities:

- A program utilizing an SGML parser that supports SGML's optional markup min-imization features could easily expand the *pressmin.sgm* file. And it is worth not-ing that the sample document is a completely valid SGML document, with no surprises.
- Web browsers traditionally are far more lax in what they'll accept than SGML parsers, recognizing that many people create documents that are far from valid SGML. These people might well be dismayed to discover that their documents would not open in a Web browser.

Example 25 — Stop the Presses!

Panorama takes the Web context very seriously, and is, accordingly, optimized for full SGML documents that may not be valid — or even close. Because of this unpredictability, the Panorama parser is less likely to believe that the appearance of one element should automatically close off the previous "sibling" element. In any case it is always best to validate your documents with any of the popular free or commercial SGML tools to prepare them for posting to your Web site or internal SGML browsing environment.

But wait, there's more...

Later, if you are keen on typing in SGML markup or if you have a collection of consistently created text files, you may wish to avail yourself of other minimization techniques. (There are several.) The standard SGML reference texts cover the subject in depth; I refer you to the *Bibliography* (p. 449).

What's Content?
What Appears Magically?

Goal of the Example:

Even while we're exploring new applications, we must not lose track of the fact that there still remains much to learn regarding the creation and processing of full SGML. This section introduces several new concepts and revisits some old friends.

- *Generated Text*: a name for those parts of the display of information which are produced by publishing or browsing software. You've seen them all around you. The page number on the bottom of this page didn't appear in the source file. (I can guarantee it — I'm looking at it. You're looking at something quite different.) The word "Example" at the beginning of this section and the number that follows it weren't in the source file. Numbers or bullets on lists are generated.
- *Multiple style sheets*: make clear that the rules (for generating numbers, for example) or the actual fixed generated text do come from somewhere. In the traditional realm of typesetting, the specification of generated text came from processing instructions accompanying a manuscript. In modern times, they *should* come from style sheets or similar mechanisms. This allows generated text to be altered or updated (as you'll see in the sample files). Compare this with first generation Web browsers that decide, on your behalf, which element types have numbers automatically created. (Only LI inside of OL, in case you were wondering.)
- A *New Set of Common Element Type Names*: throughout this book there has been a presumption of the usefulness of common names for element types, even though the DTDs in which they're contained may be vastly different. We used HTML generic identifiers (GIS) scattered in and amongst specialized GIS for

revision control, for electronic review, for metadata, and so forth. This chapter, however, has already introduced a new "family" of element types, including PARA, NOTE, EMPH1 and EMPH2, LIST1 and LIST2. In this example, we continue to employ those as the basic structural element types.

• *Continued and Extended Use of "Information Content Tagging"*: you'll see that *minutes.dtd* uses a large number of generic identifiers which explicitly describe what they do — ACTION, ATTENDS (for attendees at the meeting), MOTION, LOCALE, STATUS, and so on. They are interwoven with the publication-structure element types and provide a more valuable alternative to them. (You could, for example, create an "Action Item Summary" using a traditional list element, but it's more useful as a reminder for the next meeting to have it recognizably distinct, using an ACTSUMM element, which in turn consists of one or more ACTION elements.)

Goal of the Application:

I'm a strong believer that, whenever plausible, markup should follow information around throughout its existence. I've written earlier about the transformative powers of markup as content moved from aerospace engineers to technical writers. This section provides a far simpler example; markup that supports the brief life cycle of a document as it moves from being the agenda for an upcoming meeting to becoming the minutes of the same meeting. (One can imagine the extension of this principle: information marked up in a Request for Proposals document turns into the core of the response. The same marked-up content becomes a Request for Quotation, then a Specification, then a Test Procedures Manual, and so forth. The information-content markup stays consistent throughout — the low-level publication-structure element types stay the same, the high-level element types change as needed.

The application includes what amounts to two DTDs in one: a small set of element types which can be used to create the agenda for a meeting, and a much richer set for the minutes of the same meeting. The intention is that, where appropriate, an efficient minutes-taker could simply edit the agenda to create the skeleton for the minutes. As a lazy minutes-taker, I can attest to the downright usefulness of this straightforward approach (and application).

Example 26 — What's Content? What Appears Magically?

Is Influenced by/Builds on:

A number of the basic element types for this DTD come directly from the press release application. At the same time, it builds on our previous discussions of *content-oriented markup*.

In addition, this application builds on a DTD for minutes originally created for meetings of the SGML *Open* Board of Directors.

Stored on the Accompanying Disk as:

Sample DTD: *minutes.dtd*

Sample Instance: *agenda.sgm* and *minutes.sgm*

Step by Step:

The sample files record the agenda and the minutes for a meeting that never took place. Both the DTD and the SGML encoding for the two sample files are reprinted in the following pages, along with two formatted versions of each.

The DTD is the model of simplicity:

```
<!ENTITY % emphs     "em | emph1 | emph2 ">
<!ENTITY % text      "%emphs; ">
<!ENTITY % heads     "h1 | h2">
<!ENTITY % lists     "list1 | list2">
<!ENTITY % special   "motion | action ">
<!ENTITY % paracon   "%text; | q ">
<!ENTITY % paratyp   "para | bq | note | %heads;">

<!ELEMENT minutes (head, body)>
<!ELEMENT head    (group, mtgtype?, date, attends, locale, mtgnum?)>
<!ELEMENT body    (open?, item*, adjourn?, actsumm?)>

<!ELEMENT open    (#PCDATA)>
<!ELEMENT item    (topic, (%paratyp; | %lists;| %special;)*)>
<!ELEMENT adjourn (mover, second)>
<!ELEMENT actsumm (action+)>
```

```
<!ELEMENT (%paratyp;) (#PCDATA | %paracon;)*>
<!ELEMENT (%paracon;) (#PCDATA)>

<!ELEMENT (%lists;) (lhead?, litem)+>
<!ELEMENT lhead     (#PCDATA | %paracon;)*>
<!ELEMENT litem     (#PCDATA | (para | %lists;)*)>

<!ELEMENT attends   (name, affil?, officer)+>
<!ELEMENT motion    (mover, second, content, discuss?, vote)>
<!ELEMENT action    (num?, descr, assignto, duedate?, status?)>

<!ELEMENT (topic|descr)                   (#PCDATA | %paracon;)*>
<!ELEMENT (name|affil|officer)            (#PCDATA)>
<!ELEMENT (num|assignto|duedate|status)           (#PCDATA)>
<!ELEMENT (group|mtgtype|date|locale|mtgnum) (#PCDATA)>
<!ELEMENT (mover|second|content|discuss|vote) (#PCDATA)>
```

Figure 48. The tree view illustrates the overall structure of the DTD *for meeting agendas and minutes.*

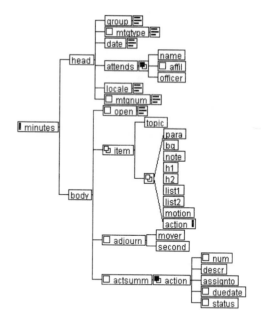

Example 26 — What's Content? What Appears Magically?

A Meeting's Agenda

An examination of the sample agenda introduces the concept of generated content:

```
<MINUTES>
<HEAD>
<GROUP>The Dadaist Movement</GROUP>
<MTGTYPE>Agenda: Organizational Meeting</MTGTYPE>
<DATE>16 Sept 1915 1800h</DATE>
<LOCALE>Terrace Cafe, Zurich</LOCALE>
</HEAD>
<BODY>
<ITEM><TOPIC>Approval of Previous Minutes (None)</TOPIC></ITEM>
<ITEM><TOPIC>Discussion of Proposed Name</TOPIC>
<NOTE>(Tzara proposes <EM>Dada</EM></NOTE></ITEM>
<ITEM><TOPIC>Establishment of Constitutional Committee</TOPIC></ITEM>
<ITEM><TOPIC>Membership Policies and Procedures</TOPIC></ITEM>
<ITEM><TOPIC>Publications and Exhibition Schedule</TOPIC></ITEM>
<ITEM><TOPIC>Other Business</TOPIC></ITEM>
</BODY>
</MINUTES>
```

As you can see in the formatted examples, generated headings, item identifiers and other typographic effects can be quite easily adapted to suit the tastes of different audiences. A comparison of the printed samples exposes some of the options available to you in the generation of content.

Figure 49. In the first sample, horizontal rules are generated for the start and end of the HEAD element. "Where:" comes from the LOCALE element. Automatic numbering is associated with the ITEM elements.

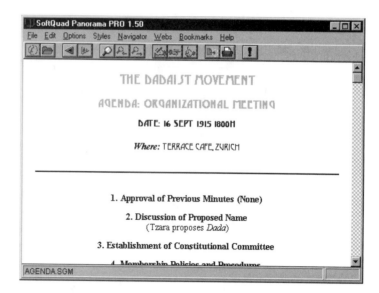

Figure 50. The diamond-shaped typographic ornaments are generated for the start and end of GROUP elements, as well as the HEAD element. "Location:" is generated for the start of the LOCALE element. In this version, the the text "Item:" is generated for the start of ITEM elements.

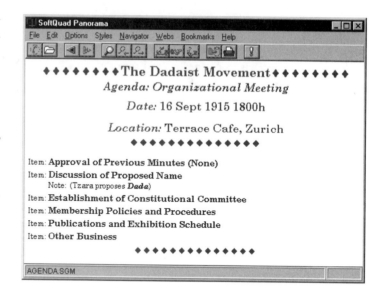

Example 26 — What's Content? What Appears Magically?

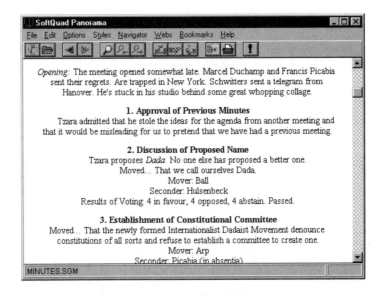

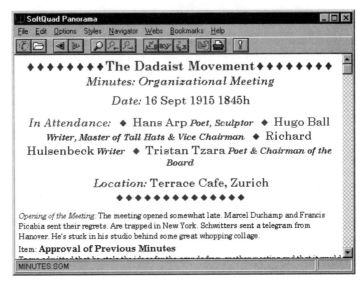

A Meeting's Minutes

The sample instance of the minutes of the meeting are a fair bit longer than the agenda, but well worth the effort to study it.

```
<!DOCTYPE minutes PUBLIC "Agenda and Minutes">
<MINUTES><HEAD>
<GROUP>The Dadaist Movement</GROUP>
<MTGTYPE>Minutes: Organizational Meeting</MTGTYPE>
<DATE>16 Sept 1915 1845h</DATE>

<ATTENDS>
<NAME>Hans Arp</NAME>
<AFFIL>Poet, Sculptor</AFFIL>

<NAME>Hugo Ball</NAME>
<AFFIL>Writer, Master of Tall Hats</AFFIL>
<OFFICER>Vice Chairman</OFFICER>

<NAME>Richard Hulsenbeck</NAME>
<AFFIL>Writer</AFFIL>

<NAME>Tristan Tzara</NAME>
<AFFIL>Poet</AFFIL>
<OFFICER>Chairman of the Board</OFFICER>
</ATTENDS>

<LOCALE>Terrace Cafe, Zurich</LOCALE>
</HEAD>

<BODY>
<OPEN>
The meeting opened somewhat late.
Marcel Duchamp and Francis Picabia sent their regrets.
Are trapped in New York.
Schwitters sent a telegram from Hanover.
He's stuck in his studio behind some great whopping collage.
</OPEN>

<ITEM>
<TOPIC>Approval of Previous Minutes</TOPIC>
<PARA>Tzara admitted that he stole the ideas for the agenda
from another meeting and that it would be misleading for us to pretend
that we have had a previous meeting.</PARA></ITEM>
```

Example 26 — What's Content? What Appears Magically?

```
<ITEM>
<TOPIC>Discussion of Proposed Name</TOPIC>
<PARA>Tzara proposes <HEAD>Dada</HEAD>.
No one else has proposed a better one.</PARA>
<MOTION>
<CONTENT>That we call ourselves Dada.</CONTENT>
<MOVER>Ball</MOVER>
<SECOND>Hulsenbeck</SECOND>
<VOTE>4 in favour, 4 opposed, 4 abstain. Passed.</VOTE>
</MOTION></ITEM>

<ITEM>
<TOPIC>Establishment of Constitutional Committee</TOPIC>
<MOTION>
<CONTENT>That the newly formed Internationalist Dadaist Movement
denounce constitutions of all sorts and refuse to establish
a committee to create one.</CONTENT>
<MOVER>Arp</MOVER>
<SECOND>Picabia (in absentia)</SECOND>
<DISCUSS>No discussion was held.</DISCUSS>
<VOTE>Unanimous.</VOTE>
</MOTION></ITEM>

<ITEM>
<TOPIC>Membership Policies and Procedures</TOPIC>
<MOTION>
<CONTENT>That the newly formed Internationalist Dadaist Movement
denounce policies and procedures and formally censure our colleague
Tzara for creating this agenda.</CONTENT>
<MOVER>Duchamp (in absentia)</MOVER>
<SECOND>Picabia (in absentia)</SECOND>
<DISCUSS>No discussion was held.</DISCUSS>
<VOTE>Unanimous.</VOTE>
</MOTION></ITEM>

<ITEM><TOPIC>Publications and Exhibition Schedule</TOPIC>
<PARA>Now we're getting to the important stuff.
Tzara and Picabia intend to found as many publications as possible,
starting, naturally, with a periodical to be entitled <EM>Dada</EM>.
Suggestion to establish a gallery to host exhibitions,
lectures and entertainments.</PARA>
<ACTION>
<DESCR>Find a location for the Cabaret Voltaire.</DESCR>
<ASSIGNTO>Tzara  and Hugo Ball</ASSIGNTO>
```

```
<DUEDATE>October 15</DUEDATE>
</ACTION></ITEM>

<ITEM><TOPIC>Other Business</TOPIC>
<MOTION>
<CONTENT>That we never record minutes again.
In fact, that we destroy all records of this meeting.
That we become famous.
That we become reckless.
That we counter justice with dada.
That we counter truth with dada.
That we counter minutes with dada.</CONTENT>
<MOVER>All</MOVER>
<SECOND>All</SECOND>
<VOTE>Unanimous.</VOTE>
</MOTION></ITEM>

<ADJOURN>
<MOVER>Duchamp (in absentia)</MOVER>
<SECOND>Schwitters (in Hanover)</SECOND>
<VOTE>Unanimous</VOTE>
</ADJOURN>
</BODY>
</MINUTES>
```

Bonus:

To fully appreciate what the generated text is doing for you in this application, be sure to examine both sample documents using both style sheets available in the browser.

EXAMPLE 27

Turn off the Lights!

Goal of the Example:

We have managed to portage through an awful lot of forest without running into the SGML construct known as the general entity. Given how remarkably useful entities are, this is somewhat remarkable. This example aims to rectify that terrible injustice.

At the same time, the example also serves to introduce us to the SGML NOTATION keyword, which lets us indicate in a document instance, that an element type is encoded in a non-SGML notation. A bitmap graphic, for example, might be in GIF or WMF or BMP.

Goal of the Application:

- To incorporate figures and illustrations into a slide presentation using standardized SGML mechanisms.

Is Influenced by/Builds on:

The publication-structure element types come directly from the press release and minutes applications. The content-specific markup is minimal in the application; there is just a small of amount of tuning for a simple slide show. (You could, for example, readily transform the agenda for a meeting into a slide or set of slides.)

The attributes for the ART element type come more or less directly from the *Association of American Publishers* set of three DTDs, the first major public SGML application in the world.

Stored on the Accompanying Disk as:

Sample DTD: *slideset.dtd*

Sample Instance: *slides1.sgm*

Step by Step:

A *slideset* consists of an optional TITLE followed by one or more SLIDE elements:

```
<!ELEMENT slideset  (title?, slide+)>
<!ELEMENT slide     (head, (%special; | %paratyp; | %lists;)*)>
```

A SLIDE must begin with a HEAD — our display software is counting on there being a HEAD in order to generate the *Table of Slides* as a navigator for our slidesets. The remaining content is to be marked up using the same set of element types that we've been exploring throughout this chapter, with the major exception of two new ones, FIGURE and ART.

Example 27 — Turn off the Lights!

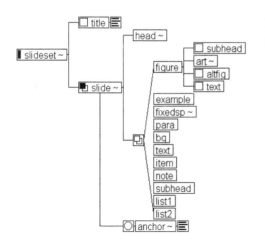

Figure 53. The tree view illustrates the overall structure of the DTD for slides.

As you can well imagine, FIGURE and ART are used for images that are created using drawing, or engineering software. These pictures are certainly not stored as SGML — nor should they be. Graphic data formats — we call them notations — are optimized for the work they need to do, for speed of display or transmission, for fidelity of color. It is the task of the SGML structure of your document to ensure that information accompanies your content that allows processing systems to find, manipulate (if necessary) and display or print the images, irrespective of their notations.

What allows full SGML documents to readily incorporate contents in non-SGML data is the idea of the entity reference, a reference surrounded by delimiters (so it can be readily recognized) to an entity of some kind. You'll notice that the document fragment below begins with a pair of entity declarations in a declaration subset which enable, respectively the &dtd; and &pool; entity references. In this case, both of the declarations have the keyword SYSTEM, which indicates that they have system-specific location names — "dtd.bmp" and "pool.bmp". These are the filenames your software will know to use to find the images in the current folder. If you intended to interchange the images, or make them part of a bundled collection of files and images, you would use existing standardized mechanisms to accomplish that.

The NDATA keyword indicates that the entity being declared has content which is not SGML but some other notation, and the final parameter, BMP is a *data content notation* which has previously been declared, either here in the declaration subset, or, more likely, in the DTD. (We'll examine it in a moment.)

```
<!DOCTYPE SLIDESET PUBLIC "SoftQuad Slideset"[
<!ENTITY dtd  SYSTEM "dtd.bmp"  NDATA BMP>
<!ENTITY pool SYSTEM "pool.bmp" NDATA BMP>
]>
<SLIDESET WHERE="SGML 96"        WHEN="DEC 2, 1996"
          CREATOR="YURI@SQ.COM" SECTION="WEBSGML">
<SLIDE><HEAD>SoftQuad Inc.</HEAD>
<SUBHEAD>Working to bring you full SGML browsing,
on and off the World Wide Web</SUBHEAD>
<TEXT>Prepared By </TEXT>
<TEXT>Yuri Rubinsky </TEXT>
<TEXT>For </TEXT>
<TEXT>Universal Communication</TEXT>
<TEXT>January 1996 </TEXT></SLIDE>
<SLIDE><HEAD>Table of Contents</HEAD>
<ITEM>All You Need to Know about SGML </ITEM>
<ITEM>Standalone SGML Browsing & SGML on the Web </ITEM>
<ITEM>New Capabilities for Browsers </ITEM>
<ITEM>What Are HTML and SGML?</ITEM>
<ITEM>A Slightly Different Notion of a Document</ITEM>
<ITEM>The Information Pool</ITEM>
<ITEM>Small Steps to SGML on the Web </ITEM>
<ITEM>Reasons to Have SGML on the Web </ITEM>
<ITEM>For further information... </ITEM></SLIDE>
[several other slides are not presented here.]
<SLIDE><HEAD>A Slightly Different Notion of a Document </HEAD>
<SUBHEAD>Two Parts; No Surprises </SUBHEAD>
<FIGURE><ART FILE="DTD">
<ALTFIG>The figure is of a box labelled
"The Document" which includes two other boxes,
labelled "DTD" and "Instance".</ALTFIG>
<TEXT>The DTD and the Instance together
comprise the SGML document </TEXT></FIGURE></SLIDE>
<SLIDE><HEAD>The Information Pool</HEAD>
<SUBHEAD>Create Once, Store Once, Use Often</SUBHEAD>
<FIGURE><ART FILE="POOL">
<ALTFIG>The illustration shows a database in the center,
labelled SGML Data Pool, with a caption on the left
reading "In from multiple sources" and on the right
reading "Out to CD-ROM, paper, Internet, anything".</ALTFIG></FIGURE>
</SLIDE>
[several other slides are not presented here.]
</SLIDESET>
```

Example 27 — Turn off the Lights!

When we encounter the FIGURE, we're ready for it. We've declared a name for the *external entity* called for by the ART element's `file` attribute:

```
<FIGURE>
<ART FILE="DTD">
```

As we'll see in the DTD fragment below, the FIGURE element type has been declared as containing ART, followed by an optional "alternative" description of the artwork enclosed in an ALTFIG element type. This allows people who have visual disabilities or computers that don't allow the display of graphics to be offered a description of the graphic they cannot see:

```
<ALTFIG>The figure is of a box labeled
"The Document" which includes two other boxes,
labelled "DTD" and "Instance".</ALTFIG>
<TEXT>The DTD and the Instance together comprise
the SGML document</TEXT></FIGURE>
```

The TEXT element type also contained within FIGURE acts as a caption for the image. You'll find that the caption and the alternative figure description are vastly different. In fact, it is a good exercise always to use the ALTFIG element type (and, in HTML, to use its equivalent, the `alt` attribute declared for images). You'll find that describing an image in such a way that someone who can't see it can, nonetheless, get the benefits of any information it may contain is a useful skill.

Here's the full declaration for FIGURE. The optional SUBHEAD acts as a figure title and is expected to be rendered (on screen or in print) larger than a TEXT element:

```
<!ELEMENT figure     (subhead?, art, altfig?, text?)>
<!ELEMENT art        EMPTY>
<!ELEMENT altfig     (#PCDATA)>
<!ATTLIST art sizex     NUTOKEN #IMPLIED
              sizey     NUTOKEN #IMPLIED
              unit      (i|c|p|u|m|n|v) i
              file      ENTITY #REQUIRED>
```

ART is empty. We know that it is likely to be stored in a notation that an SGML processing system will not read natively. All that remains is that the attributes include enough information that such a system will know what to do. The secret is in the file attribute. Naturally, it's REQUIRED, since without the name of the artwork file there is no point in having an ART element in your document. The keyword ENTITY indicates that the value of the attribute will be a reference to a declared entity. This allows us to include more information in the entity declaration. Let's revisit it:

```
<!ENTITY dtd SYSTEM "dtd.bmp" NDATA BMP>
```

In fact, although NDATA is an SGML keyword (meaning non-SGML data), you cannot simply use the word "BMP" as if you can plausibly expect the SGML system to know what to do with that. Elsewhere, you must create a *notation declaration* to establish BMP as meaningful. We do that in the DTD:

```
<!NOTATION BMP PUBLIC
"+//ISBN 0-7923-9432-1::Graphic Notation//NOTATION Microsoft Windows Bitmap//EN">
```

Here we've established an equivalence between the name BMP and the *formal public identifier* for a notation. In this case, the FPI refers to a reference text that defines the Windows Bitmap file format. We've now gone as far back as we need to. Let's examine the steps in logical order:

- We declared a notation, expressing clearly what it is, or how to process it, in a way that software application builders can readily understand and/or implement.
- We declared an external entity, creating an entity name to encapsulate all the information we might know about the graphic we wish to include in our document:
    - how to find it (a system or public name)
    - whether or not it's represented in SGML
    - if not, the notation it employs, using a notation name we've previously declared in a notation declaration
- We used that entity name to actually place the non-SGML data entity in our document. All we needed was the entity name itself — that small handful of characters represents all the accumulated information listed above.

Example 27 — Turn off the Lights!

In the notation declaration above, the middle parameter is PUBLIC. This means that we're describing the notation in a system-independent manner. Obviously, anyone can go to the book with the ISBN given above and learn about the BMP format. A PUBLIC keyword in a declaration is a loud, public statement that the means of identifying the location of the item being declared has no machine or system dependencies. If you try to use it on another machine, you won't have to change the entity declaration.

The alternative keyword is SYSTEM. We could create a declaration for another graphic notation thusly:

```
<!NOTATION GIF SYSTEM>
```

This declaration effectively says, "Your system knows how to deal with this." A variation of that use would be:

```
<!NOTATION TEXT SYSTEM "C:\WINDOWS\NOTEPAD.EXE">
```

This declaration effectively says, "Only your system knows how to deal with this, and here's where it will find the viewing software to examine any entity declared to have the TEXT notation."

The Compleat DTD

Following, for completeness, is the complete DTD. You'll notice that it includes some element type declarations that weren't used in this example. In particular, there is an ANCHOR that will be used in Example 29 (*Jumping from Slide to Slide*) on page 273. The attributes on SLIDESET are a variation on those introduced in Example 21 (*What You See is the Tip of the Information Iceberg*) on page 185:

```
<!NOTATION BMP PUBLIC
"+//ISBN 0-7923-9432-1::Graphic Notation//NOTATION Microsoft Windows Bitmap//EN">

<!NOTATION GIF SYSTEM>

<!ENTITY % emphs    "em | emph1 | emph2 ">
<!ENTITY % text     "%emphs; ">
<!ENTITY % heads    "subhead">
<!ENTITY % lists    "list1 | list2">
<!ENTITY % special  "figure | example | fixedsp">
```

```
<!ENTITY % paracon "%text; | q ">
<!ENTITY % paratyp "para | bq | text | item | note | %heads;">

<!ELEMENT slideset (title?, slide+)>
<!ATTLIST slideset where   CDATA #IMPLIED
                   when    CDATA #IMPLIED
                   creator CDATA #IMPLIED
                   section CDATA #IMPLIED>

<!ELEMENT slide (head, (%special; | %paratyp; | %lists;)*)>
<!ELEMENT head  (#PCDATA | %paracon;)*>
<!ATTLIST (slide|head) ID ID #IMPLIED>

<!ELEMENT (%paratyp;) (#PCDATA | %paracon;)*>
<!ELEMENT (%lists;)   (lhead?, litem)+>
<!ELEMENT (%paracon;) (#PCDATA)>

<!ELEMENT lhead (#PCDATA | %paracon;)*>

<!ELEMENT title (#PCDATA)>
<!ELEMENT litem (#PCDATA | (para | %lists;)*)>

<!ELEMENT figure (subhead?, art, altfig?, text?)>
<!ELEMENT art EMPTY>
<!ATTLIST art sizex NUTOKEN #IMPLIED
              sizey NUTOKEN #IMPLIED
              unit  (i|c|p|u|m|n|v) i
              file  ENTITY #REQUIRED>
<!ELEMENT altfig (#PCDATA)>

<!ELEMENT example CDATA>
<!ELEMENT anchor (#PCDATA)>
<!ATTLIST anchor IDREF IDREF #IMPLIED>

<!ELEMENT fixedsp EMPTY>
<!ATTLIST fixedsp sizey NUTOKEN #IMPLIED
                  unit (i|c|p|u|m|n|v) i>
```

The FIXEDSP element type can be used to insert vertical space in your slides.

Example 27 — Turn off the Lights!

Bonus:

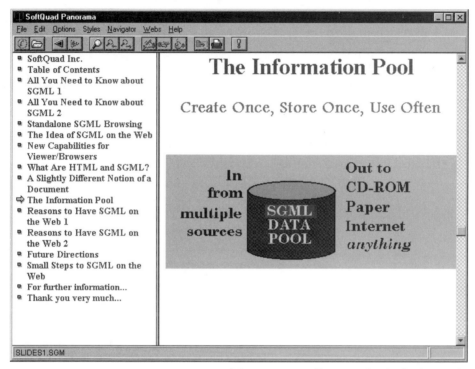

Figure 54. Examining slides1.sgm, you will see several styles for the sample presentation, including one for printing. Notice that the two graphics are in different formats, as you've seen above: &dtd; is declared as using the BMP notation, and &pool; is declared as GIF.

But wait, there's more...

In this example, you scrolled though the slides in the sample file and used the navigator to make your way through. In Chapter 8 (*You Can Get There From Here*) opposite, learning about different types of links, you'll find ways to create a "Next" icon, and to build a hypertext table of contents.

In this chapter you were introduced to entities as a way of incorporating artwork into your SGML documents. In addition, there is a whole chapter (albeit a short one) devoted to general entities that are used to:

• provide a mechanism for text replacement
• incorporate entire files
• incorporate external entities, but with the additional zing of nesting entities.

❧ CHAPTER 8

You *Can* Get There From Here

The brain makes connections. Period. That's what it does. The human brain — we flatter ourselves by making species-chauvinist distinctions — seems more interesting that the animal brain because it seems capable of subtler connections.

A small animal hears a twig snap and scampers away. The sabre-tooth tiger drawing on the cave wall is seen by the human eye and recognized as standing for prey, or danger, or spirits.

Jewish and Christian Biblical writing is particularly interesting (compared to other contemporary works from the same neighborhoods) because present events are connected to prophesies that foretold them, and to similar previous incidents, and are let stand for imminent other events.

I taste pineapple-orange ice cream and remember the summer when I was eleven years old, and if I'm feeling expansive, I go on to remember the beach and the lake and then other great ice-cream-related moments.

What's your point?

We are capable of far more interesting connection-making than the simple one-dimensional, one-directional pointing we get in HTML today. The ways we really use information aren't limited. We point in all directions and make decisions about which path to follow based on cues and clues of all sorts. You may have noticed that words in sentences follow each other, as do pages in books and moments in time. We constantly struggle between the multi-directional hypertext links we're capable of following and the linear nature of what we're able to do.

In books, tables of contents, indexes, cross-references, footnotes and other such tricks are our traditional, tested, tried and true methods of overcoming the straight lines of time and print. The display of information on computer screens has adopted the same (or very similar) techniques without doing much to enhance them — except to add speed, really.

Here is the list of basic HTML hypertext linking capabilities available today.

- *The Anchor element type:* absolute and direct link via unique names for another document, to part of another document.
- *The* LINK *element type:* chain a sequence of linked documents.
- rel/rev *attributes:* name link types and relationships.
- *The* BASE *element type:* use the current location to generate relative anchor addresses.

We've discussed all but the last of these in Chapter 4 (*Exploring* HTML *with a Flashlight*) on page 89.

For this chapter, then, it seems important that one part of a book's introductory section on sophisticated hypertext linking is about the need to design and implement a richer suite of pointing mechanisms — at least as rich as books, scraps of paper, scribbled notes in margins, and our fingers give us today.

Elsewhere I have written about how one associates element types with styles for display or printing. One of SGML's great strengths is that *how* a piece of content is marked up — this is a footnote, for example — can be separated from what is generally called its *semantics*, how it looks, what it does, what it means to be marked up in a certain way, in any specific context.

For many element types, this is a completely reasonable — even refreshing — approach. Sometimes, however, you may create a piece of text (or graphic) knowing that it has a *hypertext link relationship* of some kind to another piece of text (or graphic or video clip or whatever). What you want is to have the DTD offer you a choice of appropriate markup for your needs that carries with it a semantic association of "linking".

This chapter illustrates two approaches:

- Use of the SGML attribute value keywords ID and IDREF to indicate a hyperlink relationship between two pieces of information, the anchors of the hyperlink.)
- Use of HyTime, the ISO standard (built upon full SGML) that offers a conceptually rich set of mechanisms for various types of hypertext, as well as multimedia encoding.

❧ EXAMPLE 28

Anchors, Links, Targets, Buttons, Icons, We Got It All

Goal of the Example:

Perhaps needless to say, the historic invention of the ID/IDREF mechanism predates its use for representing traversable hyperlinks in SGML documents. Its first use was for cross-references. By way of example, here are two parts of a document instance in which one section refers to another:

```
<SECTION ID="LINKTYPE">
<TITLE>Example: What Was That Link I Saw You With?</TITLE>
<SUBSECT1><TITLE>Goal of the Example:</TITLE>
<P>What can you really do with an element type called LINK? [...]</P>
</SUBSECT1>
```

```
<SUBSECT1 ID="MULTIWAY">
<TITLE>Links are Content. No, Links Are Styles</TITLE>
<P>Stop. You're both right. As we saw previously,
<XREF IDREF="LINKTYPE">, you often know, at the time you're
creating content, not only that you want Item A to refer to Item B,
but also how you want to display the nature of their relationship.</P>
```

Once typeset, appearing in the finished pages of a book, the second half of the example might well be:

```
Stop. You're both right. As we saw previously, in the section entitled
"What Was That Link I Saw You With?" (page YY), you often know, ...
```

We've seen generated text before, so we're not entirely surprised by this capability, but much has happened here:

- the XREF element was replaced first with the words "in the section entitled", then
- the value — *not* of the referenced element (that is, not the ID that matched its IDREF) — but of the TITLE element within that SECTION, and
- fixed text appeared, saying "(page" (including the the space after "page", followed by
- the page number where the title appeared, and the closing ")".

The generality of the algorithm we've stepped through is worth noting. This procedure would work for any TITLE element within a containing element with an id. Presumably if the reference were to a CHAPTER, the fixed text "section entitled" would be replaced with "chapter entitled", and so on.

The algorithm, which is part of the processing specification for the document type, could be altered at any time, just as we often change other aspects of style sheets in the browser). Another version of the output generated from the same SGML source file might be:

```
Stop. You're both right. As we saw previously, in chapter XX [pp YY-ZZ],
you often know, ...
```

With this example, we see why the IDREF is pointing to the containing element, not to the TITLE. The (reasonable) presumption is that we've pointed at the structural unit of content that matches the topic we're now revisiting.

The ID/IDREF mechanism has a long and glorious tradition, allowing us to attach arbitrary points in a publication to figures, tables, footnotes, citations, glossary definitions, maps. As we move the same documents into electronic delivery, we're really engaged in simply, once again, modifying the processing specification for our idref attributes.

As you'll see in examples in this chapter, while you have a great deal of flexibility in how you choose to process ID/IDREF connections, modern Web browsers aren't yet capable of the rich processing semantics of print. On the other hand, clicking on a book page doesn't get you anywhere.

Example 28 — Anchors, Links, Targets, Buttons, Icons, We Got It All

Goal of the Application:

Tiny, trivial DTDs have their place. This one explores *all* the possibilities available to you in a basic SGML browser using *only* the ID/IDREF mechanism to represent hyperlink relationships.

By applying processing rules (here through style sheets, which we could describe as a special case of processing specifications) and without changing the underlying documents, you have a panoply of presentation choices for the simplest of links.

Is Influenced by/Builds on:

Nothing. This is your basic five-line DTD.

Stored on the Accompanying Disk as:

Sample DTD: *semantid.dtd*

Sample Instance: *semantid.sgm*

Step by Step:

We've come back almost to where we began, to the most basic of relationship representation mechanisms. The application is designed only to illustrate the attachment of hypertext linking semantics to TARGET and POINTER element types. To make the links work, we need unique identifiers on each TARGET and references to them on the POINTER elements, which serve as both anchors and hyperlinks. Also allowing an optional unique identifier on the POINTER is a bonus that will support processing distinctions later.

```
<!ELEMENT document (target | pointer)*>
<!ELEMENT (target | pointer) (#PCDATA)>
<!ATTLIST target   id     ID #REQUIRED>
<!ATTLIST pointer  id     ID #IMPLIED
                   idrefs IDREFS #REQUIRED>
```

Our first surprise is the IDREFS keyword, which you've not seen used in the previous examples. Not surprisingly, its task is to indicate to the parser that multiple values are allowed for the idrefs attribute, separated by spaces, tabs or carriage returns.
   The document itself is the soul of simplicity, brevity and wit:

```
<DOCUMENT>
<TARGET ID="T1">This is the first of the targets.</TARGET>
<TARGET ID="T2">This then would be the second.</TARGET>
<TARGET ID="T3">And this would be your third target element.</TARGET>
<TARGET ID="T4">This then would be the fourth target.</TARGET>
<TARGET ID="T5">This then would be the fifth
which is pointed at but does not point back.</TARGET>
<TARGET ID="T6">And this is target number six,
the final one of this episode.</TARGET>
<POINTER ID="P1" IDREFS="T1">
This is pointer one, pointing at TARGET one.</POINTER>
<POINTER ID="P2" IDREFS="T2">
This is pointing at target two and is being pointed back at.
Just click on the "Hi! I'm a target!" icon.</POINTER>
<POINTER ID="P3" IDREFS="T3">
This is being pointed at from target three.
(Although if you click here, traversal is still possible.
It just doesn't reveal itself to be an anchor.)</POINTER>
```

Example 28 — Anchors, Links, Targets, Buttons, Icons, We Got It All

We will be using the third POINTER's unique identifier to distinguish it from the others. Normally, if you wanted to have a set of links with slightly different capabilities, you would invent element types with different names and assign them different properties. (As you see from the example, however, they could have identical attributes. You might also want to restrict the use of certain kinds of links and anchors to certain parts of your DTD.)

```
<POINTER ID="P4" IDREFS="T4 T5 T6">
This is pointing at the last three targets,
still using the ID/IDREF mechanism.
To see the attributes, choose Show Tags from the Options menu
and then click on any of the little boxes.</POINTER>
```

The structure of our final anchor is the same, but now we are taking advantage of the IDREFS keyword to point at more than one target anchor. If we had used IDREF in our attribute list declaration, an SGML parser would have told us that more than one idref value is an error.

Bonus:

Inevitably, this example counts on the capabilities of the software that interprets it: It must do, because, as you've seen, all of the TARGET and POINTER element types are marked up identically. The differences among the traversal capabilities are based purely on the application of style sheets.

Figure 56. The style sheets distinguish among the anchors in two ways — they apply colors and traversal capabili-ties based on the id *attribute value, and, just to show off, the color formatting of the sixth target in the "Color Varia-tion" style sheet is based solely on the fact that it's the last* TARGET.

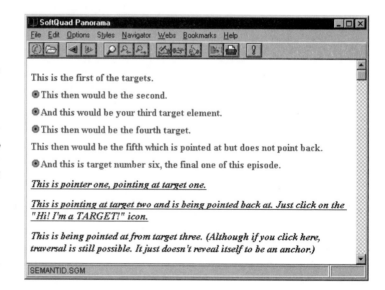

But wait, there's more...

You'll see a practical variation of the multiple semantic interpretations of ID/IDREF capability in the Example 29 (*Jumping from Slide to Slide*) opposite, coming to this chapter next.

❧ EXAMPLE 29

Jumping from Slide to Slide

Goal of the Example:

In Example 27 (*Turn off the Lights!*) on page 253, you saw a slideset presentation in which you used either the navigator or the scroll bar to move through what really was one long file of slides. The current example, though still a collection of slides in one file, adds two hypertext linking mechanisms to the slideset.

 The example also includes a brief explanation of where unique identifiers come from: automatic generation and author generation.

Goal of the Application:

- To support a table of contents capability for a slide presentation.
- To support a simple, clickable "Next Slide!" capability.

Is Influenced by/Builds on:

I would be lying to you if I pretended for a second that this isn't exactly the same SLIDESET DTD we saw in the previous chapter with the addition of one element type and some unique identifier attributes. In fact, the missing pieces were in the DTD all along; we just didn't describe them. As promised, we'll get to see how the ANCHOR is used in this example.

Stored on the Accompanying Disk as:

Sample DTD: *slideset.dtd*

Sample Instance: *slides2.sgm* and *slides3.sgm*

Step by Step:

A *slideset*, you will recall, consists of an optional TITLE followed by one or more SLIDE elements:

```
<!ELEMENT slideset (title?, slide+)>

<!ELEMENT slide    (head, (%special; | %paratyp; | %lists;)*) +(anchor)>
```

As we saw in the last chapter, a SLIDE must begin with a HEAD — our display software is counting on there being a HEAD in order to generate the *Table of Slides* as a navigator for our slidesets. The remaining content is to be marked up exactly as the slides were in the previous chapter, with the exception of ANCHOR, which appears as an inclusion. An ANCHOR may be used *anywhere* within the slide to create a link to any other slide (or, more commonly, to its HEAD). The attributes make that clear:

```
<!ATTLIST (slide|head) ID    ID #IMPLIED>

<!ATTLIST anchor       idref IDREF #IMPLIED>
```

Several software packages expect the target anchor of a link traversal to be highlighted when you traverse that link. Accordingly, if the entire next SLIDE in a sequence carries the ID (and is therefore the target anchor), then the entire next slide will be highlighted. When you examine the slideset samples in Panorama, you'll see the effect with highlighted HEADs. You'll see how the anchor is used in the following example.

Example 29 — Jumping from Slide to Slide

In practice, here are two slides acting as if they are a slideset:

```
<SLIDESET><SLIDE><HEAD ID="WHATARE">What Are HTML and SGML?</HEAD>
```

There are two ways to generate unique identifier attributes:

- By hand, as in the example: Obviously, "WHATARE" is the author's idea of an easy-to-remember identifier for this slide. You can rely on your own memory (or on software that tracks unique IDs) for small documents or small collections. If you were intending to mix and match sets of slides in order to create customized presentations, then you could readily end up with two slides with the same "unique" identifier. Your SGML parser would identify the problem only when the slides were merged into one larger document.
- Automatically: Your SGML software may be able to maintain a list of IDs and assign them in an algorithmic fashion as needed. For example, lists might be assigned an ID such as "L1", paragraphs "P1", with the numbers simply incremented as new identifiers are needed. As soon as paragraphs get moved around or documents are heavily revised, the numbers will not mean anything to a human, but at least you can be sure that the IDs are not duplicated.

```
<ANCHOR IDREF="TWOPARTS"></ANCHOR>
<TEXT><EMPH>HTML:</EMPH> a set of elements whose associated display
characteristics and capabilities are built into HTML browsers.</TEXT>
<TEXT><EMPH>SGML:</EMPH> a language for creating sets of elements
to which you attach rich style sheets for interpretation by an
SGML browser or viewer.</TEXT>
<FIXEDSP SIZEY="3" UNIT="V"></SLIDE>
```

The IDREF points to the next slide. Note that ID values do *not* have to be created before they are used, but they *must* appear somewhere in the document. The next slide's ID matches the IDREF of the previous ANCHOR. The combination creates the effect of a "Next" button.

```
<SLIDE>
<HEAD ID="TWOPARTS">A Slightly Different Notion of a Document</HEAD>
<SUBHEAD>Two Parts; No Surprises</SUBHEAD>
```

The "fixed space" element type is an instruction to the display or printing software, asking, in this case, for a blank vertical space equivalent to three lines of text. HTML includes a BR or "line break" element type which is often used in quantity to achieve this effect. Here, since there are no SGML presentation packages, FIXEDSP is used to ensure that each slide gets a full screen to itself (without the next one's title showing up at the bottom).

Full SGML viewing software that interprets the ID and IDREF combination as linked objects readily offers a clickable list such as the "Table of Contents" page of the sample slideset in *slides2.sgm*:

```
<SLIDE><HEAD>Table of Contents</HEAD>
<TEXT><ANCHOR IDREF="NEED1"></ANCHOR>
     The 90-Second SGML Introduction</TEXT>
<TEXT><ANCHOR IDREF="STAND"></ANCHOR>
     Standalone SGML Browsing & SGML on the Web</TEXT>
<TEXT><ANCHOR IDREF="NEWCAP"></ANCHOR>
     New Capabilities for Browsers</TEXT>
<TEXT><ANCHOR IDREF="WHATARE"></ANCHOR>
     What Are HTML and SGML? Why Use Them?</TEXT>
<TEXT><ANCHOR IDREF="STEPS"></ANCHOR>
     Small Steps to SGML on the Web</TEXT>
<TEXT><ANCHOR IDREF="INFO"></ANCHOR>
     For further information...</TEXT>
</SLIDE>
```

Bonus:

The two sample files that accompany this application, *slides2.sgm* and *slides3.sgm*, are identical in every way *except for the Table of Contents markup*. While *slides2.sgm* uses empty anchors (shown as arrow icons), *slides3.sgm* incorporates the text of the titles from the table of content entries right in the anchors.

What you'll notice, then, is that the entire entry is an anchor that links to the matching slide. In fact, we could have created an empty element type to include on each slide. That way nothing would have been highlighted when we traversed a link to a new slide.

Example 29 — Jumping from Slide to Slide

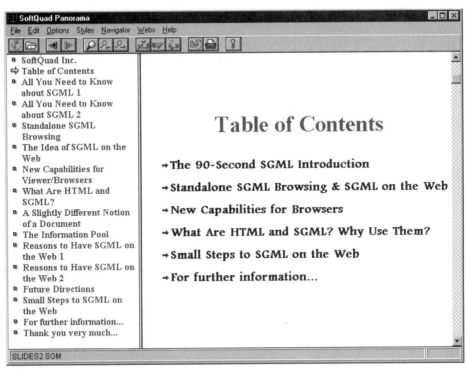

Figure 57. The example file slides2.sgm uses empty anchors for the Table of Contents markup, and the links are represented on the screen with small arrow icons

Figure 58. The example file slides3.sgm incorporates the text of the titles from the table of content entries right in the anchors. The entire entry is an anchor that links to the matching slide.

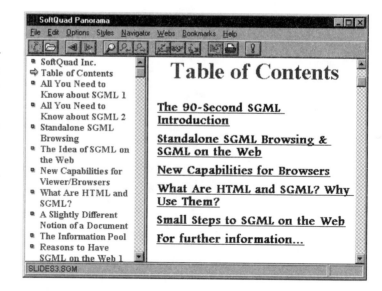

But wait, there's more...

We'll revisit the slideset application again when we talk about general entities in Example 38 (*Multiple Sources for One on-the-fly Document*) on page 353. That discussion focuses on pulling together a slide presentation from several sets of slides — without touching the originals!

The Low Low End of Computer-based Training

Goal of the Example:

Information-content markup combined with very simple hypertext linking can go a long way towards creating an interactive training mechanism. The DTD uses the basic ID/IDREF keywords to link user-choice buttons to the next part of the test or to material to be reviewed. This demonstrates once again the interesting relationship between markup and the occasionally arbitrary processing associated with it — in this case, the need to make the answers or instructions invisible until called for. This example also turns out to be the appropriate place to editorialize for a moment on how futile it is to design an SGML application without thinking about how it will interact with the software that you'll use with it, and how wrong it is to think only about the software.

Goal of the Application:

- To support interactive, multiple choice testing, where each answer is a link to further information (including the fact that you may have chosen the right answer).

Is Influenced by/Builds on:

The sample DTD in this section is like nothing else I know of. It exploits the ID/IDREF capabilities we've been discussing, and is otherwise a pure information-content markup application for simple computerized multiple choice tests. I don't expect anyone to use it as is, but it may serve as an example for blending into more specific applications.

Stored on the Accompanying Disk as:

Sample DTD:	*llecbt.dtd*
Sample Instance:	*llecbt.sgm*

Step by Step:

In the creation of the interactive tests, each element to which you might later want to refer needs to be given a unique id attribute value. As always, the appropriate attribute definition list declaration will have used the keyword ID in order to let the SGML parser know to check for uniqueness.

Here is the DTD for the training module:

```
<!ELEMENT lesson - - (h1, (learn | test)*)>
<!ELEMENT test   - - (p | (question, (answer, choice)*)*)*>
```

Figure 59. The tree view illustrates the overall structure of the DTD for low-level computer based training.

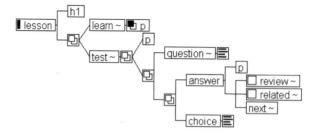

Example 30 — The Low Low End of Computer-based Training

We've not yet run into a content model quite like the one for TEST. The multiple asterisks, once you parse the parentheses, mean, "A test consists of any number of explanatory or introductory paragraphs interspersed with sets of questions-with-choices-and-answers. A question may be followed by any number of choice-and-answer combinations."

Eagle-eyed readers have noticed that the element type declaration puts ANSWER before CHOICE, and I keep talking about them in the other order. This brings up one of the Great Issues of Our Time: *How do you include elements in your documents to exploit the capabilities of the software you're thinking of using without unduly narrowing the general usefulness of the application?*

You'll see in a minute why these two elements appear to be in the wrong order. Let's continue through the DTD first:

```
<!ELEMENT answer - - (p, (review?, related?, next))>
```

REVIEW and RELATED, pointers to the original or further lessons respectively, are optional because they're not needed if your test subject chose the correct answer; NEXT is required because of a presumption that there is always going to be either another question or a concluding statement of some kind. (It would be unusual, this application designer decided, to have an interactive test that simply ended in the middle of an answer.)

```
<!ELEMENT learn - - (p+)>
```

This is the lesson portion. In real life it might be a bit more complex, what with having examples and subheadings and emphasis, and so on.

```
<!ELEMENT (h1|p|question|choice) - -  (#PCDATA)>
<!ELEMENT (review|related|next) - o  EMPTY>
```

These are empty since they are really only pointers. They are an example of "typed links". You'll see in the demonstration file that each gets its own generated text and has a different role to play in the interactive test.

Here are the attributes to take care of the pointing:

```
<!ATTLIST (question|learn|test) id    ID    #REQUIRED>
<!ATTLIST (review|related|next) idref IDREF #IMPLIED>
```

The document instance, stored on the disk in *llecbt.sgm*, contains a handful of questions and multiple choice answers. Only the first has been reprinted here:

```
<LESSON>
<H1>Learning about Multiplication</H1>
<LEARN ID="L1">
<P>Those things on either side of the x get multiplied together.
That's about all there is to it.
Well, I might mention that a good rule of thumb is
that most of the time when you multiply numbers together,
the resulting number is bigger than either of the ones
you started with. There are exceptions, but we'll get
to those later.</P>
</LEARN>
```

The id is associated with the entire lesson portion of the document. We'll be referring back to this whenever the test-taker needs to review the lesson.

We could link to entire tests (as you'll see immediately below) but for the purposes of the example, link only to the QUESTION element types:

```
<TEST ID="T1">
<P>By now you should be able to answer the following questions:</P>
<QUESTION ID="Q1">How much is 2 x 12? </QUESTION>
```

Here's where it gets confusing. Remember we're seeing pairs of answers-and-choices, and the answer includes the links that you can traverse having chosen an answer. The actual answer someone chooses (inside the CHOICE element) appears right after the ANSWER element with which it's associated.

This is where the trade-off came between what might have been a cleaner model in the DTD and the functionality I was looking for in my software application. I happened to know that the software I wanted to use for this test has a feature that allows you to *hide any element behind a clickable icon* (including all its subelements). I wanted each of the answers to disappear behind the square icon representing the good old-fashioned square into which we wrote an "X" when we did multiple choice questions using pencil and paper. Further, I wanted the square to appear to the *left* of the answer, so the appearance would be most like the paper version of such tests. This meant that the ANSWER element had to appear in the browser *before* the CHOICE. I made that choice.

Example 30 — The Low Low End of Computer-based Training

Such decisions are commonplace in SGML applications. We all like to think they're not, and we recognize that the best applications will choose to optimize the value of the data in preference to the happenstance of the feature set of the software you happen to be using today. But software applications are all different, and every one has strengths and weaknesses. You may have made large investments in order to achieve certain functionality. You often don't want your hands tied to the high-level goal of data independence when it means not exploiting your current system to the fullest. The example is here to remind you that you have such a choice.

Anyone who creates content today for the World Wide Web is likely to be consciously or unconsciously making the choice already: Do I optimize my data for one browser's extensions knowing that they're likely to fail in another browser, or most other browsers? Do I need to decide today that certain contents will be "bold" or "italic" forever instead of a more generic "emphasis"? Do I spend money converting thousands of complex tables into the simplistic table model currently in vogue on the Web, and thereby knowingly trade the value-added markup in my data for the broad distribution that the Web offers?

Back to our sample instance where the CHOICE comes after its matching ANSWER:

```
<ANSWER>
<P>Wrong. You must have fallen asleep in yesterday's class.</P>
<REVIEW IDREF="L1">
<RELATED IDREF="L2">
<NEXT IDREF="Q2">
</ANSWER>
<CHOICE>16</CHOICE>
```

We could have (and perhaps should have) used a different form of forward-pointing link in order to avoid locking each question into an actual sequence. I would feel more comfortable with this application if it let us pick and choose the lessons and the test questions from a big pool and create customized tests. Far better to *not* have to assume that the NEXT pointer will always go from the element with the id of "Q1" to "Q2".

```
<ANSWER>
<P>Correct! You may go on.</P>
<NEXT IDREF="Q2"></ANSWER>
<CHOICE>24</CHOICE>
```

Bonus:

Bring up the copy of Panorama, which accompanied this book, and open *llecbt.sgm*. Now fire up any other SGML software you may happen to own and open the same file. What you see is the following:

- In Panorama, with the default style sheet, certain element types have disappeared behind the multiple choice buttons. When you choose an answer to a multiple choice question, you're taken immediately to a separate small window that tells you if you're right or wrong and may take you to a remedial exercise. This is semantic processing associated with those element types through the style sheet mechanism. (The same could have been accomplished through other means, by the way; this is how Panorama chooses to implement such mappings.)
- In any other piece of SGML software, you simply see the questions, answers and comments on the screen. As far as computer-based training goes, a lot of the fun goes out of it when you can see which answer is the right one.

If you were the author of the electronic test, the second representation would be your preferred display. Fair enough, you need to see the questions and answers to create the test. If you are taking the test, however, it only makes sense displayed as Panorama displays it. The lesson here is distressingly fundamental: the software tools need to interpret the SGML markup *not simply according to what the markup means, but also the context in which it is being viewed.*

Example 30 — The Low Low End of Computer-based Training

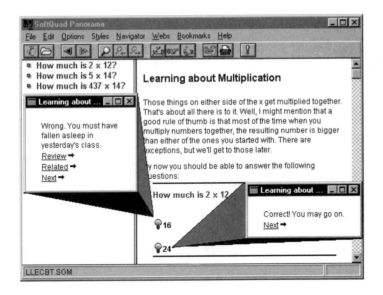

Figure 60. Notice that there are two pop-up windows shown in the same area as the navigator. The topmost pop-up is the result of a mouse click on the icon in front of the wrong answer; the lower one from a click on the correct answer. (We cheated to create this picture in the book!)

But wait, there's more...

Notice the assumption in this example that all the questions, answers and lessons are in one document. In fact, for a real computer-based training application, you would be likely to have a collection of separate entities containing repeated lessons and test questions. In that case you would use HyTime constructs to link together test fragments stored in multiple sources.

You may be thinking that we've teased you with references to HyTime quite long enough. As luck would have it, the next three examples will tell you how to use some of its capabilities.

Cranking up the Power

with HyTime Contextual Links and Named Locations

Goal of the Example:

The example in this section introduces:

- one HyTime link type
- one HyTime location addressing mechanism.

Goal of the Application:

For this entire book, we've assumed World Wide Web linking is limited to what HTML gives us. For most intents and purposes, this is the anchor element type and its graphic equivalent the ismap attribute — links that are traversable in only one direction, from one object to another. The originating anchor of a link can be in text or a region in a clickable image. Other than actually running computer scripts or performing database queries, the other anchor can only be an entire file, or an element within that file with a unique identifier stored as the value of the name attribute. (If this all seems fuzzy to you, revisit Chapter 4 (*Exploring* HTML *with a Flashlight*) on page 89.)

Notwithstanding how much has been accomplished on the Web with this simple model of hypertext linking, there's more fun to be had, with link types only slightly more complex than the HTML anchor element.

This basic HyTime application introduces:

- two-way linking between documents
- one-to-many linking among documents
- two-way linking at the level of uniquely identified elements
- one-to-many linking at the level of uniquely identified elements.

Is Influenced by/Builds on:

This basic HyTime application is built directly on HyTime, the ISO/IEC International Standard 10744:1992, the *Hypermedia/Time-based Structuring Language*, and continues the development of the streamlined version of HTML that we developed in Chapter 4 (*Exploring* HTML *with a Flashlight*) on page 89.

Stored on the Accompanying Disk as:

Sample DTD: *hybasic.dtd*

Sample Instance: *hybasic.sgm*

Example 31 — Cranking up the Power

Step by Step:

Put a little indirection in your life.

Think about the difference between street addresses and phone numbers. I telephone you, not knowing you're no longer at your old address. If you've moved only a short distance, in all likelihood you'll still have the same phone number and I'll never know you've moved. Even if you move far, I'll get a synthesized voice telling me your new number. Luckily, I know your name. If I have no phone number for you, I look for your name in the directory, and it points me to your phone number. This way I don't have to keep track of either your address or phone number, so long as I remember your name and you don't change it.

I go to look for a book in a reference library. I use the book title (or author name) to find a number in the card catalog; that number matches a number on the spine of the book. There's a middle ground for these two systems; the shelves have a small notice pinned up that tells me which numbers are sitting on which shelves. I am, in fact, grateful that the catalog does *not* tell me exactly which shelf the book is on, because I wouldn't believe it. A card catalog entry that said, "Third shelf from the window, fourth from the top, seventh book from the left-hand end," is bound to be wrong.

The two parts of the search need to be separated, more in keeping with the phone system mode. The sought-after book or individual has an identifier *and* the identifier has an address (which in the case of the phone system, is actually the phone number), which is maintained separately.

The maintenance is really the key.

Avid readers may recall that the HTML anchor element type takes an href attribute whose contents is the combined name of a computer, file system and actual document. *That's what Web browsers use to find things, and they count on the address not changing.* But lots of documents do move, and the current URL-based system fails too often to remain credible as the Web moves forward.

Anchors that float!

In the current sample, the HTML portion of the DTD is unchanged except for one new declaration and the introduction of an inclusion to the BODY element type. We first met inclusions in the MODREQ application in Example 22 (*The Combined Joys of Electronic Review and Machine Processing*) on page 191.

```
<!ENTITY % float "clink|nameloc">
```

FLOAT (or something very similar, such as I.FLOAT) is a traditional name for a parameter entity that contains inclusions. This is a clean way to gather up a list of element types so as not to clutter up the element type declaration inclusion parameter where it will be used:

```
<!ELEMENT body    (div+ | (%block;)+)    +(%float;)>
```

Explanation: CLINK and NAMELOC may appear *anywhere* in the BODY of a document conforming to this DTD. Of the floating element types, CLINK is the critical one. We will look at examples of the use of NAMELOC element types later in this example, and at related location addressing methods, *data location addressing* (DATALOC) and *tree location addressing* (TREELOC), in the next example. They all work with and complement CLINK.

CLINK, short for "contextual hyperlink" and pronounced "Sea Link", is a HyTime architectural form. A contextual hyperlink is defined as:

> A hyperlink that occurs "in context", meaning that one anchor of the link is the link element itself. In an interactive application, the self anchor can be accessed externally from adjacent elements or data in the document hierarchy.

The other element types in %float; are where the *addressing* work gets done. CLINK's linkend attribute makes that clear — all that attribute is doing is pointing elsewhere:

```
<!ELEMENT clink - - (#PCDATA)>
<!ATTLIST clink   HyTime  NAME   #FIXED "clink"
                  linkend IDREFS #REQUIRED>
```

Example 31 — Cranking up the Power

The SGML Parser and HyTime Engine

You've seen, throughout this book, examples of the work that an SGML parser does, validating the instance against the rules established by the DTD and ensuring the uniqueness and the existence of the identifiers. The use of HyTime presupposes similar capabilities, checking for a different kind of conformance, and resolving hypertext links *across documents* instead of just within the current document.

So far, I've stressed the separation, observed by SGML convention, between the markup and its interpretation, or semantics. But you've seen, throughout, that *software applies semantics*. It must — you expect and deserve capabilities and display characteristics to be associated with markup.

One area that calls out for particular semantic handling is hypertext. If I'm creating an SGML document and linking one piece of content to another, I may want to express the fact of that link and perhaps some details about it within the document. I will be interchanging it with other people, or sending it to a processing system, and there is a reasonable school of thought that says the *hypertext linking semantics* are more fundamental to the information than the point size or color or amount of indent.

HyTime, then, is the formal specification, using the language of full SGML, of a large set of "standardized semantics", a way of saying, "I mark this up as a *related lessons* element type, but really it's one type of link." HyTime declares a set of architectural forms — specific semantics for any element types, including the attributes they need to work — and also explains how to use them in *any* DTD.

A HyTime "engine" is software that understands the requirements of the HyTime Standard. It is the cousin of the SGML parser, doing work that is beyond the scope of the parser, and ensuring the integrity of the document markup from the point of view only of the HyTime requirements. For example, does a link have at least two anchors? If you've said you're linking to other content somewhere, is it an element of the type you declared it should be?

The CLINK attributes

A CLINK is a binary link; that is, it has two anchors, one them is the CLINK element itself. The CLINK attributes are minimal. The first, the hytime attribute is used anywhere, in any SGML application, to tell your software (assuming it knows about HyTime) that the element type that it is associated with *conforms to* a HyTime architectural form. In this case, the declaration is telling us that our element type called CLINK happens to be a HyTime CLINK. The name of the element type could have been anything we wanted; because of the attribute, HyTime software would know to treat it as a CLINK.

The linkend (or "anchor address") attribute has a declared value of IDREF, which we've seen earlier in this chapter. Here it tells us that a CLINK must have exactly one linkend since the CLINK itself is the other anchor.

```
<!ATTLIST clink  HyTime   NAME    #FIXED "clink"
                 linkend  IDREF   #REQUIRED>
```

Remembering the *semantid.dtd* with which we began this chapter, you can see that the declaration for POINTER was not very different from this new declaration for CLINK:

```
<!ATTLIST pointer id      ID      #IMPLIED
                  idrefs  IDREF   #REQUIRED>
```

Yes, it has an optional id attribute that's there only if we need to point to or for other reasons uniquely identify a POINTER. (In the *semantid.sgm* sample file, we used that possibility to allow us to format some anchors differently from others based on their identifiers). We could readily add this attribute to CLINK if we needed to, without changing its real functionality. The serious difference between the two declarations comes down to the presence or absence of the hytime attribute, our mechanism for telling the system that the element type being declared conforms to the architectural form for CLINK.

A HyTime application, knowing that an element type conforms to a CLINK architectural form, will, upon opening a document, build internal representations of the instances of that element type optimized for displaying and traversing the links.

Example 31 — Cranking up the Power

Addressing using NAMELOC

The *hybasic.dtd* includes two forms of addressing. The first one, built on the NAMELOC architectural form, is an extended version of the ID/IDREF mechanism we've already examined.

```
<!ELEMENT nameloc - - (nmlist)*>
<!ATTLIST nameloc  id     ID   #REQUIRED
                   HyTime NAME #FIXED "nameloc">
```

The value of the ID of the NAMELOC is what the linkend attribute of a CLINK element points to. We're used to anchors which point to unique identifiers. That's still going on here; the difference is that what's being pointed at *isn't the target anchor itself, but something which points to the target anchor*. This indirection allows us to build lists of things to point to and allows us to establish separate attributes for each of the target anchors. (Some may be whole documents, for instance, some may be partial documents, or graphics. All of those can be aggregated together into a list of references inside one uniquely identified NAMELOC.)

Notice that NAMELOC — which stands for "Named Location Address" — may contain one or more occurrences of a NMLIST. NMLIST (the "Name List" architectural form) contains a list of either the unique IDs of elements in a document or entity names. Here's the big step forward from the way we've been using ID previously: Now the ID values can be either local to the current document or be sitting in an external document. The name of the external entity (or entities) is captured as the *contents* of a NMLIST element. We'll get to that in a moment. First the relevant declarations:

```
<!ELEMENT nmlist - - (#PCDATA)>
<!ATTLIST nmlist  HyTime    NAME   #FIXED "nmlist"
                  nametype (element | entity) element
                  docorsub  ENTITY #IMPLIED>
```

The SGML parser, as you may recall, looks to see that any attribute declared as an IDREF matches an ID elsewhere in the same document. But here, the IDs of the target anchors are listed as the data content of the NMLIST element type. The parser will not complain, therefore, if the identifiers for the target anchors don't match IDs in the current document. This is what allows us to point to IDs in other documents. This will become clearer in the document instance:

```
<!DOCTYPE HTML PUBLIC "Basic HyTime 1"[
<!ENTITY doc1 SYSTEM "hybaslnk.sgm" NDATA SGML>

<!ENTITY doc2 SYSTEM "agenda.sgm"   NDATA SGML>
<!ENTITY doc3 SYSTEM "plainbod.sgm" NDATA SGML>
<!ENTITY doc4 SYSTEM "rev-ata.sgm"  NDATA SGML>
]>
```

The document type declaration points us to the public identifier "Basic HyTime 1", which is the application declared in our *hybasic.dtd*. In the declaration subset, we extend the DTD with four new entity declarations, one for each of the external documents to which we will be pointing in our sample files. The SYSTEM keyword here could be replaced with PUBLIC if we were using a machine-independent name for the external documents. In this case, however, I've used the file names exactly as they're stored on the disk that accompanies this book. Notice that they could be *any* kind of external file, graphic, video, text, anything. Therefore we need to add another keyword, NDATA to tell the software what data "notation" they're represented in. In this case, they're in SGML. In the DTD itself we've included a notation declaration for SGML.

The document continues, identical to any previous documents we've examined, until we reach the CLINK element:

```
<HTML>
<HEAD>
<TITLE>No Document Is an Island</TITLE></HEAD>
<BODY>
<DIV><H1>No Document Is an Island, At Best They're Peninsulas</H1>
<P>The first step ... </P>
<H2>The Real Point of This Sample</H2>
<P>You were wondering when I'd get around to this. </P>
<P>This is a link that uses <I>nameloc</I> to address
an editorial entitled <CLINK LINKEND="DOCLINK1">"Keep the
Identifiers Apart from the Addresses"</CLINK>.</P>
```

Example 31 — Cranking up the Power

The linkend attribute has an IDREF value. Accordingly, it *must* be to a unique identifier in the current document. And indeed it is, the ID of a NAMELOC element:

```
<NAMELOC ID="DOCLINK1">
<NMLIST NAMETYPE="ENTITY">doc1 </NMLIST>
</NAMELOC>
```

The NAMELOC can be *anywhere* in the document. If you examine the entire sample file, you'll find that I've grouped all the NAMELOCs together at the end of the file. They could appear at the top or with their respective CLINKs, or wherever you find convenient.

So the NAMELOC id value matches the CLINK linkend. This associates the entire content of the NAMELOC with the CLINK. Here that content consists only of one NMLIST. It could have been multiple NMLISTs, and the NMLIST could have included a longer list of entities to which it points. Here it points only to the "doc1" external entity (the file called *hybaslnk.sgm*). We know that the content of the element, "doc1" is indeed the name of an entity (and not an ID of an element) because the nametype attribute is set to "entity". (The other choice was "element", and would have meant that the content was a unique identifier.)

The next example takes the other approach:

```
<P>This link uses <I>nameloc</I> to address the
<CLINK LINKEND="ZEITLINK">second last paragraph of
the same document</CLINK>.</P>
```

The IDREF value "zeitlink" points to another NAMELOC:

```
<NAMELOC ID="ZEITLINK">
<NMLIST DOCORSUB="DOC1" NAMETYPE="ELEMENT">zeit</NMLIST></NAMELOC>
```

The real work is going on in the attributes of NMLIST. The job of the docorsub attribute is to let us know the name of the document that contains the name of the anchor we're referencing. You've not seen an ID value of "zeit". The reason for that is that it only exists in the document called *hybaslnk.sgm*, the one we declared as "doc1". By setting the nametype attribute to "ELEMENT", we've told the HyTime software that "zeit" is to be treated as an ID. By setting the value of docorsub to "doc1", we've told the HyTime software that "doc1" is where "zeit" exists.

Note   Let me be perfectly frank. This is the most complicated stuff in the entire
           book. I've promised you "small, small steps" in moving beyond HTML, and
           these are larger steps than elsewhere. I have a simple recommendation,
           however, which is that you learn about these capabilities the same way I
           did — take the sample files, copy the pieces that you need into your own
           documents, and use the same entity names and unique identifiers as the
           examples, substituting only the names of the files that you're creating. We
           are not used to thinking quite as indirectly as HyTime lets us, and the real
           value will be apparent only after you see how easily you can build up lists
           of anchors (instead of the old-fashioned one-to-one linking that HTML
           gives us) and what a time-saver it is to be able to store the file names apart
           from the link itself.

Tying it Together

Alright. Deep breath. Back to the example:

```
<P>Frequently you find that from any given document there's more
than one link to <CLINK LINKEND="MAINLINK">parts of another document
(such as both the second heading and the very very end of the
same document)</CLINK>.
One useful aspect of using SGML entity names to address those anchors
is that if their file location changes -- and it does sometimes --
you put the new location only in the entity declaration
where you named that file. All links are automatically updated. </P>
```

The CLINK whose linkend attribute is the ID "mainlink" is sending us to:

```
<NAMELOC ID="MAINLINK">
<NMLIST DOCORSUB="DOC1" NAMETYPE="ELEMENT">
main endpoint
</NMLIST></NAMELOC>
```

The content of the NMLIST element type is unlimited in size. In this case it acts as if
it is a list of IDREFS, each of which is a unique identifier in the SGML document
entity "doc1". Notice that we can list those identifiers in a single NMLIST element
because they share the same docorsub and nametype attribute values. If that weren't
the case — if you wanted to add to this list identifiers in other documents — you
would simply use more than one NMLIST element, all within the same NAMELOC.

Example 31 — Cranking up the Power

We'll conclude with a similar example, but one that points to several documents instead of to several target anchors within one document. Here the CLINK element's linkend attribute points to a NAMELOC with the id "multidoc". There, the nmlist attribute "nametype" tells us the list is of entities; the content of the element tells us the entity names are "doc2", "doc3" and "doc4". These have all been declared in the declaration subset, so the system knows how to resolve them:

```
<P><CLINK LINKEND="MULTIDOC">We should end off with a flourish:
an example that points to a collection of other documents.
This is that example.</CLINK></P>
</DIV>

<NAMELOC ID="MULTIDOC">
<NMLIST NAMETYPE="ENTITY">doc2 doc3 doc4</NMLIST></NAMELOC>
</BODY></HTML>
```

Better Maintenance through Entities

Earlier in this section, you saw that we declared entities for each of the files to which links were pointing. Those declarations appeared at the top of each document, in the declaration subset:

```
<!DOCTYPE HTML PUBLIC "Basic HyTime 1" [
<!ENTITY doc1 SYSTEM "hybaslnk.sgm" NDATA SGML>
<!ENTITY doc2 SYSTEM "agenda.sgm"   NDATA SGML>
<!ENTITY doc3 SYSTEM "plainbod.sgm" NDATA SGML>
<!ENTITY doc4 SYSTEM "rev-ata.sgm"  NDATA SGML>
]>
```

There is a better way. Before each of your document instances, in the prolog where those declarations are now, simply call in a single external entity that contains the declarations of the external target entities:

```
<!DOCTYPE [
<!ENTITY % targets SYSTEM "external.ent">
%targets;
]>
```

The file *external.ent* would contain just the following:

```
<!ENTITY doc1 SYSTEM "hybaslnk.sgm" NDATA SGML>

<!ENTITY doc2 SYSTEM "agenda.sgm"   NDATA SGML>
<!ENTITY doc3 SYSTEM "plainbod.sgm" NDATA SGML>
<!ENTITY doc4 SYSTEM "rev-ata.sgm"  NDATA SGML>
```

Now you can maintain that file separately, knowing that if locations or names of files change, or if you need to add new ones, it all happens in one place.

Depending on your organization and the scale of your SGML publishing, you may want to declare the TARGETS parameter entity in the DTD, and call it in there! That way none of this ever needs to appear in your SGML document entities. This approach assumes that you have a small collection of documents, one in which you're not incurring too much overhead by loading the full set of entity declarations when you load the DTD into your computer's memory. Indeed, it's more effective to have this list loaded just once, with the DTD, than with each document. On the other hand, this means that you'll have just one set of external entities for any DTD.

You can be fancy of course. You can have multiple copies of the *external.ent* file, strategically placed so that as your software reads in the DTD, the correct list of external entities is being picked up. You can use the SGML marked section construct which we'll discuss (p. 411) in *The* SGML *Primer* (although this forces you to indicate, in the declaration subset, which "family" of DTD/entities any file belongs to). The goal remains: Find a way to declare the reference to the list as rarely as possible given the special circumstances of your electronic publishing process, and maintain the list of target files in just one place.

Example 31 — Cranking up the Power

Bonus:

Opening the sample file in a full SGML browser, you'll see that, even though the links are all marked up as CLINKS, once the attributes and contents of the NMLIST elements are taken into account, the characteristics of the links are quite different. Among them, the CLINKS in the sample file point to:

- one other file
- a uniquely identified target anchor in that other file
- multiple uniquely identified target anchors in one file (and here you'll notice that the Panorama browser automatically builds a scrolling list dialog of your choice of identifiers)
- multiple files (and here you'll notice that the *Panorama* browser automatically builds a scrolling list dialog of your choice of other documents)

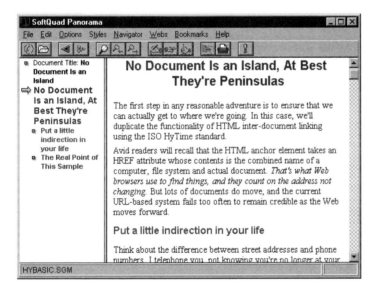

Figure 61. Open hybasic.sgm and explore the new capabilities that HyTime's contextual hyperlinks provide.

✒ EXAMPLE 32

HyTime Tree Location Addressing

Goal of the Example:

The example in this section introduces the HyTime tree location addressing mechanism which allows you or your software to identify a specific element by where it sits in the hierarchy of the document.

Goal of the Application:

You can always get what you want. This is a little known fact. Of course, I'm thinking specifically here of the case where you want to make a link to something that *doesn't have* a unique identifier. This application outlines two methods of identifying target anchors within documents where you want to point at a specific element but it has no ID attribute and you are unable to create one. (The DTD doesn't support it and/or you have no permission to alter the source file.)

Needless to say, this goal is well beyond the capabilities of HTML, and requires a tiny piece of HyTime functionality in the browsing software. Luckily such software exists.

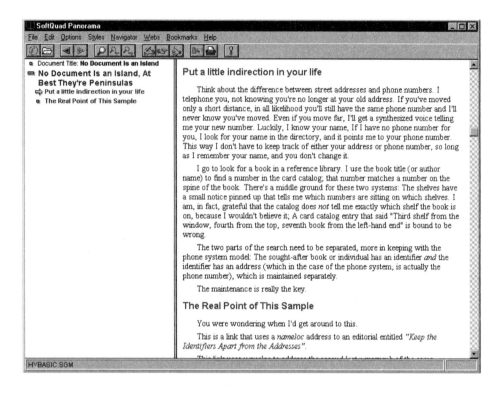

Is Influenced by/Builds on:

This application is built directly on HyTime, the ISO/IEC International Standard 10744:1992, the Hypermedia/Time-based Structuring Language, and continues the development of the streamlined version of HTML which we developed earlier.

The application builds directly on the previous section, adding to it only four new floating element types. In every other respect, the DTD remains the same.

Example 32 — HyTime Tree Location Addressing

Stored on the Accompanying Disk as:

Sample DTD: *hybasic2.dtd*

Sample Instance: *hybasic2.sgm*

Step by Step:

Declarations for Addressing Tree Locations

In the HTML section of the DTD, we add two new element type names to the declaration of the parameter entity for the "floating" elements, the inclusions which may appear anywhere in the BODY of the document.

```
<!ENTITY % float "clink|nameloc|treeloc|dataloc">
```

The examples can be very similar to the previous ones, with the added pleasure that you can now create links that address part of an element's data, even content that you cannot modify. That is, using this technique, you can point at words, phrases or whole elements even though the person who created the target document didn't put any markup at all on the phrases you wish to link to, and didn't put IDs on the elements you wish to target.

The declarations for TREELOC make clear that this is a very straightforward method of accomplishing what needs to be done:

```
<!ELEMENT treeloc - - (marklist)>
<!ATTLIST treeloc     id      ID     #REQUIRED
                      locsrc  IDREF  #IMPLIED
                      HyTime  NAME   #FIXED    "treeloc">
```

As we saw with CLINK and NAMELOC, we've used the same name for our element types as the HyTime architectural form. Here there is a #FIXED attribute value of "treeloc" whose job is to tell the HyTime software that the element type named TREELOC is in fact an instance of the architectural form called TREELOC.

Naturally you need an ID on the TREELOC; otherwise how would the CLINK be able to point to it?

The `locsrc` attribute allows us to establish any point in the document's tree structure as the starting point of the counting of the tree branches — its tree location address. This will become clearer first when we examine the document as a tree, and then, later, when we merge the TREELOC into a *location ladder*, combining it with the capabilities of NAMELOC.

```
<!ELEMENT marklist - - (#PCDATA)>
```

Here's where the work gets done. The content of MARKLIST, although declared simply as #PCDATA, is really anticipated *not* to be just any kind of character text. In fact, it will always be a sequence of numbers, separated by spaces, that count what are called the "nodes" of a tree structure.

An Instance of Treeloc

```
<!DOCTYPE HTML PUBLIC "Basic HyTime 2">
<HTML><HEAD><TITLE>Anyone Can Make a Tree</TITLE></HEAD>
<BODY>
<DIV><H1>Anyone Can Make a Tree -- and Should!</H1>
<DIV><H2>Addressing by Counting Branches</H2>
<P>This example is built on the HTML-with-Divisions application,
both because it needs a notion of containers to be meaningful,
and, from the opposite point of view, it shows off why containers
are a terrific invention.</P>
<P>I'm going to turn this entire paragraph into one end of a
linked pair of elements. Click here, and you are magically
transported two paragraphs further along, directly to the
<CLINK LINKEND="RE-TLOC">first bold word of the next
paragraph</CLINK>.</P>
<P>You need to know that there are no <I>IDs</I> on any of
the standard HTML elements in this example. We do, however,
in this part of the example still use a <I>CLINK</I> to
to traverse to an anchor.</P>
<P>And this fourth paragraph is the other anchor of the <B>link</B>
that began in paragraph two. Here's the markup that made it
possible; [...]</P>
```

The fact that certain elements contain other elements means that we could draw a picture of the relationship, and that picture would end up looking somewhat like a tree — a lopsided horizontal tree in this case:

Example 32 — HyTime Tree Location Addressing

Each specific instance of an element in the tree is a node. Towards the bottom of each branch, we get to the character data content of the element, and you notice that an element containing both PCDATA and subelements (such as the last of the paragraphs) has both character content and subelement content treated similarly. This will allow us to readily address either type.

The TREELOC element contains the MARKLIST that determines where the CLINK is pointing:

```
<TREELOC ID="RE-TLOC"><MARKLIST>1 2 1 2 5 2</MARKLIST></TREELOC>
```

Not really a whole lot of markup there. The first thing you notice is that the CLINK linkend attribute is pointing directly at the TREELOC element. As we saw above, TREELOC consists only of a MARKLIST element. By referring to the figure of the tree, you'll see that the contents of the MARKLIST have the following explanation:

- the first "1" stands for the top-level HTML document element
- the first "2" traverses the next level of the hierarchy, and gets us past HEAD to BODY
- the next "1" takes us into the first DIV element
- the next "2" skips over the H1 and gets us to the nested DIV element
- the "5" counts paragraphs (and includes the first H2, which is at the same level of the hierarchy)

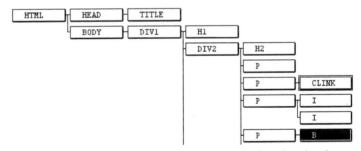

- the final "2" counts elements or *pseudo-elements*. It counts as "1" the chunk of PCDATA that begins the paragraph, as if it were an element, and gets us to the B element that we were seeking. (The pseudo-element is not shown in the diagram above.)

So, without there being an identifier on the B element in the fourth paragraph, we are nonetheless able to follow the tree structure to link to it.

Bonus:

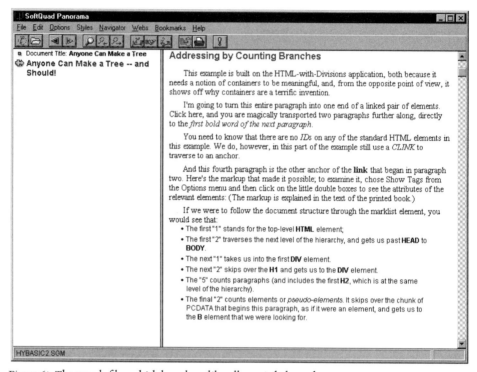

Figure 64. *The sample files, which have been liberally quoted above, show you what's going on. This style sheet is more appropriate for daily usage, having rendered invisible all the* NAMELOC, TREELOC *and* DATALOC *elements and their contents. The second style sheet shows you everything, including the contents of the HyTime elements that support the various hypertext linking mechanisms.*

This mechanism may be used in combination with the NAMELOC introduced in the previous section to point to elements in separate documents. The real power of the combined approach is that, from one document, you can create a link directly into another document without caring whether the target document has IDs on the elements you wish to link to, indeed without touching the target document.

❧ EXAMPLE 33

HyTime Data Location Addressing

Goal of the Example:

The example in this section introduces the HyTime data location addressing mechanism, which allows you or your software to identify specific words or characters within data.

Goal of the Application:

If you try sometime, you'll get where you need. This is a corollary to the little known fact from the previous example. In this case, you want to make a link to something that *doesn't even have any markup.*

This application outlines another method of identifying target anchors within the content of documents where you want to point at a specific piece of content (a phrase perhaps, or a word) that has no markup surrounding it, and you have no permission to alter the source file (whether or not the DTD has an element type you could use).

Alas and alack, HTML can offer no help, and so once more our need is met by a tiny piece of HyTime functionality.

Is Influenced by/Builds on:

This application builds directly on the previous example, adding to it only two new floating element types. In every other respect, the DTD remains the same.

Stored on the Accompanying Disk as:

Sample DTD: *hybasic3.dtd*

Sample Instance: *hybasic3.sgm*

Step by Step:

Declarations for Addressing Data Locations

There is a logical extension of our desire to point at and comment on an element in someone else's document: We may also wish to link to content that has *no markup at all!*

```
<!ELEMENT dataloc - - (dimlist)>
```

One might normally wish to have multiple DIMLIST elements within a DATALOC; for the examples, we've only allowed one.

```
<!ATTLIST dataloc  id      ID    #REQUIRED
                   locsrc  IDREF #IMPLIED
                   quantum (norm) norm
                   HyTime  NAME  #FIXED "dataloc">
<!ELEMENT dimlist - - (#PCDATA)>
```

As with CLINK, NAMELOC and TREELOC, we've used the same name for our element types as the HyTime architectural form. The #FIXED attribute value establishes that the element type named DATALOC is in fact an instance of the architectural form called DATALOC.

The ID on DATALOC allows other elements to point to it. *Remember that the* CLINK linkend *must be either the ID of the anchor, or the ID of a location address element that points to the anchor.* For instance, in the document example that follows, the link-end is the ID of the DATALOC, which in turn points to the TREELOC that establishes the path to the desired element.

As with TREELOC, the locsrc attribute allows us to establish any point in the document's tree structure as the starting point of the counting of words. To avoid having to count words all the way from the top of the document, we utilize the

Example 33 — HyTime Data Location Addressing

DATALOC in a location ladder, combined with a TREELOC, and starting to count words from the point where we leave off counting nodes on the tree. The example will make that clearer.

An Instance of Dataloc

I've reprinted only the bottom half of the sample file. The TREELOC element below, however, is counting from the start of the document — the document element.

```
<DIV><H2>Addressing by Counting Words</H2>
<P>While you have the ability to design DTDs with attributes
to hold IDs and then to create documents with all the necessary
unique identifiers, you can't always count on everyone else
doing so. But it is completely reasonable for you to expect to
be able to point at the contents of another document, either to
comment on it from your document, or to link it to another chunk
of contents somewhere.</P>
<P>The "dataloc" architectural form gives you this ability, and,
in combination with the other AFs we've been discussing, let's you
always link to that part of a document that is most likely to be
stable over time. More on the stability business later.</P>
<P>For now, let's simply create a link to the words "completely
reasonable" in the first paragraph of this section.
<CLINK LINKEND="REASON">This is that link.</CLINK>
And what follows is the markup that makes it possible:</P>
```

The TREELOC that follows is like the previous example. *Notice that the* CLINK *link-end is the* ID *of the* DATALOC *element.* The DATALOC, through its locsrc attribute, tells the HyTime software to start counting words within the location source identified by the ID "ID3.TREE". The MARKLIST gets us to the element that contains the words.

```
<TREELOC ID="ID3.TREE"><MARKLIST>1 2 1 3 2</MARKLIST></TREELOC>
```

The CLINK references the DATALOC element shown below, and whose content is the numbers "37 2". This is very simple to parse, just as you might expect. This means that the anchor is the 37th and 38th words. (That is, it is a list of words beginning at the 37th and consisting of 2 words.)

```
<DATALOC ID="REASON" LOCSRC="ID3.TREE"><DIMLIST>37 2</DIMLIST></DATALOC>
```

The example doesn't use the quantum attribute. The default is "norm", a normal *token*, where a token is simply a collection of characters bounded by a specific set of other characters. For example, we can describe words as tokens because we know they are broken up by white space and punctuation. The difference between "norm" and "word", by the way, is that "word" doesn't include punctuation.

You've seen a location ladder. The DATALOC gets its starting point by attaching itself to the TREELOC. The TREELOC, in turn, could have been attached to a NAMELOC.

Of the three types of location addressing, NAMELOC gives you the most security over time. Documents may change, and if they do, counting mechanisms based on the number of elements or the number of words may prove to be pretty flimsy. But if a unique identifier continues to exist, there is a good chance that the element it refers to has survived the edits. Pointing a CLINK to a NAMELOC (just as with pointing any IDREF to any ID), is as stable as you can hope for in the world of electronic documents. TREELOC is the next best approach, and DATALOC comes third.

In building a location ladder, it is usually a good idea to set your locsrc attribute to a unique ID if possible, and then count tree nodes from there. It is usually safest to only count words when you have to. Otherwise your links might not survive complex editing sessions — minimizing the use of word counting gives your links a fighting chance.

Example 33 — HyTime Data Location Addressing

Bonus:

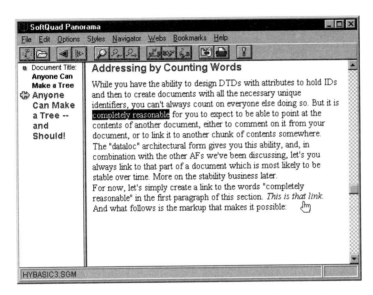

Figure 65. Click on a hypertext link and you get a "completely reasonable" response, even without additional markup to help the browser find its way to the right place.

It is worth drawing your attention to an issue of ease-of-use with regards to the various kinds of HyTime location addressing mechanisms; you've seen them here *in the raw,* but software exists whereby you simply point and click (or, perhaps, point and clink?) to create hypertext links, and in the background the software writes out all the element content and attribute values needed to make these powerful capabilities function.

So don't be alarmed. These last few examples of this chapter are here just to reassure you that there is a strong underlying foundation for the extended hypertext linking that a new generation of electronic publishing tools will bring you.

❧ CHAPTER 9
The Tiny Table Two-Step

The 10-Minute Executive Guide to Some of the Table Issues

What is a table?

A table is a sequential presentation of multiple dimensions of related information, generally ordered along one or more axes. In slightly plainer language, a person creating a table figures out a sequence that seems to make the most useful presentation of information both across the table column and down the rows.

Is this a table?
The simplest table type is a basic list — in this case unordered, and representing only one axis:

```
Pick Up Groceries:
Milk
Honey
Bread
Wine
```

If it looks like a table...

The same information starts to look more like a table — even if the amount of information (the "information quotient") stays the same — if we start adding some of the look-and-feel paraphernalia of a traditional table:

Grocery List	
1	Milk
2	Honey
3	Bread
4	Wine

In the table above, note the value of distinguishing the notion of *a table of information* — a collection of information that makes sense only because it is in a table — from *presenting* or *rendering* information as a table. The information structure of this data is still a list, but it rendered and displayed as a table.

And it acts like a table...

The distinction becomes clearer as we add a second dimension of information to what is rapidly becoming a means of data representation that is integrally related to its presentation format:

Grocery List		
Item	Description	Quantity
1	Milk	1 bottle
2	Honey	1 jar
3	Bread	2 loaves
4	Wine	2 bottles

This version still wouldn't necessarily have to be rendered as a table to make sense, but it has a visual clarity that disappears in a less formal presentation, "I need one bottle of milk, one jar of honey, two loaves of bread and two bottles of wine." And as we add more and more items, the sentence version becomes less and less readable.

And it walks the aisles like a table...

There aren't yet enough items that ordering them makes sense. You can imagine however, that if there were 30 items, alphabetical order would help, or else adding another dimension, sorting them by the aisle where they're found in the store:

Grocery List		
Aisle	Item	Quantity
1	Milk	1 bottle
1	Yoghurt	750 ml
4	Honey	1 jar
4	Bread	2 loaves
9	Wine	2 bottles
11	Carrots	2 bunches
11	Lettuce	1 head
11	Radishes	2 bunches
...	...	...

By now we've lost the possibility of presenting this in some other way. Characteristics of the contents — number of items, value of the sequence — have turned the underlying structure into a table.

Notice that I've surreptitiously added a few more tidbits of complexity. Center-alignment for two of the columns, I think we would all agree, makes no difference, is mere prettifying. We might feel more strongly about numbers being aligned on a decimal point, however, or long fractions aligning on the slash.

Line all your ducks in rows

I think we can probably agree that there are now three dimensions of information in the table. The next task is to determine whether the table we've just seen is the same as the following table, which is sorted alphabetically by item as an index to the aisles:

Grocery List		
Item	Quantity	Aisle
Bread	2 loaves	4
Carrots	2 bunches	11
Honey	1 jar	4
Lettuce	1 head	11
Milk	1 bottle	1
Radishes	2 bunches	11
Wine	2 bottles	9
Yoghurt	750 ml	1
Fowl	4 ducks	1
...	...	...

Multi-dimensional tables of information

So far, however, none of the formatting that has been done has "interfered with" or changed the meaning of the contents. It is probably safe to say that we could put the centering information in a style sheet and not feel we're losing anything from the underlying SGML markup.

But what about a table in which the formatting of spanned cells affects the meaning? What about a table in which the order of the information matters, or doesn't?

The following two examples are what might be the same information. If you think about these tables from the point of view of the price of 88 cents, you have two extreme choices:

Prices are in US dollars		Tea			Coffee		
		Earl Grey	Mint	Green	Turkish	Spanish	English
Loose	per lb	.42	.33	.38	1.23	3.32	.68
	per kg	1.01	.74	.77	3.00	7.65	1.61
	per ton	322					
In Bags	per lb	.88	.54	.55	NA	NA	NA
	per kg						
	per ton						

Tea					
Earl Grey		Mint		Green	
Loose	In Bags	Loose	In Bags	Loose	In Bags
Price per pound in US dollars					
.42	.88	.33	.54	.38	.55
Price per kilogram in US dollars					
Price per ton in US dollars					
Coffee					
Turkish		Spanish		English	
Loose	In Bags	Loose	In Bags	Loose	In Bags
Price per pound in US dollars					
	etc				

Hierarchies of information

There are hierarchies of information here. Within the domain of "Tea", is the sub-domain of "Price per pound", and within that is the sub-sub-domain of "Earl Grey", and within that is "In Bags". We could imagine this as an SGML document, with a suitable *element array* to contain it:

```
<DOMAIN>Tea<SUBDOMAIN>Price per pound
        <SUBSUBDOMAIN>Earl Grey  <SUBSUBSUB>In Bags  <ACTUAL-DATA> .88
                                 <SUBSUBSUB>Loose    <ACTUAL-DATA> .42
        <SUBSUBDOMAIN>Mint       <SUBSUBSUB>In Bags  <ACTUAL-DATA> .54
                                 <SUBSUBSUB>Loose    <ACTUAL-DATA> .33
```

Database records

The next presentation is offering the same information, but as if it comes from records in a database. Most interesting, perhaps is the idea that there is no such concept as a "span", either for rows or columns, in this version. Now the truth comes out: A span is (at least on this occasion, but perhaps always) a formatting convenience. The first table was *actually* carrying the information shown below — notice especially the disappearing content from the top left cell, the one that acted as if it spanned the whole table!

		Tea	Tea	Tea	Coffee	Coffee	Coffee
		Earl Grey	Mint	Green	Turkish	Spanish	English
Loose	per lb	U$ .42	U$ .33	U$ .38	U$ 1.23	U$ 3.32	U$ .68
Loose	per kg	U$ 1.01	U$ .74	U$ .77	U$ 3.00	U$ 7.65	U$ 1.61
Loose	per ton	U$ 322					
In Bags	per lb	U$ .88	U$ .54	U$ .55	NA	NA	NA
In Bags	per kg						
In Bags	per ton						

Making sense of information

From another point of view, there is no hierarchical structure, either real or implied. Each cell is a data point with five dimensions. This becomes clearer if we think of the previous table as if we cannot see it.

Speech synthesizers for people with visual disabilities must offer a presentation of the information such that what they hear will be meaningful at any point in the table. The same is true for those who touch Braille representations of tables of information on paper and computer pin pads.

Imagine that you are *listening* to someone reading this table, in any of the three presentations. Here's what you hear:

Tea. Coffee. Earl Grey. Mint. Green. Turkish. Spanish. English.
Loose. Per pound. 42 cents. 33 cents. 38 cents. 1.23 dollars. 3.32 dollars. 68 cents
Loose. Per kilogram. 1.01 dollars. 74 cents. 77 cents. 3 dollars. 7.65 dollars. 1.61 dollars.
Loose. Per ton. 322 dollars.
In bags. Per pound. 88 cents. 54 cents. 55 cents. NA. NA. NA.
In bags. Per kilogram.
In bags. Per ton.

Not particularly helpful, I think you'll agree. If someone unable to see the table was trying to glean information from this presentation, the listener would literally have to attempt to re-build the table in his or her mind's eye.

So, the fifth version of the same information is the way a synthesizer should present it — indeed the way anyone reading a table to someone else might do:

```
Tea: Earl Grey: Loose: Per pound: Price: 42 cents
Tea: Earl Grey: Loose: Per kilo: Price: 1.01 dollars
Tea: Earl Grey: Loose: Per ton: Price: 322.44 dollars
[...and so on to, for example ...]
Coffee: English: Loose: Per pound: Price: 68 cents
```

Table as Artwork

Earlier, I mentioned that a table is "a sequential presentation of multiple dimensions of related information" and then proceed to show you, in a number of cases, that the sequence of presentation may not matter. Yet it is also true that in many tables the sequence is critical. A table of grocery items ordered by aisle is one such example, share price fluctuation over time is another. Here's a famous table where the time axis is critical, and the eloquence of the information in other dimensions is such that we cannot imagine a reordering that would carry the weight of the data:

Figure 66. This table was created by Colonel Leonard P. Ayres for his book "The War with Germany", (Washington, D.C., 1919). The table records the numerical designation of each American armed forces division in France during World World I, when it arrived and how long it stayed. I am grateful to Edward R. Tufte's "The Visual Display of Quantitative Information" for reproducing the table and bringing it to the world's attention.

Jun	Jul	Aug	Sep	Oct	Nov	Dec	Jan	Feb	Mar	Apr	May	Jun	Jul	Aug	Sep	Oct
																8
																38
																31
															34	34
															86	86
															84	84
															87	87
														40	40	40
														39	39	39
														88	88	88
														81	81	81
														7	7	7
														85	85	85
													36	36	36	36
													91	91	91	91
													79	79	79	79
													76	76	76	76
												29	29	29	29	29
												37	37	37	37	37
												90	90	90	90	90
												92	92	92	92	92
												89	89	89	89	89
												83	83	83	83	83
												78	78	78	78	78
											80	80	80	80	80	80
											30	30	30	30	30	30
											33	33	33	33	33	33
											6	6	6	6	6	6
											27	27	27	27	27	27
											4	4	4	4	4	4
											28	28	28	28	28	28
											35	35	35	35	35	35
											82	82	82	82	82	82
										77	77	77	77	77	77	77
									3	3	3	3	3	3	3	3
									5	5	5	5	5	5	5	5
									32	32	32	32	32	32	32	32
						41	41	41	41	41	41	41	41	41	41	41
				42	42	42	42	42	42	42	42	42	42	42	42	42
			26	26	26	26	26	26	26	26	26	26	26	26	26	26
			2	2	2	2	2	2	2	2	2	2	2	2	2	2
1	1	1	1	1	1	1	1	1	1	1	1	1	1	1	1	1
Jun	Jul	Aug	Sep	Oct	Nov	Dec	Jan	Feb	Mar	Apr	May	Jun	Jul	Aug	Sep	Oct
1917							1918									

The database that might have generated this table still lives by the rules of the previous tables. The inverse of the speech synthesizer's presentation of this table is the question one might ask, "Was the third division in France in January?"

Where Does This Get Us?

In practical terms, I believe the goal has to be to create tables that can be understood as easily as if they are presented using either the last of the tea and coffee examples, or the version optimized for speech synthesis. This is *not* to suggest they should always be presented with repetitive data, but *you should be able to determine the axes of every datapoint*. And your table model should allow for that, in fact, should support it cleanly and eloquently. If possible it should encourage such clarity (in much the same way as the `alt` attribute on image elements encourages document creators to offer a verbal description of all images).

We'll see precisely the element types and attributes needed to achieve this goal later in this chapter. But first, the basics of a really simple table.

❧ Example 34

A Simple Kitchen Table

Goal of the Example:

In the world of typesetting, tables have traditionally been regarded as terrifically complicated. In days of yore, tables were known in the publishing trades as "penalty copy" because of the premiums, in time or money, that were exacted by typesetters for setting type in tables. That's fair enough — we cannot pretend that complicated tables aren't complicated to typeset. But the HTML work teaches us the important lesson that *there are an awful lot of tables you can create with very simple markup.*

Goal of the Application:

- To offer DTD support for basic tables.
- To do so in such a way that someone, without the help of an HTML table editor, could easily type in the markup needed to represent information as a table.
- To introduce the value of containers in tables, to distinguish the table headers, body and footers from each other.

Is Influenced by/Builds on:

This application builds very slightly on the initial table fragment from the early drafts of what was called (in the spring of 1994) "HTML Plus", the DTD that went on to become, under Dave Raggett's care, and with the work of the HTML Working Group, IETF Experimental RFC 1942.

Stored on the Accompanying Disk as:

Sample DTD: *simptbl.dtd*

Sample Instance: *simptbl.sgm* and *simptbl.htm*

Step by Step:

The first declaration introduces the extensions that weren't in the original HTML+
DTD. The notion of dividing the table up into three separate containing elements (all
of which have the exact same content model).

The structure is straightforward. A table consists of:

- an optional header component (the months on a sales chart, the titles rather
  than the data, the parts that get repeated if the table goes on longer than one
  page), followed by
- a required body (where the data resides), followed by
- an optional footer element type (where explanatory notes go, a legend if there
  are special symbols or abbreviations).

```
<!ELEMENT table          - -   (thead?, tbody, tfoot?)>
<!ELEMENT tbody          0 0   (tr)+>
<!ELEMENT tr             - 0   (td|th)*>
<!ELEMENT (thead|tfoot)  - 0   (tr)+>
<!ELEMENT (td|th)        - 0   (#PCDATA)*>
```

Each of those three element types consists of one or more rows. A table row, the TR
element type, consists of any number of table data cells (TD) and any number of table
header cells (TH), in any order. In practice, of course, one anticipates that all the rows
in a table will have the same number of cells (spanning cells notwithstanding — they
don't yet exist in this DTD).

Example 34 — A Simple Kitchen Table

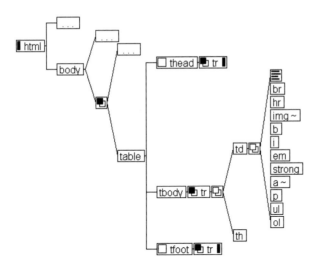

Figure 67. The tree view illustrates the overall structure of a simple table with a head, body and foot. Table rows consist of TH and TD cells that may contain text or the usual assortment of paragraphs and lists.

In practice too, one expects all the header cells of a row to appear, generally, at the left hand edge of a table. The declaration could have been as follows, requiring "zero or more table row header cells followed by zero or more table data cells":

```
<!ELEMENT tr (th*, td*)>
```

In fact, there was a concern that tables sometimes have header-type cells at the right-hand edge of the table, or occasionally anywhere within rows. The current model allows for those conditions.

Let's set the table

Here's one of the grocery tables marked up according to *simptbl.dtd*:

```
<TABLE>
<THEAD>
<TR><TH></TH>
    <TH>Grocery List</TH></TR>
```

To have the heading "Grocery List" appear in the second column of the table, we've left a blank cell before it.

There is a minimal kind of redundancy here. Table header cell, TH elements, appear within the THEAD element. The DTD is sufficiently flexible, however, that you could put TD (table data) cells into the table head too. So the THEAD is a precaution —we really do want to distinguish between cells which contain only data and those which have content that reflects the axis or dimension of information. We need to be able to see the value "4" and be able to follow either up or to the left (in similar circumstances) to determine that this value is an aisle number.

```
<TR><TH>Aisle</TH>
    <TH>Item</TH>
    <TH>Quantity</TH></TR></THEAD>
```

To most Web browsers, content marked up as a TH element type indicates to the system that you want style characteristics of boldness and centering. Placing them within a THEAD too could indicate additional refinements — perhaps a bold horizontal rule along the bottom edge of the header. And, more interesting, if the table has many rows — in a paper printout it would extend over many pages and on screen it would scroll down for so long that you'd forgotten what the column headings are — software implementors could offer a feature that says the THEAD stays in position at the top of the viewing window, and the TFOOT at the bottom, while the rows of the table body scroll down and up as the reader sees fit.

```
<TBODY>
<TR><TD> 1</TD>
    <TD>Milk</TD>
    <TD>1 bottle</TD></TR>
```

Example 34 — A Simple Kitchen Table

The carriage returns and spaces in this sample have no meaning to the SGML or HTML browser. That is, if you're more comfortable creating files in which all the TD elements for any given TR appear on one input line, go ahead. I've chosen this display to make clear the start and end of each cell and row.

```
<TR><TD> 1</TD>
    <TD>Yoghurt</TD>
    <TD>750 ml</TD></TR>
<TR><TD> 4</TD>
    <TD>Honey</TD>
    <TD>1 jar</TD></TR>
<TR><TD> 4</TD>
    <TD>Bread</TD>
    <TD>2 loaves</TD></TR>
<TR><TD> 9</TD>
    <TD>Wine</TD>
    <TD>2 bottles</TD></TR>
<TR><TD>11</TD>
    <TD>Carrots</TD>
    <TD>2 bunches</TD></TR>
<TR><TD> 1</TD>
    <TD>Duck</TD>
    <TD>2 roasters</TD></TR>
<TR><TD>...</TD>
    <TD>...</TD>
    <TD>...</TD></TR>
</TBODY></TABLE>
```

There are end-tags galore in this little sample. In practice, you can leave off the end-tags for everything but TABLE itself. The only start-tag that may be omitted is the one for TBODY, since that is a required element within the TABLE.

Bonus:

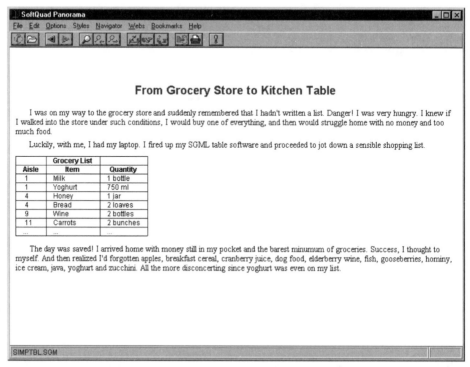

Figure 68. The sample file will work both in Panorama and in any HTML *Web browser that supports the display of tables. For use with Panorama, as mentioned in the discussion of minimization in Example 25 (Stop the Presses!) on page 231, all the end-tags should be included. If you're building the tables using any of the most popular* SGML *editing software packages, all the end-tags will be there anyway.*

But wait, there's more...

We cheated on the top row of the sample table. If you check back to the original grocery store table, you'll notice that the text "Grocery List" was in a cell that spanned all three columns of the table. In this section we simply placed the content in the second cell of the row, leaving a blank one. The next section solves this little problem.

❧ EXAMPLE 35

Throw a Little Span in the Works

Goal of the Example:

In daily life, you don't really see tables quite as simple as those in the previous section. Here we introduce four small additions to the DTD (in attributes) which create a great deal more potential sophistication in the presentation of a table — the spanning of rows and of columns.

The example also introduces a simple case of markup minimization in attribute values, one that will save you a lot of shift work.

Goal of the Application:

- To support the notion of hierarchical dimensions of information in a table.
- To continue to support tables whose markup is simple enough to generate by hand.

Is Influenced by/Builds on:

This is exactly the same application as *simptbl.dtd* with four new attributes.

Stored on the Accompanying Disk as:

Sample DTD: *spantbl.dtd*

Sample Instance: *spantbl.sgm* and *spantbl.htm*

Step by Step:

The following attributes are added to the DTD for the table cells, both header and data cells:

```
<!ATTLIST (td | th)  COLSTART  NUMBER  #IMPLIED
                     COLSPAN   NUMBER  "1"
                     ROWSTART  NUMBER  #IMPLIED
                     ROWSPAN   NUMBER  "1">
```

For a span to work, cells need to be missing. That is, if we look at the top row of the grocery store list source file, we notice that it now contains only one cell, a cell which may be said *to span three columns*. The cell that is there must carry enough information to indicate to the display software what is going on. Here's the markup for the top row:

```
<TR><TH COLSPAN=3>Grocery List</TH></TR>
```

Note   At this moment you're asking yourself, "What about the missing quotation marks?" Well done. Yes, you're right. In all the previous examples of attribute values, we've always surrounded the values with old-fashioned typewriter quote marks (which are actually inch marks or second marks; real quote marks are curly).

This is another example of SGML's markup minimization — you may leave out the quote marks when the attribute value contains only numbers and letters. One-word and one-number attribute values are the perfect candidate for this minimization feature.

Example 35 — Throw a Little Span in the Works

Later in the table, we notice that the aisle number for some of the groceries remains the same. This is a typical opportunity to use a cell that spans *rows*:

```
<TR><TD ROWSPAN=2> 1</TD>
    <TD>Milk</TD>
    <TD>1 bottle</TD></TR>
```

The first cell spans *down* over the next row. It eliminates the first cell of the next row, and its contents are perceived by the reader to apply to both the rows it spans. That is, both milk and yoghurt are in aisle one.

```
<TR><TD COLSTART=2>Yoghurt</TD>
    <TD>750 ml</TD></TR>
```

Instead of the three TD elements we expect to find in a row, this one has only two. This makes sense, as the first cell is shared with the row above. And to make the situation absolutely clear, the first TD has an attribute which states explicitly that "this cell starts in column two".

The `colstart` and `rowstart` attributes are a convenience: Some software needs this information to properly lay out spanned cells, and some software determines where each cell sits without this detail, simply by counting and calculating. To be more certain that your tables will work in a variety of SGML packages, it's best to include the information, even though it should be redundant.

Bonus:

The same file is on the disk accompanying this book with both *.sgm* and *.htm* extensions to make it convenient to view them in SGML and HTML browsers. Web browsers that support tables have already hard-wired in support for the known table element types and attributes.

Figure 69. The style sheet that comes with Panorama on the disk has already built into it a mapping that tells the software that certain cells — in this case, TABLE, TR, TD and TH — have special semantics associated with their display.

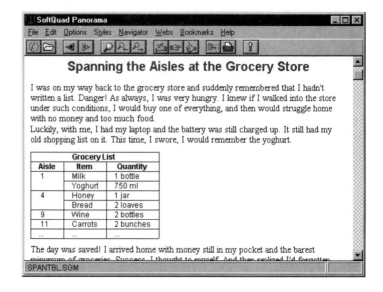

But wait, there's more...

After this exploration of a very sophisticated table capability built onto a very simple table model, we'll return next to slowly adding features to the model.

❧ EXAMPLE 36

Seeing the World through Rose-Colored Glasses

Goal of the Example:

People are often accused of seeing only what they want to see. Finally we come to an application where *this is a feature, not a bug.*

Goal of the Application:

Picture yourself recording the values of a set of gauges scattered around the factory. You have five colleagues who do the same. You each work on a custom form which has all the irrelevant cells grayed out in a table of gauges and times.

The results are recorded on a master form.

In the old days the person who created gauge-checking procedures built the master form, using publishing software, and then painstakingly created the grey backgrounds for the non-applicable cells.

In this hypothetical production, the SGML publishing software currently creates all seven versions of the paper form from one source file. (That is to say yours, your five colleagues, and the master form.) Now the company wants to display just the *relevant* previous recorded value for the same gauges to the person collecting the data. But the source file contains all the data, and everyone agrees that they shouldn't need to build an application just to separate out the data customized per datataker.

Is Influenced by/Builds on:

The datataker application is built directly on top of David Raggett's table proposal. For the purposes of this book, the tables have been embedded into the Simplified HTML application and markup added specifically to support the customizable versions required by the application.

Stored on the Accompanying Disk as:

Sample DTD: *datatkr.dtd*

Sample Instance: *datatkr.sgm* and *datafull.sgm*

Step by Step:

We are about to bring a rich structure to the contents of all table cells, both data and heading cells, beginning by changing the content model for the two types of table cell, TD and TH.

The basic HTML table model declares:

```
<!ELEMENT (td | th) (%text;)>
```

%text; references a parameter entity incorporating all the normal paragraph-like element types. We'll declare a new parameter entity for the set of cells — in this case six, but there could have been any number — where each cell is designed to include information that is meaningful for only one of the people charged with collecting or verifying the data from the gauges:

```
<!ENTITY % dt-cell "dt1|dt2|dt3|dt4|dt5|dt6">
```

Example 36 — Seeing the World through Rose-Colored Glasses

The TABLE itself is the very basic table we've seen before. The principle at work in the datataker cell markup can be applied to the contents of any cell in any table, no matter how rich the parent table's model may need to be. In this example, there are no column or row spans. Nothing in the example precludes them; I left out absolutely anything I could get away with in order to focus on just the datataker capability.)

```
<!ELEMENT table    - -  (tr+)>
<!ELEMENT tr       - O  (td | th)*>
<!ELEMENT th       - O  (%dt-cell; | #PCDATA)*>
<!ELEMENT td       - O  (%dt-cell; | #PCDATA)*>
<!ELEMENT (%dt-cell;) - - (#PCDATA)>
```

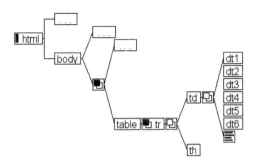

Figure 71. The tree view illustrates the overall structure of a table. In this DTD, table cells can contain text, but are expected to contain DT1, DT2, DT3, DT4, DT5 or DT6 elements with the data values recorded by the respective datatakers.

In every instance of a datataker table, certain information (such as the row and column headings or general instructions) must appear in all the tables. It might have seemed natural to create an element type called ALL, for example, but on closer examination, we can decide that, by default, the contents of any cell that contains just PCDATA is to be printed. Surrounding that content with markup indicates the information is to appear *only* on the version of the table geared to that datataker. (Content that appears within a DT1 element is to show up just on the table for Datataker One.)

But here's the wrinkle: The tables start out their lives *without* content. They're supposed to show the datatakers where to place their numbers. There are several ways one could accomplish this — here are two of them:

- Generate text associated with each of the DT1, DT2, etc. family of element types. Associate that text with a specific style sheet geared to each datataker. (This is the approach taken in the sample files.)
- Write a processing procedure whereby, in the table printed or displayed for Datataker One, only cells that contain a DT1 element are left blank. The rest are grayed out or have a large X printed in them.

There are many possibilities. Here is the document instance to exploit this capability:

```
<TABLE>
<TR><TH>POST</TH>
    <TH>TIME</TH>
    <TH>RECORD VALUE</TH>
    <TH>VERIFY VALUE</TH></TR>
```

The first row, immediately above, contains only headings for the columns. The second and remaining rows, start with two columns of TH elements, headings for each row (which are sometimes called "stub cells"), followed by the data cells to be filled in by the datatakers. Notice that heading cells too might have been surrounded by the DT markup, indicating that the instructions (or times, in this case) are to appear only on one printout.

```
<TR><TH>A</TH>
    <TH>9:15</TH>
    <TD><DT1></DT1></TD>
    <TD><DT3></DT3></TD></TR>
```

The markup above shows the cells in the second row that are to be filled in by Datatakers One and Three respectively. At this point they have no content.

Example 36 — Seeing the World through Rose-Colored Glasses

```
<TR><TH>B</TH>
    <TH>12:15</TH>
    <TD><DT2></DT2></TD>
    <TD><DT3></DT3></TD></TR>
<TR><TH>C</TH>
    <TH>15:15</TH>
    <TD><DT1></DT1></TD>
    <TD><DT3></DT3></TD></TR>
<TR><TH>D</TH>
    <TH>18:15</TH>
    <TD><DT2></DT2></TD>
    <TD><DT3></DT3></TD></TR>
</TABLE>
```

Sample screens will make clear what's going on:

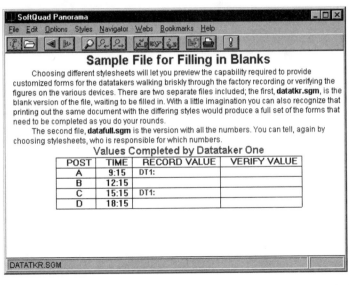

Figure 72. Here is the master table, ready to filled in by datataker one.

Let's further assume that, either automatically or by hand, all the numbers from the various datatakers are collated together onto one "Master Table". Interestingly, with *no additional markup*, the master table can also be used to generate versions that display the input only of a specified datataker. Here's the master table and then the work of Datataker Two:

Figure 73. Here is the work of data-taker two.

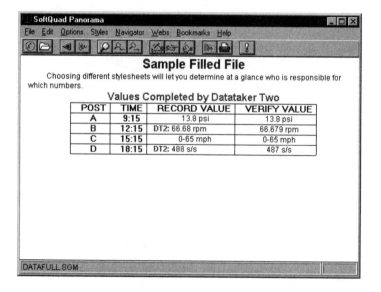

Bonus:

The sample files and style sheets on the accompanying disk illustrate the workings of the datataker application. Be sure to apply all four style sheets and examine both the *datatkr.sgm* and *datafull.sgm* sample files. The first is the empty one demonstrating an application for people filling in the data that they're gathering — one can imagine a small, portable digital device geared to the input requirements of the specific environment; the second displays all the reported numbers.

Example 36 — Seeing the World through Rose-Colored Glasses

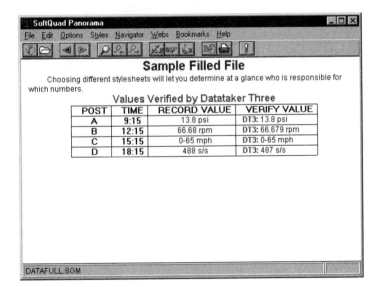

Figure 74. This is the work of data-taker three.

But wait, there's more...

Don't lose track of the fact that the datataker example relies entirely on the processing of the data to create the custom presentations. Marked sections offer a more sophisticated mechanism for indicating which content belongs to which version. We'll discuss (p. 411) the marked section capability in The SGML Primer.

The Powers of Axis/Axes

Goal of the Example:

In a chapter whose beginning claims to introduce the issues of *table* versus *tableau* (to paraphrase the French philosopher François Chahuneau), it seems disconcertingly regressive to end up with examples of tables where there is no distinction between the two. Luckily we have a fighting chance, using the axis/axes attributes on header and data cells, to make a little bit of semantic hay here.

Goal of the Application:

- To support a useful richness of table display.
- To support the "synthesized voice" or database construction/deconstruction of tables as outlined in the overview at the beginning of this chapter.

Is Influenced by/Builds on:

The section explores a subset of table functionality. The rowspan/colspan attributes and the axes/axisname constructs come to HTML (and to this example) from the work of the *International Committee for Accessible Document Design* (ICADD), the developers of techniques for making electronic texts available to the visually impaired.

Stored on the Accompanying Disk as:

Sample DTD: *htmltbl.dtd*

Sample Instance: *htmltbl.sgm*

Step by Step:

The axis attribute (short for "assigned axis name" may appear on any column or row head cell and covers the synthesized voice requirement (as described early in this chapter) for alternative text to be provided if the cell content is too long to appear in the voiced header. It functions like the alt attribute used in HTML for images. The identifying name for each axis may be stored here for use in Braille or voice. The software that I'd like someone to create will pick up values from the axis attributes of the TH and place them into the TD cells which they affect. Where tables are populated from databases, axis is the key to the source of the row or column of data.

Few people are likely to take the time to use the axis and axes attributes as they were intended if they're building tables by hand. Their value comes from their automated use, from software built specifically to populate the axes attributes of data cells with the axis value of every header cell that affects that data.

Example 37 — The Powers of Axis/Axes

To start with the tea and coffee example from earlier in the chapter, we would build the markup for the relevant cells by examining the table as presented:

Prices are in US dollars		Tea			Coffee		
		Earl Grey	Mint	Green	Turkish	Spanish	English
Loose	per lb	.42	.33	.38	1.23	3.32	.68
	per kg	1.01	.74	.77	3.00	7.65	1.61
	per ton	322					
In Bags	per lb	.88	.54	.55	NA	NA	NA
	per kg						
	per ton						

Here are parts of the marked-up version of the first three rows:

```
<TABLE>
<THEAD>
<TR><TH COLSTART="1" COLSPAN="2" ROWSPAN="2" AXIS="US DOLLARS"
        VALIGN="MIDDLE" ALIGN="CENTER">Prices are in US dollars</TH>
```

I've made a somewhat arbitrary decision here about the contents of the unusual first cell in the table. At the beginning of the chapter, I talked about the "dimensions of information" represented by the column and row structure of a table. In fact, this version of the table (in which "Price per pound/kilogram/ton in US dollars" breaks the table with a full-width row), shows that a dimension of information can be present without appearing in the traditional way you expect. Sometimes it might be implied by the title, or hiding in a footnote. In this case, I'm taking the position that "Prices are in US dollars" is one dimension of the data in all the cells we see. (Imagine another possibility: that the table continues on for several pages, broken into sections with a thick horizontal rule, and the next part begins with "Prices are in ECU" in the top left corner.) Accordingly, a "synopsis" of the value of the cell contents is captured in the attribute axis.

As we go through the sample table, you will see that the content of *each* TH *element* is captured the same way. For convenience, I've decided that each axis name be an SGML name, unbroken by spaces. This could have been built into the DTD by declaring the axis attribute to have a declared value of NAME.

```
<TH COLSTART="3" COLSPAN="3" AXIS="TEA">Tea</TH>
<TH ALIGN="CENTER" COLSTART="6" COLSPAN="3" AXIS="COFFEE">Coffee</TH>
</TR>
```

Reading the body of the table, concentrating on the axis values, will free us up from caring about row and column spanning attributes. Those will become irrelevant, as we'll see when we examine the data cells. But, while we're still examining the TH cells, the spanning values carry crucial information — they let us know which rows or which columns will pick up these values. In the case above, the colspan value of three, combined with the colstart value of 6, tells us that the axis "coffee" applies to all the data cells (the TDS) in columns 6, 7 and 8. We'll see that this is true:

```
<TR>
<TH COLSTART="3" AXIS="EARLGREY" AXES="TEA">Earl Grey</TH>
<TH COLSTART="4" AXIS="MINT" AXES="TEA">Mint</TH>
```

Oddly, some of the TH elements contain both axis and axes values. The axes attribute's role is to carry the value of the axis names that apply to it. As you can see here, the content of a TH element may indeed represent a subset or subtype of another TH. In this case, "mint" is an axis on its own and also has the same relationship to "tea" that a data cell will.

```
<TH COLSTART="5" AXIS="GREEN" AXES="TEA">Green</TH>
<TH COLSTART="6" AXIS="TURKISH" AXES="COFFEE">Turkish</TH>
<TH COLSTART="7" AXIS="SPANISH" AXES="COFFEE">Spanish</TH>
<TH COLSTART="8" AXIS="ENGLISH" AXES="COFFEE">English</TH>
</TR></THEAD>
```

Example 37 — The Powers of Axis/Axes

We now start on the "stub cells", the headers that appear to the left (or occasionally to the right) of the data. Some DTDs formalize this construct by distinguishing between header cells that appear atop a column from header cells that appear at the edge of rows. I recommend you recommend this by building it into your DTDs.

The *International Committee for Accessible Document Design* (ICADD) application, for instance, has a content model for table rows that appear in the table body of "optional **stubcell** followed by zero or more **substubcells** — this distinction allows you to have "subtotal" rows formatted differently from "total" rows — followed by any number of data cells." Strictly speaking, if people have done a good job of marking up a table, you can determine if a cell is a rowstub cell from its context. If the TH cell is in a TBODY, then it should be a rowstub. Column headers should all be TH within THEAD.

Stub cells have two major goals: Most generally, they allow for the possibility that the stub cells of a very wide table may be fixed in position as a user scrolls to the right or may be repeated on several pages in printing. At the same time, they facilitate the ability of Braille and computer voice software to determine the row heads that affect any individual cell in order to manipulate the order in which they appear. That is, TH elements marked up as TDS offer no clue to software that they carry information that affects or describes the entire row.

```
<TBODY>
<TR><TH VALIGN="MIDDLE" COLSTART="1" ROWSPAN="3"
        AXIS="LOOSE">Loose</TH>
    <TH VALIGN="MIDDLE" COLSTART="2" ROWSPAN="1"
        AXIS="PRICEPERLB" AXES="LOOSE">per lb</TH>
```

We're now moving into the data section of the table. You'll see that the value of the axes attribute of every TD cell is a list of every row and column head that applies to it. From the point of view of software, speaking anthropomorphically, it has looked to the left and grabbed the axis value of every TH in its path, and done the same looking up to the top of the table:

```
<TD COLSTART="3" AXES="USDOLLAR TEA EARLGREY LOOSE PRICEPERLB">.42</TD>
<TD COLSTART="4" AXES="USDOLLAR TEA MINT LOOSE PRICEPERLB">.33</TD>
<TD COLSTART="5" AXES="USDOLLAR TEA GREEN LOOSE PRICEPERLB">.38</TD>
<TD COLSTART="6" AXES="USDOLLAR COFFEE TURKISH LOOSE PRICEPERLB">1.23</TD>
<TD COLSTART="7" AXES="USDOLLAR COFFEE SPANISH LOOSE PRICEPERLB">3.32</TD>
<TD COLSTART="8" AXES="USDOLLAR COFFEE ENGLISH LOOSE PRICEPERLB">.68</TD>
</TR>
<TR>
<TH COLSTART="2" AXIS="PRICEPERKG" AXES="LOOSE">per kg</TH>
<TD COLSTART="3" AXES="USDOLLAR TEA EARLGREY LOOSE PRICEPERKG">1.01</TD>
<TD COLSTART="4" AXES="USDOLLAR TEA MINT LOOSE PRICEPERKG">.74</TD>
<TD COLSTART="5" AXES="USDOLLAR TEA GREEN LOOSE PRICEPERKG">.77</TD>
<TD COLSTART="6" AXES="USDOLLAR COFFEE TURKISH LOOSE PRICEPERKG">3.00</TD>
<TD COLSTART="7" AXES="USDOLLAR COFFEE SPANISH LOOSE PRICEPERKG">7.65</TD>
<TD COLSTART="8" AXES="USDOLLAR COFFEE ENGLISH LOOSE PRICEPERKG">1.61</TD>
</TR>
```

Example 37 — The Powers of Axis/Axes

Bonus:

The sample files created for this section are best viewed with an HTML browser which supports the table extensions discussed here. You will see spanning and axis support in the Panorama browser which accompanies this book. One interesting view is of *htmltbl.sgm* using the style sheet called "Show us what you can do with your Axes!", where "axes" is the plural of "axis", not a reference to the tools of either loggers or rock guitarists.

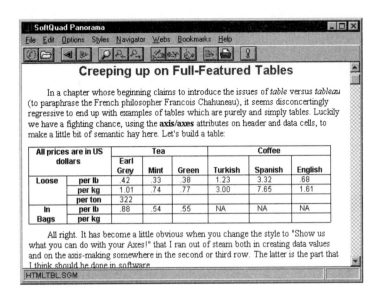

But wait, there's more...

To further explore HTML tables, see the Web site maintained by the *World Wide Web Consortium (http://www.w3.org)* and follow the links to the HTML working group papers.

To learn the latest thinking about SGML tables in general, get in the habit of attending the *Graphic Communications Association's* SGML conferences.

☙ PART IV

Struttin' Your Stuff

CHAPTER 10

Running on Entities

You've met two types of entities thus far: The first is the Parameter entities — used primarily in DTDs and the second type is the General entity, used so far only to include graphic images.

We've seen Parameter entities in almost all the examples in the book:

```
<!ENTITY % heading "h1 | h2 | h3 | h4">
<!ENTITY % list    "ul | ol">
<!ENTITY % font    "b | i">
```

Within a DTD, a parameter entity can be used to invoke whole sets of declarations. A typical use would be for a collection of special characters (where general entities represent typographic necessities such as acute accents or bullets) or for DTD fragments (such as a set of table element declarations used across a suite of related DTDs). The most commonly used ones are those standardized by ISO; a long and very useful list is incorporated into DTDs by declaring them first and then immediately calling for their inclusion with an entity reference:

```
<!ENTITY % ISOlat1 PUBLIC "ISO 8879-1986//ENTITIES Added Latin 1//EN" >>
<!ENTITY % ISOpub PUBLIC "ISO 8879-1986//ENTITIES Publishing//EN">
%ISOlat1;
%ISOpub;
```

In this example, sets of character entity declarations are being identified with their PUBLIC identifiers. You can also point directly to your copies of the files using the SYSTEM keyword. The ISO character sets are publicly available.

Parameter entities also have a role to play in marked sections which we discuss (p. 411) in *The SGML Primer*.

General entities have been used thus far only to include graphic images in SGML documents. The slideset application, for example, incorporates BMP and GIF images through a `file` attribute with a keyword of ENTITY.

As we saw, entities can be accessed by placing entity references in text:

- *Parameter entity references* are opened and closed in markup by the % and ; delimiters respectively, as in:

```
<!ELEMENT (%heading;) (a | %text;)*>
```

- *General entity references* are opened and closed in markup by the & and ; delimiters respectively, as in:

```
It was No&euml; and Fran&ccedil;ois was expecting presents.
```

Entity references cause the entity to be accessed by the SGML parser. If they are SGML entities, they will be parsed after they are accessed. An entity name could also appear in an attribute value or in data content. These are not technically "entity references". The entities are accessed, if at all, by the application or other semantic processor (such as a HyTime engine).

This chapter concentrates on the second of the entity types, the general entity, in several of its guises.

Multiple Sources for One on-the-fly Document

Goal of the Example:

We have previously seen anchors in one document referred to anchors in other documents by declaring those documents as external entities, and using the entity names in a NAMELOC element. As you will recall, we began by declaring the external entities:

```
<!DOCTYPE HTML PUBLIC "Basic HyTime 1"[
<!ENTITY doc1 SYSTEM  "hybaslnk.sgm" NDATA SGML>
<!ENTITY doc2 SYSTEM  "agenda.sgm"   NDATA SGML>
<!ENTITY doc3 SYSTEM  "plainbod.sgm" NDATA SGML>
<!ENTITY doc4 SYSTEM  "rev-ata.sgm"  NDATA SGML>
]>
```

In this section, we use exactly the same mechanisms to declare external entities, but in this case we incorporate them directly into the source document we're creating.

Goal of the Application:

In Example 27 (*Turn off the Lights!*) on page 253, you saw a slideset presentation in which you used either the navigator or the scroll bar to move through what really was one long file of slides. In Example 29 (*Jumping from Slide to Slide*) on page 273, you used two hypertext linking mechanisms to travel through the slideset. Now, finally, you put these techniques together with the high-level "pointing" capability of entity references, and we build a presentation out of component parts of any length.

Is Influenced by/Builds on:

This application uses the *slideset.dtd* from Example 27 (*Turn off the Lights!*) on page 253. We add two new lines to the DTD to declare and then incorporate a list of entity declarations pointing to the component sets of slides.

Like all of the applications in this chapter, the application described here is not DTD-dependent in any way. The techniques it describes will work in any SGML conforming software using any DTD.

Stored on the Accompanying Disk as:

Sample DTD: *slidents.dtd*

Sample Instance: *slidents.sgm*

Example 38 — Multiple Sources for One on-the-fly Document

Step by Step:

Laziness is the mother of invention. Time-saving and cost-cutting techniques arise from someone saying, "There must be a better way to accomplish this. A way that is less boring, or less expensive, or less harmful."

In my case, I've finally caught on that many of the presentations I give are simply a mix-and-match collection of pieces of other presentations. What I really want is a piece of software that lets me choose which chunks to include, sequence them easily, build a table of contents, and let me add event-specific content or slides. I almost have this today, thanks to the notion of the external entity, and the files on my laptop computer.

For today's show, we are going to create a slide show that consists of an opening slide followed by sets of slides that fit together smoothly into a presentation.

We'll start by declaring a set of four entities, each standing for a small set of two to five slides:

```
<!ENTITY sgml SYSTEM "sl-sgml.sgm" --Two-slide Intro to SGML-->
<!ENTITY brows SYSTEM "sl-brows.sgm" --Introduces SGML browsing-->
<!ENTITY web SYSTEM "sl-web.sgm" --HTML, SGML & the Web-->
<!ENTITY end SYSTEM "sl-end.sgm" --For further info/Thanks-->
```

We can declare these entities in one of several ways:

1. in the DTD
2. in the declaration subset before the document instance
3. in an external entity which we then "call in" to the DTD through a parameter entity reference, or
4. in an external entity which we then call in to the declaration subset through a parameter entity reference.

Let's choose the third method. The entities that were declared above comprise the entire contents of the external file *slideset.ent*. These entity declarations point to the slide presentation fragments that may be chosen and re-ordered for any specific presentation. In the DTD, we add these lines:

```
<!ENTITY % sl-ents SYSTEM "slideset.ent">

%sl-ents;
```

This mechanism allows them to be available to anyone using the DTD. For some purposes (for example, if a number of people share the DTD but they don't share the slideset fragments), you may prefer to move the two lines to the declaration subset before each document.

Leaving the two lines in the DTD, and being careful with relative or fixed path names allows each person to create his or her own set of declarations in a file stored locally, and always called *slideset.ent*.

Meanwhile in the Document Instance...

To implement the document instance becomes pretty darn simple now. The hard work has been done. Here's the entire contents of an instance (presented as a template for you to modify) which uses two of the four available slide set fragments:

```
<!DOCTYPE SLIDESET PUBLIC "Slides Stored in External Entities">
<SLIDESET>
<SLIDE>
<HEAD>Mix and Match Slide Show</HEAD>
<TEXT>Here's Where You'd Fill in the
Specific Information for Today's Talk</TEXT>
<FIXEDSP SIZEY="3">
<PARA>And maybe your name here.</PARA>
<PARA>Your affiliation here</PARA>
<PARA>The date; you know, all the regular stuff.</PARA>
</SLIDE>
&sgml;
&end;
</SLIDESET>
```

You could add new slides in and around the entity references, you could add references to the other two slideset fragments that have been declared (&brows; and &web;) and of course you can modify the template file so that it always starts off with *your* name and affiliation.

Software in which you view the sample file will resolve the entity references and show you the full contents of the presentation you've created. I encourage you to do some mix-and-matching of the slides. Declare new entities, modify the template, have a good time.

Example 38 — Multiple Sources for One on-the-fly Document

Bonus:

For many of the examples in this book, seeing them work in Panorama really was gilding the lily. You had learned the lesson or seen the point anyway. But for *slidents.sgm* the value becomes apparent *only* when you see the entity references resolve themselves into one coherent slide show.

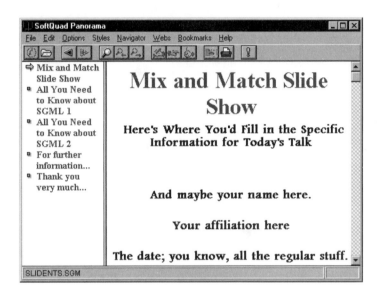

But wait, there's more...

In our next example, as if the thrill of pulling together streams of documents wasn't enough, we add automation. Example files will have a reference to an *undeclared* text entity which will be resolved instantly, as we display the files.

Automatic Text Generation for Automotive Manuals

Goal of the Example:

To show off the power of general text entities when they are declared on the fly, as needed, by a document management source such as a database.

Goal of the Application:

Here's a legend about lawyers. Once upon a time, in a kingdom far away, there was an automobile manufacturer that produced 40 different types of cars, with 40 different sets of manuals for maintaining and repairing these cars. The car owners needed to be advised what to do and when. Mechanics needed to know how. While parts of the manuals were very very similar, there really were 40 different ones. You couldn't send a *Buick LeSabre* manual to the owner of a *Cadillac Seville* car (or vice versa even).

Secretly, the creation of those manuals was both more complicated and less complicated than one might imagine. On the less complicated side of the equation was the idea that certain text was common to all of the manuals. Somewhere, each manual included the idea that you should fasten your seat belt before going anywhere. The lawyers insisted on this, and also insisted that only they could really decide the exact wording for paragraphs that might imply legal liability on the part of the manufacturer. (This made the technical writers happier, not sadder.)

Is Influenced by/Builds on:

Like all of the applications in this chapter, this application is not DTD-dependent in any way. The techniques it describes will work in any SGML conforming software using any DTD. More formally, however, this is an adaptation of a design created by Wendy Freeman of *SoftQuad*, with Terry Sadlier of *General Motors Photographic*, for GM's *Electronic Bookshelf* Project.

Stored on the Accompanying Disk as:

Sample DTD: *autotext.dtd*

Sample Instance: *autotext.sgm* and *au-henry.sgm*

Step by Step:

Imagine that your name is Henry Buick. You work in the *Buick* division of a major car manufacturer, documenting the inner workings of a car called *LeSabre*. When you log on to the computer in the morning to begin work on the chapter of the owner's manual you're writing, the document management system retrieves it — it's all SGML of course, and the chapter begins with a document type declaration which includes a declaration subset which in turn includes a set of entity declarations. The document, therefore, is of the form:

```
<!DOCTYPE manual PUBLIC "Auto Text"
[
<!ENTITY UCdiv   "Buick"      -- "Upper case division name" -->
<!ENTITY UCcar   "LeSabre"    -- "Upper case car name" -->
<!ENTITY ACdiv   "BUICK"      -- "All capitals division name" -->
<!ENTITY ACcar   "LeSABRE"    -- "All capitals car name" -->
<!ENTITY ICPdiv  "Buick's"    -- "Initial cap possessive division" -->
<!ENTITY ICPcar  "LeSabre's"  -- "Initial cap possessive car" -->
<!ENTITY ICPLdiv "Buicks"     -- "Initial cap plural division" -->
<!ENTITY ICPLcar "LeSabres"   -- "Initial cap plural car" -->
]>
```

Example 39 — Automatic Text Generation for Automotive Manuals

Throughout the document, as you write, you reference those entities:

```
<BODY>
<DIV><H1>Welcome to Your New &UCcar;</H1>
<P>Congratulations on choosing to purchase a &UCdiv; &UCcar;.
You've made the right decision. This is the very car that people have
been using as an example in books about the World Wide Web!
In fact, to be specific, this is <I>the very car used as an example
of an automatically reconfigured entity reference!</I> We know you'll
enjoy many happy years of cruising the Web and driving this car.</P>

<P>You should also be aware that the &ICPcar; browser defaults to SGML.
If you wish to use a plain vanilla HTML browser, you'll need to set
the <I>browse</I> variable in the car's cruise control <B>ini</B> file
to the browser of your choice. As of model year 1997, all &UCdiv; &ICPLcar;
come with an SGML browser as standard.</P>
</DIV>
</BODY>
```

You can imagine precisely what will happen when the instance is sent to a printer or to a display device: The required text will be substituted for the entity references, and the text will read quite normally:

```
Welcome to Your New LeSabre

Congratulations on choosing to purchase a Buick LeSabre.
You've made the right decision. This is the very car that people
have been using as an example in books about the World Wide Web!
In fact, ...

You should also be aware that the LeSabre's browser defaults
to SGML...
```

This all seems perfectly reasonable. But don't forget the one subtle detail in the beginning of this chapter: the manufacturer makes some 40 different cars and models. All of their owner manuals use identical or very similar text. They are using a database to feed out the text to the stable of writers!

Remember that the entities were declared in the declaration subset after Henry logged in. In fact, *all the same entities had already been declared, in the* DTD!

```
<!ENTITY UCdiv    "Division">
<!ENTITY UCcar    "Car">
<!ENTITY ACdiv    "DIVISION">
<!ENTITY ACcar    "CAR">
<!ENTITY ICPdiv   "Division's">
<!ENTITY ICPcar   "Car's">
<!ENTITY ICPLdiv  "Divisions">
<!ENTITY ICPLcar  "Cars">
```

You, on the other hand, work in the Cadillac division, and are busy writing the owner manual for the new Seville. When you receive the text from the database for your task today, the declaration subset is similar, but different:

```
<!DOCTYPE manual PUBLIC "Auto Text"
[
<!ENTITY UCdiv    "Cadillac">
<!ENTITY UCcar    "Seville">
<!ENTITY ACdiv    "CADILLAC">
<!ENTITY ACcar    "SEVILLE">
<!ENTITY ICPdiv   "Cadillac's">
<!ENTITY ICPcar   "Seville's">
<!ENTITY ICPLdiv  "Cadillacs">
<!ENTITY ICPLcar  "Sevilles">
]>
```

Just for the record, your software is clever enough so that you don't actually see all these declarations. You use the entity references, and the substitutions are built in to the display. You know only that the legal boilerplate text that you received from the database seems *already* to have in it all the right names of your division and the car you're describing today.

Oh those lawyers, what will they think of next?

Example 39 — Automatic Text Generation for Automotive Manuals

Bonus:

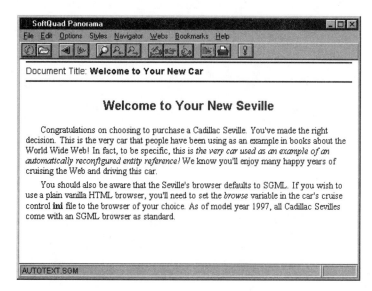

Figure 78. Open autotext.sgm in Panorama.

There is no database software on the CD ROM that accompanies this book. Accordingly, we have to cheat a little to get the effect that this application is supposed to provide. The file called *autotext.sgm* has the entities already declared for you. The file called *au-henry.sgm* is the same file except with the declarations set for Henry who works in the Buick division. (We're pretending that these are the two files released by the document management system for editing work by each of you.) Opening both will show you the effect —*Not one character in the body of the document instance was changed.* All that did change was the part that was generated automatically by the database based on your login account and your indicating which car you were planning to work on.

Figure 79. Open au-henry.sgm in Panorama.

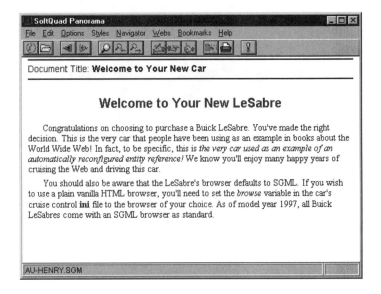

Figure 79. Open au-henry.sgm in Panorama.

But wait, there's more...

In our next example, as if the thrill of pulling together streams of documents and declaring the contents of general text entities on the fly weren't enough, we add a nestedness component; for example, external entities that we include will have a reference to an *undeclared* general text entity that will be resolved instantly, as we display the files.

Make Your Own Nest and Lie in It

Goal of the Example:

We have the opportunity to go further with entities. We have seen that:

- automatic substitutions can be made for entity references acting as replaceable text in documents — a kind of power and automation that we know about in programming languages but we're not used to seeing in text
- we gain control over component pieces of content by calling them into a document as fragments, also with entity references.

Now we get to put the two techniques together and support general entity reference nested within external entities. This gives us, in fact, the ability to establish text variables within reusable document fragments.

Goal of the Application:

The application in the previous example expressed one extreme example of the role played by SGML text entities — to save the high costs of content customization by exploiting the power of a database to declare new entities on the fly. The application in this section is another extreme. This one expects you to personally declare the entities that are needed to make it work, but from there on, the software takes over, saving considerable time for the humans involved.

Is Influenced by/Builds on:

Like all of the applications in this chapter, the Ruby-Throated Double-Nested Entity application is not DTD-dependent in any way. The techniques it describes will work in any SGML conforming software using any DTD.

Stored on the Accompanying Disk as:

Sample DTD: *html2ht.dtd*

Sample Instance: *rubydemo.sgm* is the basic demo file which you should edit and save under the name *fred.sgm*; *rubyinst.sgm* is the set of instructions (which matches the "Step by Step" section here); *rubytest.sgm* is a sample of the magic trick as completed by you.

Step by Step:

As with any good magic trick, you'll have to take a few minutes to set this one up. For a start, you'll need to find the source file for the demo document. It is part of your Panorama distribution that came with this book, in the folder called *Demos*, with the name *rubydemo.sgm*.

Move to that folder and open the file. You'll see from the declaration subset that a number of external entities have been declared. This allows you to refer, to files which also exist in the current folder.

```
<!ENTITY copydemo  SYSTEM  "copywrit.sgm">
<!ENTITY fanclub   SYSTEM  "fanclub.sgm">
<!ENTITY statment  SYSTEM  "statment.sgm">
```

Example 40 — Make Your Own Nest and Lie in It

You'll notice one other declaration. Unlike the external entities above, this is an internal SGML entity, and is a kind of short form, or variable, where whatever's between the quote marks replaces a reference to the entity named in the declaration. This one, "author", is the fun one. Replace the name "George Meteskey" in the replacement text parameter of the entity declaration with a name of your choice. That's an entity reference for the famous *author* of the fictional books that star in this demo.

```
<!ENTITY author CDATA "George Meteskey">
```

Note   All of these general entities are referenced in your text simply by preceding them with an ampersand (so the software knows it's an entity name) and following them with a semi-colon.

You need to know that you can insert any of the boilerplate text chunks anywhere in the document by typing an entity reference. Type in the &copydemo; reference, for example, right after the next paragraph in the demo version of the file. You could add &statment; to this document too. When you load the file into a full SGML browser, each entity reference will disappear, replaced by the entity itself. We've put in the &fanclub; reference as an example.

Fine. Add in the other external entities, save the file with your changes, and open it with an SGML browser. When you view the sample file, if you don't see the boilerplate text in position, please look at the "Tested Sample Source" file *with your changes already in place*, in the folder as *rubytest.sgm*.

How the Trick Worked

Full SGML allows not just one level of entity replacement but nested levels! The file inclusion mechanism is actually a generalized replacement capability. All three of the included files contained an entity reference of their own — the &author; entity reference. When you declared a value for that entity in the declaration subset in the SGML document entity (the one which you saved as *fred.sgm*), that declaration took effect for all the nested entities too, as they all contain parts of the same document.

As far as uses for this kind of capability go, imagine a self-updating document on the server which is nonetheless customized for each reader. Or a copyright notice shared by a whole series of files or books which gets updated, at year-end, with the new date in only one place.

Figure 80. Open rubydemo.sgm in Panorama.

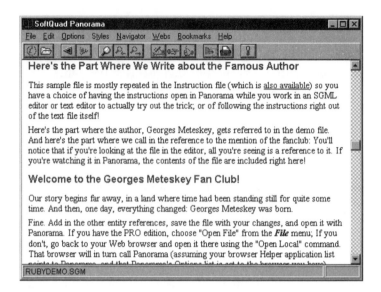

Figure 81. Open fred.sgm in Panorama.

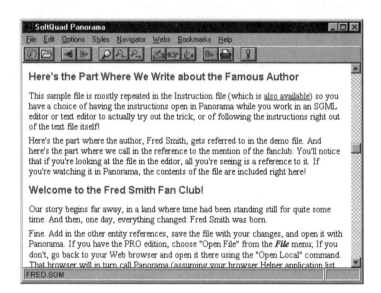

❧ Chapter 11

The Absolutely Critical Next Step

Until recently, every HTML browser has known just what markup would be coming its way. Between the *http protocol* and the MIME type as well as the *.htm* or *.html* extension on the filename, it was pretty clear that the browser would be receiving an HTML document. This meant that the browser had to know how to display <TITLE>, <H1>, <P>, *et cetera*, and what actions might be provoked by <LINK> and <A>.

So, even if you just extend HTML with one new element or attribute, the browser won't know until it sees the actual start-tag in the document that something new is coming. Traditional HTML-only browsers take the only sensible course of action — they ignore markup they don't recognize. This is good news: It means the document will still display.

But the bad news is that you were probably hoping for a lot more. You add a new element to a document for a reason — either because you want it to be displayed differently, or to have new hypertext linking properties, or to be processed in some other way. Instead it is ignored. Clearly you need a way to let a Web browser know "this is not plain vanilla HTML — it's been augmented in specific ways".

Full SGML provides a mechanism to do precisely this — the combination of the document type definition and the document type declaration — so that with SGML, *you make the rules.*

Document Type (DOCTYPE) Declarations

SGML, as you've seen already, is all about not being surprised. Computer software always wants to know what is coming next, whether it treats something as an instruction, or as data content.

Let's imagine a very simplified version of an HTML DTD.

```
<!ELEMENT html          (head, body)>
<!ELEMENT head          (title, link?)>
<!ELEMENT (title|link)  (#PCDATA)>
<!ELEMENT (body)        (h1|h2|h3|p|a)*>
<!ELEMENT (h1|h2|h3|p)  (a|#PCDATA|b|i)*>
<!ELEMENT (a|b|it)      (#PCDATA)>
```

Let's further imagine that you now wish to use this DTD with a full SGML browser. You construct a file:

```
<HTML><HEAD><TITLE>Simple Sample</TITLE></HEAD>
<BODY>
<H1>This Example is about Declaration Subsets</H1>
<P>This sample doesn't include the critical piece to let a
system know you're using a special version of an HTML DTD.</P>
<P>For this we need only read on.</P>
</BODY></HTML>
```

This is the question: How would a browser (or any other software) know which document type definition (DTD) is associated with this instance of a document type? Full SGML answers that question with one answer that appears as two mechanisms. The answer: treat the whole thing as one document. That is an odd answer if you are used to thinking of these as two separate components. But that is how SGML works: The DTD and instance together comprise the document.

Mechanism one: *Declare* the relationship of DTD and instance with a document type declaration. The task of any SGML markup declaration is to declare a match between one item (represented by one *parameter*) and another parameter, which often consists of a whole set of components. (Frequently other parameters are involved too.)

Therefore, to connect the instance with the DTD, type the document type declaration before the instance:

```
<!DOCTYPE html [
<!ELEMENT html        (head, body)>
<!ELEMENT head        (title)>
<!ELEMENT title       (#PCDATA)>
<!ELEMENT (body)      (h1|h2|h3|p|a)*>
<!ELEMENT (h1|h2|h3|p) (#PCDATA|a|b|i)*>
<!ELEMENT (a|b|i)     (#PCDATA)>
]>
<HTML><HEAD><TITLE>Simple Sample</TITLE></HEAD>
<BODY>
<H1>This Example is about Declaration Subsets</H1>
<P>This sample doesn't include the critical piece to let
a system know you're using a special version of an HTML DTD.</P>
<P>For this we need only read on.</P>
</BODY></HTML>
```

We now have, for the first time in this book a complete SGML document in a single entity. This is effectively what the SGML parser always sees.

Of course when the same DTD is used for multiple instances, as it normally is, this isn't very practical. One shouldn't be required to always duplicate DTDs if they're going to be used frequently, or maintained in one central place, to avoid any risk of errors creeping in. Fortunately, SGML's own entity mechanism has come to the rescue. In the examples in the book, we were able to keep the DTD in an entity apart from the SGML document entity in which the instance begins. How? Because the DOCTYPE declaration is also an entity declaration in disguise — and an entity reference as well. Let's take a closer look at it.

HTML documents frequently omit the document type declaration (even though HTML-only browsers will support it). If you want to use HTML documents with a full SGML browser, however, you'll need to advise the browser which markup to expect by adding a declaration, normally in one of the following formats, at the top of each relevant file:

```
<!DOCTYPE doctypename PUBLIC "machine-independent DTD name">
```

or

```
<!DOCTYPE doctypename [actual DTD]>
```

Here "doctypename" is the document element type name, the highest-level element type in the hierarchy of element types declared in the DTD. (In the case of the HTML DTD, for example, the highest-level element type is called HTML.)

The remainder of the parameters are those you will find in typical external entity declarations, as described in Chapter 10 (*Running on Entities*) on page 351. The entry being declared contains the DTD (strictly speaking, the "external subset" of the DTD). That entity is referenced immediately before the closing delimiter of the DOCTYPE declaration.

The example with square brackets is just as it appears: "[actual DTD]" means that you can insert between the square brackets the entire text of a DTD, even if it goes on for hundreds of lines.

These two techniques — referencing the DTD and including the DTD — may be combined in a third option:

```
<!DOCTYPE doctypename PUBLIC "machine independent DTD name"
[local additions to the DTD]>
```

This approach can be quite exhilarating. You can extend any DTD by creating new markup in this internal declaration subset (anything between the square brackets). The public identifier points to the external declaration subset, which is parsed after the internal one.

Public Identifiers

One normally creates a public identifier for a DTD that is to be shared so there can be no confusion. There are two kinds: formal and informal. In our example then:

```
<!DOCTYPE HTML PUBLIC "xxxxxx">
```

where xxxxxx is the public identifier we'll give to the sample variation DTD we created earlier. There is a specific syntax for all formal public identifiers (illustrated here by the FPI for the HTML 3.2 DTD):

```
"-//W3C//DTD HTML 3.2//EN"
```

In the example, the components of the FPI are:

- The hyphen-slash-slash, which indicates that the owner of this *public text* is unregistered. (A "+" followed by the two slashes would indicate that the owner identifier is registered according to the rules of ISO 9070, the standard for the registration of public text owner identifiers.)
- The owner identifier, in this case "W3C", the World Wide Web Consortium.
- A keyword that indicates which SGML construct the FPI identifies, in this case a DTD, but the keyword could also have been DOCUMENT (for an entire SGML document, ENTITIES (for an entity set), TEXT (for reusable text portions in an SGML text entity), or one of nine others.
- A description or name for the "public text", in this case, a name for the DTD.
- After the last pair of slashes, the language used in the public text.

There is a less useful but simpler form of public identifier as well — an informal public identifier obeys only one rule. It must be unique in the realm for which it is declared. For example, the public identifiers of the DTDs used as examples in this book are no more than one word; each uniquely identifies its sample application within the closed world of this book. You would not want to use these public identifiers too far afield since there is nothing built in to ensure their uniqueness in other domains.

To that end, by the way, each DTD in this book includes a comment stating its formal public identifier. If you want to build files that point unambiguously to the specific DTDs in this book, in your document type declarations, use the FPIs given at the top of each DTD. (We guarantee their uniqueness by building in the International Standard Book Number (ISBN) for the book, which is guaranteed unique within the realm of published books. Having done that, it's easy to guarantee uniqueness with respect to the book.)

Finding DTDs in Daily Life

Imagine that you and I work on two different operating systems and have, naturally, working directory structures peculiar to our habits and thought processes. One day we each receive 40 SGML documents from our friend Jack, whose computer uses a third operating system. We have all agreed to use the same DTD, the infamous Noah's flood DTD of which we each have a copy. (You have one too; see Appendix A.)

You have your copy in your DTD directory with the rest of your DTDs. I have my copy in my *flood project* folder with the rest of the material for the book on which we're collaborating.

Your copy: /home/den/daniel/DTD/flood.dtd.

My copy: mymachine:yuri:flood-project:working.dtd

The documents themselves include a document type declaration, typed by Jack who created these files, and which might be something like:

```
<!DOCTYPE SYSTEM "C:\jack\research\tools\ae\dtds\floodproj.dtd">
```

The trouble is that if I don't have a folder on my C drive called *jack* (with a *research* subfolder, and so on), my software will never find this DTD.

Well in fact, Jack is smarter than that. He's shipped us the files with a public identifier instead of one that is so obviously dependent on his personal file structure. Each document actually reveals its association with the flood DTD by beginning with the declaration:

```
<!DOCTYPE flood PUBLIC "-//DTD SQ SGML Primer - flood DTD//en">
```

This is considerably better, but how exactly does this help? Well, it keeps the system-dependent location out of the document and replaces it with a *system-independent* name. Now, any form of simple catalog — like a library card catalog — can be used to find the current location of the named DTD.

Of course, I actually do have the file stored in a specific location on my computer; you have it stored in some location on yours. Moveover, each of us has several software tools we'll use to process and work with those instances (and therefore with the DTD). It would be nice if they all used the same catalog format.

The SGML Open Entity Catalog

In 1994, SGML *Open*, the consortium of SGML vendors (and major users too, although most members today sell SGML software and/or services) published a technical resolution — TR001-1994 — on this subject. (The resolution was created by one of its technical committees and voted on by the members).

The resolution establishes a format for a file whose name is *catalog*, which must be resident in a folder where any SGML application will know to look. Its job is very straightforward. Tell the SGML software where to find an entity declared with a public identifier. The format would be (on your example machine):

```
PUBLIC "-//DTD SQ SGML Primer - flood DTD//en"
       "/home/den/daniel/DTD/flood.dtd"
```

Three additional details:

- The second parameter, */home/den/daniel/DTD/flood.dtd* doesn't need to be a full path. If all your SGML applications know to begin looking in a specific working directory, the entry in the *catalog* could be, for example:

```
PUBLIC "-//DTD SQ SGML Primer - flood DTD//en" "flood.dtd"
```

- The first parameter, as it appears in these examples, is a formal public identifier. A public identifier is legitimate even if informal. The following is a legal *catalog* entry (and assumes everyone knows what *flood.dtd* refers to).

```
PUBLIC "flood.dtd" "c:\jack\research\tools\ae\dtds\floodproj.dtd"
```

Which also means this is legitimate:

```
PUBLIC "flood.dtd" "flood.dtd"
```

where, by coincidence everyone publicly calls it the *flood.dtd* and you've placed your copy of it in the working directory of your SGML application(s).
- Remember that the *catalog* file is *not* normally interchanged. (Only the SGML documents are, with or without the DTD.) The second parameter will always reflect the capabilities of *your* software.

This means that if you have a full SGML browser and the DTD is actually stored elsewhere, you could use a World Wide Web Uniform Resource Identifier to point to it. In traditional URL form then, a legitimate *catalog* entry would be:

```
PUBLIC "-//DTD SQ SGML Primer - flood DTD//en"
       "http://www.sq.com/catalog/flood.dtd"
```

As you extend existing DTDs (including HTML) or create new ones, you'll need to enter their locations into your *catalog*. The sample disk that came with this book has already done that for you. The *catalog* entries are of the form:

```
PUBLIC "machine independent DTD name" "system specific storage location"
```

For example:

```
PUBLIC "Plain Text"                       "..\DTDs\plaintxt.dtd"
PUBLIC "Plain Text Plus Links"            "..\DTDs\plainlnx.dtd"
PUBLIC "Plain Text with Headings"         "..\DTDs\plainhds.dtd"
PUBLIC "Plain Text with Links and Headings"  "..\DTDs\plainlah.dtd"
PUBLIC "Plain Text with HTML Headings" "..\DTDs\plainhx.dtd"
PUBLIC "Plain Text with Lists"            "..\DTDs\plainuol.dtd"
[...]
```

That's all, folks!

There are no more example applications in this book. No more sample files to type in. No more SGML party tricks to amuse and bewilder your friends. The accompanying CD ROM contains SoftQuad Panorama and all of the sample files that are discussed in the forty examples. The *Bibliography* (p. 449) lists other books on SGML that may help you further down the road to publishing on the World Wide Web using full SGML.

This is it — the moment we have all been waiting for. We have the taken small steps needed to get comfortable with developing SGML applications. We have worked with applications that are simpler than the simplest HTML and we have gone beyond. Now it is time to step out on your own.

❧ Appendixes

❧ Appendix A

The SGML Primer

SoftQuad's Quick Reference Guide to the Essentials for the Standard: The SGML Needed for Reading a DTD and Marked-Up Documents and Discussing Them Reasonably.

Jumping In

This primer offers an introduction to SGML markup — the stuff that adds *intelligence about itself* to content — and to document type definitions (DTDs), the sets of declarations and strategies that application designers use to describe the structures of types of documents — memos, for example, or technical manuals, or corporate financial reports.

To get the bigger picture, begin with SGML: *The End-User's Eye View* (p. 380).

Or you can jump right into the specifics with *How Declarations Work* (p. 389) and *The DTD for a Primer Booklet* (p. 391).

While parts of this Primer were created using SGML, the sample DTD was created only to illustrate the vocabulary and syntax of markup declarations.

Treat this document as very basic. Its job, in any situation, whether conference or cocktail party, is to help you recognize and quickly disarm SGMLese.

Conventions Used in This Primer

Four basic typographic conventions are used to explain and illustrate SGML constructs throughout this appendix. Sample document instances appear either as ASCII text or in the on-screen form used by SoftQuad Author/Editor, an SGML-sensitive wordprocessor.

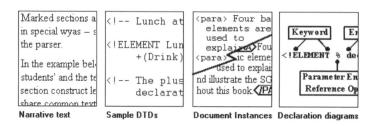

| Narrative text | Sample DTDs | Document Instances | Declaration diagrams |

SGML: The End-User's Eye View

The Standard Generalized Markup Language is necessarily sophisticated —it is providing a much-needed service by allowing the exchange of information *at any level of complexity* among software, hardware, storage and presentation systems (including database management and publishing applications) without regard to the manufacturer's name on the label. And it is doing all this with the authority of an International Standard. At the same time, SGML's strength is that it reflects the way people work today while nudging us all gently towards new concepts of information handling.

Two Ways of Looking at the Document's Structure

In general, people who create the component pieces of electronic documents are actually thinking of them in two ways at once:

- They are files — as many as are needed to build the final document — on a computer or on several computers. There may be a file with a title page, a portion of a spreadsheet that gets printed as part of Chapter Two, a graphic of an organization chart that shows up in Chapter Six, and a lot of text in various chunks. This collection of separate files — or storage entities — comprises what one generally thinks of as the document, or what, for the purposes of SGML, is termed the SGML *document*. These entities can be any size, created by any kind or number of pieces of software, resident on any number of computers. (They need not even be files; they could be database objects, parts of files, or any other form of storage.) Parts may be shared with other documents but, they may be thought of together, as the *entity structure* of a single document.

- At the same time, if you were to look at the table of contents of our imaginary book, you would see no reference to the file that contains the spreadsheet, or the file with the title page, and so on. Those storage entities are ignored when considering the *logical structure*, a hierarchical structure of objects such as chapters and tables and paragraphs that comprise the document's element structure. Sometimes the elements and the entities correspond — the logical element "table" may be the external entity "spreadsheet" — but often they don't.

Two Kinds of Content

In any communication, two levels of information are being passed: what we think of as the content, and other, subtler information, about that content. That other information — boldface in a book, underlining on a hand-written memo, shouting in a face-to-face conversation — may be thought of as markup. Its job is to express information (in general reflecting hierarchical structure) that is useful to a human or computer for processing the content.

SGML makes exactly the same distinction, dividing what is contained in a document into content, or data (made up, naturally, of *data characters*, which are the letters of the alphabet, the numbers, punctuation, and so on) and markup (made up of *markup characters*, which, by an important coincidence, are also letters, numbers, punctuation characters).

Markup is not a new idea. Traditionally, designers marked up raw manuscripts with instructions to a typesetter who did whatever was required to make titles appear big, bold and centered, to make paragraphs a certain width with an indent, and so forth. Those instructions would appear as a string of gibberish, meaningful only to the machine being used to set the type. Often they would contain "control-codes" that could baffle and halt anyone else's typesetting system.

At the same time, those instructions, embedded in the flow of text, guaranteed the long-term *uselessness* of the information. If it was to be revised and republished, it had to go to the same typesetting system, which would probably be outdated by the time of the revision. If someone wanted to change the design, it meant someone (generally someone else) having to go into the files to edit every occurrence of whatever cryptic instructions made the title 36-point bold Times Roman centered.

Using computerized global search-and-replace techniques couldn't work because the same instructions might appear in a variety of places that were not logically related. If you wanted to turn every foreign language term from italic to bold, you would accidentally but automatically convert all the italic book titles and emphasized text too.

(I've written this section in the past tense, but, in fact, *procedural markup* — whereby an operator uses cryptic machine-dependent instructions to tell a system to perform an action such as switch fonts, embolden, center — is still the prevalent technique today. Not for long. *Descriptive markup*, its opposite, identifies the elements within the document instance which make up its logical structure and solves many of the problems listed above.)

Two Improvements on Old Style Markup

SGML begins by defining a *character set*, generally based on the ASCII standard characters, which can be sent, safely, to any system. Peculiar and special characters (bullets and boxes, math symbols and so forth) are turned into ASCII representations — entity references — that get converted by the receiving system into whatever it needs to reproduce those characters. This means no peculiar "control" or "alternate" characters are used.

The second improvement came about as the creators of SGML's precursor GML (of which, more in a moment) realized that the places where markup traditionally had to be inserted in a document matched the elements of its logical structure. For example: text size changed because a title had begun; a typeface changed because an emphasized term appeared; a horizontal line was drawn to set off a table or chart.

GML then went the next step and said "All markup will be logical, and instead of cryptic codes, element type names (lodged inside tags) can be inserted into text to indicate the beginnings and ends of logical objects."

From the user's point of view, then, we know that markup will be mixed in with the data and that all of it will be represented using standard characters which are available consistently on all (or nearly all) computers.

Separating the Wheat from the Other Wheat

Clearly it's crucial to distinguish between the two types of characters, data characters and markup characters. This is done in SGML by inserting delimiter characters which let software recognize that certain characters should be read in TAG mode (and perhaps specific actions taken or translations made into typesetting languages) and others in CON (for content) mode and passed over to the application for processing.

Characters used as delimiters must be carefully chosen: They shouldn't show up too often in regular content. ISO 8879 describes a base set which includes open and close angle brackets to set off start-tags (the < > characters with the name of an element type inside) and an ampersand followed by a name followed by a semi-colon to set off entities such as graphic images or special characters (• for instance).

What Does It All Mean? How Does It All Work?

This is not madness. All databases have to have an internal representation that indicates where the "name" field (for example) ends and the "address" field begins. Each wordprocessing or desktop publishing software product has some internal markup language that initiates centering or emboldening and so on. The tricky part was in coming up with an approach to markup that would allow interchange among all of them. The solution dates back to the late 1960's and to SGML's precursor, IBM's "GML" (Generalized Markup Language).

Prior to the creation of GML, attempts were made to develop "generic coding", a system of universal, machine-independent codes whereby, for instance, <P> would always mean "paragraph", and <H1> would always indicate a "first-level heading". The intention was to specify a set of element types that would work for a very large number of documents.

The principle of generic coding is sound, but the objective was essentially unachievable: There are simply too many types of documents with too many different types of elements in them.

And a second problem appeared: What about mistakes? Is there some way that the computer can help ensure that element type names are keyed correctly? Can it help with the more difficult task of checking that users keyed in the codes in the right places?

Interestingly, there was one answer to both problems, and it came from the world of computer databases. To create a database, one first defines a "schema" that states what data elements can occur and in what order. The inventors of GML — Charles Goldfarb, Ed Mosher and Ray Lorie — did not create a set of standardized codes, but a language for entering codes in documents in accordance with a schema, known as a document type definition (or DTD).

Charles Goldfarb took this idea a step further in SGML, which includes a language for declaring the DTD itself. In SGML, a set of markup declarations defines precisely those types of elements (and other constructs — we'll get to them) needed for one document or, more usually, for a group of similarly structured documents.

The element type specifications — formally called element type declarations — have two critical functions: They indicate the "official" name of an element type, which will appear inside delimiters as a tag (<CHAPTER> for example); and they describe what each element may contain, the content model.

A "chapter" might be described as starting with a "chapter title" which would be followed by any number of "paragraphs", perhaps interspersed with "headings". The element type declaration for this example would be:

```
<!ELEMENT chapter (chptitle, (para|heading)+)>
```

SGML provides the rules — formally called a syntax — for this declaration. Any SGML system would recognize an element type declaration because it begins with <!ELEMENT. SGML software would recognize the comma as meaning "followed by", the vertical bar as "or" (as in "paragraphs or headings") and the plus sign as "one or more". The parentheses provide grouping, just as they do in elementary school arithmetic. The > ends the declaration of this element type.

Now the next step would be to go on and declare the contents of CHAPTER subelements, CHPTITLE, PARA and HEADING. We can do them together if they have the same content model.

```
<!ELEMENT (chptitle | para | heading) (#PCDATA)>
```

The SGML keyword, PCDATA, is recognized by the system as meaning that CHPTITLE, PARA and HEADING don't have any subelements of their own. Rather, they contain what is termed parsed character data — the actual letters, numbers, punctuation and special characters that make up data content.

At this point the user would create the document, based on the relationships and using the markup defined in the DTD, set off from the character data with appropriate delimiters:

```
<CHAPTER>
<CHPTITLE>My Summer Vacation</CHPTITLE>
<PARA>It was a dark night, not stormy at all,
no hint of a storm, really .......</PARA>
<PARA>A pirate ship appeared on the horizon... </PARA>
...</CHAPTER>>
```

As you may have guessed, tags that begin with the </ (the open-angle-slash) delimiter are end-tags. The content of the "chapter title" is fully contained between its start- and end-tags.

In addition to declaring the element type names and allowed contents, the DTD may also include declarations of entities, the storage objects described earlier which contain machine-independent coding for the bullets, special characters or external files which each system will have its own way of incorporating on screen or on paper.

Sometimes there's not enough information just in an element type name to allow it to be used in accordance with some individual requirements. Perhaps we want the chapter's opening paragraph to be classified as top secret. An attribute for a paragraph might be defined as follows:

```
<!ATTLIST para secrecy (topsec|public) "public">
```

The "public" in quotes represents the *default value*. A default value ensures that all paragraphs in which the user doesn't specify "topsec" or "public" will have the value "public" anyway.

```
<PARA SECRECY=TOPSEC>It was a dark night, not stormy at all,
no hint of a storm, really ...
<PARA>A pirate ship appeared on the horizon ...</>
```

Notice that in some circumstances markup minimization can be used to save some keystrokes. (As examples, the first paragraph's end-tag has been omitted since the next paragraph's start-tag implies the end of the first paragraph element. In addition, the element type name "para" has been omitted from the `</>` and, much subtler, quotation marks have been left off from around the attribute value of "topsec".) There are various minimization techniques available for end-tags as well as for start-tags and attribute specifications.

In an SGML Document, There are No Surprises

Picture the many levels at which life is made easier by SGML. You tell someone you're sending an SGML document. They know:

- That it may begin with an SGML declaration. This tells a receiving system exactly which character set, which delimiters and which optional SGML features are being used (along with much other information).(Markup minimization, for example, is something that different systems may or may not support. Often the SGML declaration will be left out, when both the sending and receiving systems have the same SGML environments.
- That it will then contain a prolog with a document type declaration subset, the formal collection of element type, attribute list, entity and other declarations that tell a system exactly what markup to expect. Often the full set of declarations for the document type definition will be replaced by one line which states

that the DTD is shared as public text or is already available on the receiving system.

• That it will then contain a document instance. This is what we intuitively think of as the document itself, the actual data content with the actual markup.

Every step has been smooth. Because the system is SGML, each component establishes the values and parameters for the following one. The only markup that appears has been declared in the document type declaration. The syntax of the declarations has been indicated by the SGML declaration. And the standard defines that.

The real benefit of this flow is that computers can follow it to check whether documents follow the rules designed for them. SGML (in spite of being human-readable) is a computer language and is very precise. This means that a computer program — a validating SGML parser — can read the SGML declaration and learn its syntax rules, then read the document type declaration and learn the vocabulary rules of the markup, and then determine whether the document instance meets those rules.

Once I Send Information Out to be Processed, What Happens?

"Determining whether the document instance meets those rules" is validation. It can happen automatically. By a computer. And as far as ensuring that the content you're sending to a database or to the typesetter or making available on-line won't hiccup or burp, it can't be beat.

The parser's job is to read in SGML and separate the data content from the markup. It recognizes when markup has been minimized and will expand that. If your content includes references to the spreadsheet for Chapter Two and the graphic of the organization chart for Chapter Six, it will instruct the system how to find those entities. If the graphic is in some special data content notation produced by a drawing program, the parser will tell the system how to have the image brought in (in this case to be displayed or published). If your content includes special directions for your processing system in its own internal language — SGML calls these *processing instructions* — they will be passed right through to the application. If you've used the SGML marked section construct to indicate that some parts of your document are not to appear in this version, the parser will know not to send them on. If you're using the SGML comment declaration construct to pass notes and messages back and forth among the writers and editors, the parser will know whether to send them on to the receiving application too. All this and more.

All this and more, and most important, invisibly. This list — and it is only part of what a parser and an SGML *system* do — represents actions you can count on, without human involvement (except, of course, to clean up human errors, a process made considerably easier than it might be by the rules, established in the DTD and enforced by the sending application).

What Do You Mean "Enforced"?

A new generation of software is appearing and will continue to appear, software that lives and breathes SGML, that takes advantage of the DTD to guide users in building documents that are well-structured; that takes advantage of the structure to give users functionality that we never had before.

Soon, if you're a user, much of what you've learned in this overview will become second nature to you, the complications masked behind intuitive interfaces but with SGML's powerful and flexible constructs at your fingertips.

Your World Wide Web browsing software will read and exploit SGML structures. (SoftQuad Panorama, included with this book, is an example of such software.) Your database software will have an option to import and export SGML files, as will your wordprocessor and hypertext creation software. Who knows, perhaps even your spreadsheet software, which has already figured out import and export with relational databases, will realize that "named cells" are already marked up! This new generation of software will work directly with DTDs and offer you a logic-driven, structure-based, objects-and-attributes-based approach to information handling far richer than the templates and style sheets and index card interfaces of today.

In the opening of this appendix, I mentioned SGML's value for the "exchange of information at all levels of complexity". Because this standard was designed as a language for building applications — through the creation of new DTDs and the extension of existing ones such as HTML — it offers a strong foundation for such a lofty ambition.

How Declarations Work

The fundamental principle of any computer language — and of any standard — should always be *No Surprises*. SGML lets people analyze the storage, retrieval and processing requirements of collections of related or similar documents (classes of documents), and create all the mechanisms necessary to describe the structures of those documents using formal markup declarations.

Simply put, markup declarations create or establish the markup used in the document to set off structures clearly and unambiguously.

Declaration Parameters

SGML declarations are generally of the form:

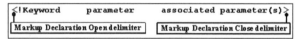

The first parameter always establishes a name that may henceforward be used to indicate, reference or represent the contents of the other parameters. (It's no different from saying "Let x have a certain value or meaning, so that I can now use x in my work.")

The keyword can be any one of:

- DOCTYPE which assigns the name in the first parameter to a set of declarations. These declarations may be right there enclosed in square brackets or in another file identified in the next parameter (or in a combination of these places). This set comprises the document type declaration subset, and may include any of the other kinds of markup declarations.
- ELEMENT to declare an object class (element type) within the logical structure of the document; here the first parameter is declared to have as content everything in a following parameter, the content model. (For example: a "chapter" is declared to have content which consists of "title followed by any number of paragraphs.")

- ATTLIST to associate an element type with a set of characteristics that may be applied to one specific instance of that element. (For example: A FIGURE element is associated with an unique identifier so that references to it can calculate its page number or show it in a separate window.)
- ENTITY to allow a short string of text to stand for a longer string, or to point to a file stored externally to the current file. (For example: Let "tsp" be used as shorthand for *The* SGML *Primer*)
- NOTATION to associate the first parameter, which names a data content notation for non-SGML data (CGM for graphics, for example; SCORE or "MIDI Files" format for music or whatever), and the second parameter which instructs the system in how to handle such notation.
- SHORTREF to name a set of associations between short strings of characters (or a single character) and markup.
- USEMAP to activate the set of SHORTREFS named in the first parameter with the element type(s) named in the second one. (The SHORTREF and USEMAP declarations are not covered in this book. These constructs are most useful when you attempt to use SGML with typewriters or old-fashioned word-processors or in *retrofitting*, the turning of old electronic files into SGML-encoded text. Software tools designed specifically for creating or editing SGML can avoid them.)

The exception to the declaration structures described here is the comment declaration which begins and ends with two hyphens, instead of a keyword.

In the following section, a fictional DTD that describes this booklet and a sample document instance created with this DTD illustrate how markup declarations are written and how they work together to define the structure of a document such as this booklet.

The DTD for a Primer Booklet

The SGML Primer, of which this appendix contains only a portion, started life as a 36-page booklet. It has since been pressed into duty on the Web, using both HTML and the simple DTD with which it was first published. Although that DTD was not used to produce this book, it is still instructive to consider it here.

The DTD begins with the document type declaration which assigns the name "booklet" to the set of markup declarations, the document type declaration subset, which follows. Since certain kinds of entities must be declared before they can be used, it is customary to list all entity declarations together at the beginning of the DTD.

Each type of declaration is illustrated in a declaration diagram and explained in greater detail in the following sections. Comment declarations can help clarify a DTD. This DTD, for example, strings together some of the declarations that describe this booklet.

```
<!DOCTYPE booklet
[
<!ELEMENT  booklet - - (title, (text|DTD|instance|diagram)*)>
<!ENTITY   tsp          "The SGML Primer" -- the title we'll use -->
<!ENTITY % declars      "element|attlist|entity|notation">
<!NOTATION pict SYSTEM "pictView">
<!ELEMENT  DTD          (%declars;) -- parameter entity shorthand -->
<!ATTLIST  DTD          type  (silly|serious) serious>
<!ELEMENT (title|instance|%declars;) (#PCDATA)>
<!ELEMENT  diagram      EMPTY>
<!ATTLIST  diagram      graphic NOTATION (pict|cgm) #REQUIRED>
<!ELEMENT  text         (para)*>
<!ELEMENT  para         (#PCDATA|quote|emph)*>
<!ELEMENT (quote|emph) (#PCDATA)>
]>
```

The Document Instance

The sample document instance which follows contains the text of the document incorporating the markup as specified in the Booklet DTD.

Why the term "document instance"? Because we are referring to a particular document which is one instance of the many possible documents that could be created in accordance with the Booklet DTD.

Markup within the document instance is called descriptive markup. Descriptive markup identifies the elements within the document instance which make up its logical structure.

Note the element type names in the document instance below are, naturally, the names declared as markup in the DTD. In this illustration tags represented as icons.

```
(BOOKLET) (TITLE) The Document Instance (/TIITLE)
(TEXT) (PARA) The sample document instance which follows contains
    the text of the document incorporating the markup as specified in the
    Booklet DTD. (/PARA)
(PARA) Why the term (QUOTE) document instance (/QUOTE) ?
    Because we are referring to a particular document which is one instance
    of the many possible documents that could be created in accordance
    with the Booklet DTD. (/PARA)
(PARA) Markup within the document is called
    (EMPH) descriptive markup (/EMPH) . Descriptive markup identifies
    the elements within the document instance which make up its
    logical structure. (/PARA)
(PARA) Note the tag names for elements in the document instance below
    are naturally, the names declared as markup in the DTD....(/PARA) (/TEXT)
    (/BOOKLET)
```

Element Type Declarations

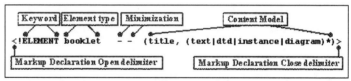

The element type declaration above defines the element type to be BOOKLET and the content model to be a TITLE followed by the subelements: TEXT or DTD or INSTANCE or DIAGRAM. The "|" says "OR". The "*" says that the subelements can appear zero or more times. Thus the subelements can occur and recur in any order — DIAGRAM could precede TEXT; DTD follow INSTANCE; TEXT can be repeated many times interspersed with DIAGRAM or DTD subelements — which is already what happens in the booklet.

Element Type

Within the element type declaration, the first parameter indicates the name of the element type. Element type names consist of one *name start character* followed by zero or more *name characters*, up to 8 characters in total. In the *concrete syntax* used in this book, name start characters are "a–z" and "A–Z". Name characters are "a–z", "A–Z", "0–9", "." (period), and "–" (hyphen). Names are not case sensitive.

The element type name parameter may consist of one element type name, or a group of elements type names.

Minimization

SGML's optional markup minimization features allow markup in the document instance to be significantly reduced by a variety of techniques including shortening or omitting tags when the parser can infer them from the content model of the current open element.

Two extra characters, entered between the name parameter and the content of the element type declaration, define whether or not a tag can be omitted. The first character represents the start-tag; the second character represents the end-tag.

These minimization symbols are:

O   (the letter, not the number zero) to indicate that the tag *may be* omitted under certain clearly defined circumstances; (It is possible for the start-tag to be omissible on some but not all occurrences of a particular element type.)

-          (a hyphen) to indicate that the tag is required.

Following is an example

```
<!ELEMENT flood   - - (water+, rainbow)>
<!ELEMENT rainbow - O EMPTY>
<!ELEMENT water   O O (rain & (lightng, thunder))>
```

FLOOD has required start- and end-tags. WATER sometimes needs neither: The start-tag on the first water can be omitted because WATER is required in a FLOOD. Each new WATER start-tag will imply the previous WATER end-tag until the last one where the RAINBOW start-tag also forces the WATER end-tag. Because start-tags can be omitted only where the element type is required, the parser will not infer a WATER start-tag from the start-tag of its three subelements.

Since RAINBOW has no content — it's just a placeholder for terrific visuals and maybe some orchestral music — it can't have an end-tag.

Content Model

Element content is described in a content model. A content model contains one model group, which is made up of any or all of:

- element types specified as allowable or required in this declaration;
- element types permitted in elements in which the current element is allowable, and specified as *flowing through* to all subelements; these are called inclusions or *inclusion exceptions.*
- raw data (signified by the keyword #PCDATA).

Summary of Occurrence Indicators

?	optional — element type or model group appears once or not at all
*	optional and repeatable — element type or model group may appear zero or more times (*that is*, not at all or any number of times)
+	required and repeatable — element type or model group appears once or more.

Summary of Connectors

,	sequential — (*e.g.* a, b, . . . a must be followed by b; b is followed by . . .) Note: in a,b?, a *may* be followed by b.
&	"and" — all the element types must occur, but may appear in any order (*e.g.* "a, b, c" and "c, b, a" are permitted among other possibilities)
|	"or" — any one of the element types or model groups must appear (*e.g.* a | b means either a or b).

The Flood DTDS: Before and After

```
<!-- Public document type definition for floods
     before God's promise to Noah -->

<!ELEMENT flood (water+)>
<!ELEMENT water EMPTY>

<!-- The first word in this declaration tells us we're
defining an ELEMENT, a structural object which may contain
other objects, information (generally in the form of letters
and numbers), or nothing. The + is an occurrence indicator
which says that "one or more" of these must appear in the
element type being defined. -->

<!-- A FLOOD element, therefore, may contain any "number"
of WATERs and may, in fact, go on forever. WATER, in turn,
must be defined. Here we're indicating that WATER has no
subelements and contains no information. It is an
EMPTY element type). -->

<!-- Notice there are no minimization symbols. Unless "omittag"
is expressly requested in the SGML declaration, the symbols may
be left out. -->
```

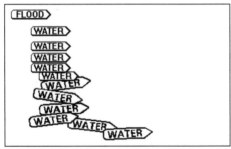

Before

```
<!-- DTD for floods after God's promise to Noah -->

<!ELEMENT flood           (water+, rainbow, (dove|goose)?)>
<!ELEMENT (rainbow|dove) EMPTY>
<!ELEMENT water           (rain & wind & (lightng, thunder))>
<!ELEMENT               (rain|wind|lightng|thunder) (#PCDATA)>

<!-- When God promised that never again would a flood go
on forever, the DTD had to be re-written. Now SGML
connectors appeared on the face of the earth.>

<!-- The comma indicates "sequence", that WATER must be
followed by a RAINBOW element, which means the flood is
incomplete without one. The question mark says the bird
following the RAINBOW is "optional".-->

<!-- In the name group (DOVE|GOOSE) the vertical bar
means "or". Only one or the other may appear. In the
content model for WATER, the ampersand
says "all these must occur, in any order"
(LIGHTNG-followed-by-THUNDER always appear in that
order, either before or after WIND and RAIN. -->
```

```
FLOOD>
WATER> RAIN> </RAIN
WIND > </WIND LIGHTNG > </LIGHTNG
THUNDER> </THUNDER </WATER
WATER> LIGHTNG > </LIGHTNG
THUNDER> </THUNDER WIND > </WIND
RAIN> </RAIN </WATER
WATER> WIND > </WIND RAIN> </RAIN
LIGHTNG > </LIGHTNG THUNDER>
</THUNDER </WATER
WATER> WIND > </WIND LIGHTNG >
</LIGHTNG THUNDER> </THUNDER
RAIN> </RAIN </WATER
RAINBOW > </RAINBOW
DOVE> </DOVE
</FLOOD
```

After

397

Comments

SGML has a way to insert comments into both DTDs — where they generally are used to help give an overall structure to the DTD and to provide minimal explanation of its use — and document instances — where they're used to carry messages for or amongst document creators and editors.

When you print out a DTD, you expect to see the comments. When you process an SGML document instance, either for publication or display, you expect the comments to disappear. In either case, when you look at markup, you should expect to see any comments that have been inserted.

Comments in the DTD

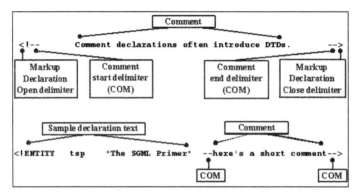

An SGML parser does not process anything in a markup declaration that is placed between the two pairs of hyphens which make up a comment's delimiters. Accordingly, comments provide a way to pass valuable information "behind the scenes".

Comments may stand alone in the DTD as the only content of a declaration or they may appear almost anywhere inside other markup declarations. They allow developers to add notes in the text as to why certain decisions were made and can give guidance to others who have to use the DTD.

You can have as many comments as you want within a single markup declaration — there are often several in attribute list declarations — but each comment must be enclosed within pairs of hyphens.

You cannot put comment delimiters (--) inside a comment.

A sample application riddled with comments accompanies this section.

Comments in Instances

Comment declarations may also appear inside a document instance. They're recognizable for starting with an markup declaration open delimiter (an open angle bracket followed by an exclamation mark) followed by the comment delimiter (--), and ending with the comment delimiter followed by a markup declaration close delimiter (close angle bracket).

Within the comments, authors and editors, a team of writers, clients — anyone interested in the document — can converse or leave messages for themselves or others. The parser knows to ignore these; they will never be output in final form.

```
<CHARNAME>Romeo:
<SPEECH><P>My dear?</P></SPEECH>
<CHARNAME>Juliet:
<SPEECH>
<P>At what o'clock to-morrow shall I send to thee?</P></SPEECH>
<!-- DIRECTOR'S NOTE:
PERHAPS IT WOULD BE FUNNY TO HAVE HER CARRY AN ALARM CLOCK. -->
<CHARNAME>Romeo:
<SPEECH><P>At the hour of nine.</P></SPEECH>
<CHARNAME>Juliet:
<SPEECH><P>I will not fail; 'tis twenty years till then.
I have forgot why I did call thee back.</P></SPEECH>
```

Software can determine whether to treat comments specially during input. In the following SoftQuad Author/Editor example, the comment appears boxed on the screen.

```
CHARNAME Rom. /CHARNAME
SPEECH  P My dear? /P /SPEECH
CHARNAME Jul. /CHARNAME
SPEECH  P At what o'clock to-morrow shall I send to thee? /P /SPEECH
```

DIRECTOR'S NOTE: perhaps it would be funny to have her carry an alarm clock.

```
CHARNAME Rom. /CHARNAME
SPEECH  P At the hour of nine. /P /SPEECH
CHARNAME Jul. /CHARNAME
SPEECH  P I will not fail; 'tis twenty years till then. I have forgot
  why I did call thee back. /P /SPEECH
```

Input

It is converted to SGML syntax to send to a publishing system, where SGML requires that it be ignored. In the output sample (which imitates the effect of sending the file to typesetting or screen display software), the "Director's Note" disappears:

Rom.
    My dear?
Jul.
    At what o'clock to-morrow shall I send to thee?
Rom.
    At the hour of nine.
Jul.
    I will not fail; 'tis twenty years till then. I have forgot why I did call thee back.

Output

Attribute Definition List Declarations

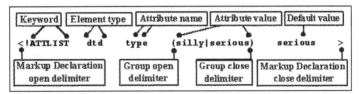

A declaration that begins with the word ATTLIST allows you to qualify an element type by declaring a list of its attributes. The DTD for the following menu avoids the declaration of a new element type for every kind of dressing on the salad. The attribute definition list declaration is attached to an element type and is composed of one or more attribute definitions. Every attribute definition is composed of a name, a declared value and a default value.

```
<!-- Lunch at the steakhouse -->

<!ELEMENT lunch (meal)+ -- one meal per person -->
<!ELEMENT meal  (appetiz?, steak, dessert?, custname, whopays) +(drink)>
```

The plus sign after the content model followed by one or more element type names within parentheses declares an inclusion, indicating that these element types can appear anywhere in the element type to which they are attached and in any of its subelements. You can have one or more DRINK elements any time during MEAL.

```
<!ELEMENT appetiz (soup | salad)>
<!ELEMENT soup    EMPTY --soup of the day -->
<!ELEMENT salad   EMPTY>
<!ATTLIST salad   kind    NAME                        #REQUIRED
                  dressing (french | 1000isl | bluechse) #REQUIRED>
```

The declared value for the attribute dressing is called a *name token group*, a series of values separated by a vertical bar (|). They represent the only possible values for the attribute. The declared value NAME requires a value usually comprising up to eight letters and numbers. REQUIRED means that one value must be specified for the attribute.

```
<!ELEMENT steak EMPTY>
<!ATTLIST steak cook (rare|medrare|medium) "medrare"
                side (potato|fries|rice)   "fries">
```

The value between quotes is used to force a default value in case no value is specified for the attribute.

```
<!ELEMENT dessert        (cake|applepie)>
<!ELEMENT (cake|applepie) EMPTY>
<!ATTLIST cake kind CDATA #REQUIRED>
```

CDATA means any letters, numbers, punctuation, spaces, or other special characters. This gives you the possibility of creating long and unique values for an attribute. This means you can ask for any kind of cake you want, but if the system doesn't recognize the name, you may not get it.

```
<!ATTLIST applepie hot      (hot|warm|cool) #IMPLIED
                   icecream (yes|no)        #IMPLIED>
```

IMPLIED is an equivalent for optional. The apple pie comes the way the waiter or waitress prefers unless you specify otherwise.

```
<!ELEMENT drink          (water|beer|cola)>
<!ELEMENT (water|beer|cola) EMPTY>
<!ATTLIST water kind (tap) #FIXED tap>
```

The declared value for WATER is fixed by the system. You can order any kind of fancy water you want, but all they've got here is tap water.

```
<!ATTLIST beer number NUMBER        #REQUIRED>
<!ATTLIST cola type   (regular | diet) #CURRENT>
```

Beer is ordered by NUMBER from the beer list. The default value CURRENT says that the first time a COLA element appears, a type must be specified. That value will be used for the next occurrences unless you specify another. In other words, you don't have to re-specify the type of COLA every time you ask for a refill.

```
<!ELEMENT (custname | whopays)  (#PCDATA)>
<!ATTLIST custname account ID   #IMPLIED>
<!ATTLIST whopays  charge  IDREF #REQUIRED>
```

The customer's name is not critical data within the content of a CUSTNAME element: The cashier could make a typo or use a nickname and the computer would have difficulty tracking the charge. Instead a unique identifier is requested — but only if the customer has an account. However, WHOPAYS has a required IDREF. The system knows that WHOPAYS may have the same value for many people's meals (when someone buys for the whole table) but each CUSTNAME will have a unique ID. The system will check that the value of the IDREF will be a legitimate ID. The example below illustrates only one of several MEALS in the LUNCH. A separate MEAL in the same LUNCH must include a CUSTNAME with an ACCOUNTID of "ALEXF" for the charge IDREF to work

```
MEAL  DRINK  COLA [TYPE="REGULAR"] /COLA  /DRINK
APPETIZ  SALAD [KIND="GREEN" DRESSING="1000ISL"] /SALAD  /APPETIZ
DRINK  BEER [ NUMBER="33"] /BEER  /DRINK
STEAK [ COOK="MEDRARE" SIDE="FRIES"] /STEAK
DRINK  COLA [ ] /COLA  /DRINK
DESSERT APPLEPIE [ICECREAM="YES"] /APPLEPIE  /DESSERT
CUSTNAME [ACCOUNT="MICHM"] Michael Markup /CUSTNAME
WHOPAYS [ CHARGE="ALEXF"] Alex Fixedfield /WHOPAYS  /MEAL
```

Attribute Definition List Declarations: The Parts

Name

The first parameter of any attribute definition list declaration normally names one or more element types being associated with the list. The following parameter is a set of one or more attribute definitions to be associated with the list of element types. Each definition consists of an attribute name, its declared value type, and a default value prescription.

Attribute Value

The declared value type may be a name token group, the actual values anticipated (potato|fries|rice), for example) or a keyword that specifies the sort of value that is needed:

CDATA	zero or more valid SGML *characters*
ENTITY	currently declared general entity name
ENTITIES	list of ENTITY names
ID	unique identifier
IDREF	unique identifier reference value
IDREFS	list of unique identifier reference values
NAME	string of 1–8 characters (8 is a default limit); starting with a–z or A–Z, followed by a–z or A–Z, hyphen, period
NAMES	list of NAME values; each string separated by one or more spaces, tabs or returns (separators)
NMTOKEN	same as NAME except that it can also start with 0–9, hyphen, period.
NMTOKENS	list of NMTOKEN values; each separated by a separator.
NOTATION	a *notation name* that identifies the data content notation of an element's content
NUMBER	a string of 1–8 characters consisting of the digits 0–9
NUMBERS	list of NUMBER values; each separated by a separator.
NUTOKEN	string of 1–8 characters beginning with 0–9 followed by a–z, A–Z, 0–9, hyphen, period
NUTOKENS	list of NUTOKEN values; each separated by a separator.

Default Value

An attribute's default value may be a literal string, the actual characters needed (fries for example) or a keyword. Most common keywords are #REQUIRED, which is obvious; and #IMPLIED, which means that the application will imply a value if none is specified (it effectively means optional).

General Entities

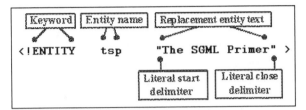

The declaration above tells the parser: When you come across &tsp; in the document instance, substitute *everything* between the quote marks including blank spaces. In this case, the substitution would result in the title of our book, "The SGML Primer".

When it comes right down to it, entities are *things*. An entity name is a short string of characters declared as standing for a longer string of characters; it may be a way of referencing a whole other marked-up file from within the current file; it may be a placeholder for a graphic or other non-SGML data that will be inserted when the document is being viewed or printed; or it may be a special symbol or character that doesn't appear on your terminal or that may have different identifiers on different systems.

Entities Automate Global Search and Replace: Because entities enable the easy substitution of one thing for another, they are extremely useful for something volatile, such as product name during the development stage.

Entities Aid Standardization: Replacement text is defined in only one place, the entity declaration. Entities are particularly useful for complicated text, scientific terms, or expressions which need fancy formatting.

Entities may be declared either in the DTD or before the instance — strictly speaking, in that part of a file which is still part of the DTD, the declaration subset. (This allows for the addition of local declarations to the DTD, which may be shared by a wide group of users.)

Entities are referenced in the document when the declared entity name is used, in context, surrounded by delimiters (& and ; respectively).

Let's start with the following declaration:

```
<!ENTITY copyr SYSTEM "c:\boilertxt\copyr.sgm" SUBDOC>
```

When &copyr; occurs in the document instance, the keyword SYSTEM alerts the system that the text to be included can be found in a file on the C: drive. The keyword SUBDOC indicates the referenced external entity is tagged SGML text with its own DTD. This means that the main DTD doesn't have to include element type (and other) declarations for constructs which appear only in the incorporated SUBDOC file. However, there's an interesting alternative: If the SUBDOC parameter isn't there, the file will be parsed just as if it had been typed directly into the document in which the entity reference appears.

The following morsel of document incorporates a boilerplate copyright notice which may be used over and over in books by many authors: (For purposes of this example, we'll assume that the SMALLBOOK DTD has been declared elsewhere.)

```
<!DOCTYPE smallbook
[
<!ENTITY copyr SYSTEM "c:\boilertxt\copyr.sgm">
<!ENTITY author     "Matthew Markup">
<!ENTITY date       "1995">
]>
<SMALLBOOK><FRONTM><TI> . . . </TI>
<AU>&author;</AU>
<PUBFM> &copyr;</PUBFM></FRONTM>
 . . .
```

The file *copyr.sgm* has no DTD of its own — all its element types must be declared in the SMALLBOOK DTD. It looks something like this:

```
 . . . . Copyright &date; by &author; . . .
```

When the book is parsed, &author; in *both* files is replaced by the name "Matthew Markup". The author's name not only appears in the book's front matter after the title, but the boilerplate text in the copyright notice is being automatically updated without ever being edited! (It is output as "Copyright 1995 by Matthew Markup".)

Accordingly, the file *copyr.sgm* may be referenced by many books, each of which declares its own replacement value for &date; and &author;.

Parameter Entities

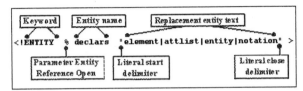

Parameter entities are used only within markup declarations. They are identified by the % sign after the keyword ENTITY.

```
<!ENTITY % declars "element | attlist | entity | notation">

<!ELEMENT DTD        (%declars;)>

<!ELEMENT (title | instance | %declars;) (#PCDATA)>
```

In the example above, the first declaration tells the parser: Let *declars* stand for everything between the pair of double quotes. Accordingly, when you come across %declars; in the DTD (that is, when you run into the entity with its start and end delimiters), act as if everything between the literals — in this case, the four subelements ELEMENT, ATTLIST, ENTITY, and NOTATION — had been freshly typed in. (Note that these element types are being used as examples only. Their names are the same as the SGML declarations they illustrate.)

There are two reasons to be particularly vigilant with parameter entities. Like all entities, they can be nested, so a replacement may have to occur within the replacement text itself, and you can get lazy. Application designers will use a parameter entity within a number of content models, and while it may be completely appropriate for many situations, unless the replacement text is examined in each of these new contexts, inappropriate structures may get built.

Note that parameter entities must be declared before they are referenced.

It's difficult to resist including the following example, if only to show off enthusiastically the use of parameter entities. This example uses an element structure that counts elements:

```
<!-- Public DTD for Noah's flood -->

<!ENTITY % m.week "water, water, water, water, water"
                 -- five working days of rain -->

<!ENTITY % m.wkend "water, water"
                   -- a two-day weekend of rain -->

<!ELEMENT flood - - (%m.week;. %m.wkend;,
                     %m.week;, %m.wkend;,
                     %m.week;, %m.wkend;,
                     %m.week;, %m.wkend;,
                     %m.week;, %m.wkend;,
                     %m.week;)>


<!ELEMENT water - O EMPTY>
```

As you can see, this DTD takes advantage of parameter entities to declare %m.week; and %m.wkend; which can now be used throughout the DTD in place of the longer constructs that appear within quotes in the declarations. The main feature of this approach is that when certain structures need to be changed, this may be done in just one place rather than each spot where the parameter entity is used. If suddenly there were a three-day weekend, only the entity declarations would have to be changed. The parameter entity construct becomes increasingly useful as you work with more complex DTDs.

Notation Declarations

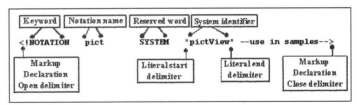

In processing an SGML file, some data may require special treatment because it has meaning other than what its characters normally mean. A notation declaration is used to specify how to interpret such data and apply any special techniques that may be required when processing the document. Typical examples would be mathematical formulae or graphics files.

The first step in using notation constructs is to identify types of data content notation that may be required, and declare them as available. The keyword NOTATION establishes that whatever parameter follows is the name of a content notation that the system will now recognize. The keyword SYSTEM associates instructions or meaning with the new notation.

```
<!NOTATION tex SYSTEM "/usr/bin/tex">
<!NOTATION eqn SYSTEM "/usr/bin/eqn">
```

The second step is to determine whether an element encoded in such a notation consists of SGML data characters or non-SGML data.

Broadly speaking, SGML data is made up of the characters you type, the same characters used for the markup and content, but, in all likelihood, with special meaning in the notation. (In the first example following, "over" has meaning to the math processor EQN. Notations that use SGML data characters can occur in external entities — or, if they have no characters that could be mistaken for delimiters, directly in the content of elements.

Non-SGML data, on the other hand, could be anything — an image produced with graphic software, a digital music recording, a clip of video. Naturally, it's unreasonable to expect to pass contents on to an SGML parser that may cause it to hiccup or crash. Accordingly, you cannot embed non-SGML data in an SGML entity. It must reside in external non-SGML data entities which can be referenced using an entity reference.

Building on the notation declarations in the previous section, here an element type (MATH) is declared with a data content notation of either TEX or EQN:

```
<!ELEMENT math (#PCDATA)>
<!ATTLIST math type NOTATION (tex | eqn) #REQUIRED>
```

In the document instance, the attribute identifies which notation to expect for this particular instance of the element type. The markup effectively says "Deal with this element's contents using a special process stored as */usr/bin/eqn.*"

```
<MATH TYPE="EQN">(3 over 4) over 10</MATH>
```

A second example demonstrates the use of a notation for *non-*SGML *data* in an external entity.

```
<!NOTATION pict SYSTEM "pictView">
<!ENTITY sysmod SYSTEM "/usr/gfx/sysmodel" NDATA pict>
```

Here the entity declaration first creates a name. One keyword says the entity is on the system (and its parameter says where the file is located). A second keyword NDATA associates the entity with a notation — one could use any declared notation at this point — and its parameter says which. By itself, the data content notation will have no inherent or obvious meaning to the system. The entity declaration is simply the standardized means to say, for example, "This drawing of the SGML System Model is represented in PICT." (Where entities need to have meaning beyond a specific system, or a machine-independent means of identification, SGML has a formal public identifier construct to accomplish this.)

The last step is to create some sort of pointer in the document where the entity is to be pulled in. The reference to *sysmod* points to an entity declaration which associates the identifiers of the System Model graphic file with the notation for PICT. That, in turn, points to a notation declaration which establishes PICT as being usable on this system. Then a software application takes over to render the PICT image.

```
<!ELEMENT artwork CDATA>
<!ATTLIST artwork filenm ENTITY #REQUIRED>
```

These declarations set the stage for the pointer in the document instance: <ARTWORK FILENM="SYSMOD">

Note that attributes for other information — scaling, cropping, positioning details, for example — can also be defined in the attribute list.

Instead of using an attribute, the entity reference &sysmod; can be placed in the document wherever it needs to be called.

Marked Sections

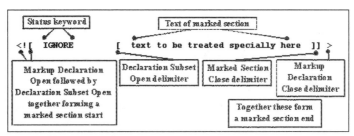

Marked sections allow for the creation of content that is to be processed in special ways — sometimes thrown away, sometimes hiding markup from the parser. In the example below, two versions of an arithmetic text book — the students' and the teacher's — are being produced from one file. The marked section construct lets you mark up text for each and lets the two versions share common text.

```
<EQUATION> 2 + 2 = <![ IGNORE [ 4 ]]> </EQUATION>
```

The parameter entity construct can be used with marked section declarations. First the appropriate parameter entities must be declared:

```
<!ENTITY % teacher "IGNORE">

<!ENTITY % student "INCLUDE">
```

Now, in the document instance, every piece of "teacher only" content is marked as such.

```
<EQUATION> 2 + 2 = <![ %teacher; [ 4 ]]> </EQUATION>
```

When it comes time to print the teacher's edition, the word IGNORE is changed to INCLUDE in the entity declaration and the parser does the rest.

(SEC)(ST) **Common Section Title**(/ST)

(P)Marked sections are a powerful feature which, by coincidence, are also great fun to use. This paragraph, which deals with the topic in general, will be common to all versions.(/P)

(.MarkSec)**[** SQ [IGNORE] **]**(P) This paragraph, which talks specifically about how marked sections are used in Author/Editor, will only appear in the SoftQuad version of this page and only when the keyword IGNORE is replaced by INCLUDE. It will mention the use of the special tag icons so users needn't worry about typing the complex marked section markup and will describe how you can toggle the versions to have only the relevant ones showing on the screen. What this means in practice is that the software takes the IGNORE keyword very seriously.(/P)(/.MarkSec)

(.MarkSec)**[**TUTOR [INCLUDE]**]**(P)The third paragraph will appear only in the tutorial version of this description, and will very carefully avoid promotion of anyone's software. Of course, it may not always be the third paragraph.(/P)(/.MarkSec)(/SEC)

Common Section Title

Marked sections are a powerful feature which, by coincidence, are also great fun to use. This paragraph, which deals with the topic in general, will be common to all versions.

This paragraph, which talks specifically about how marked sections are used in Author/Editor, will only appear in the SoftQuad version of this page and only when the keyword IGNORE is replaced by INCLUDE. It will mention the use of the special tag icons so users needn't worry about typing the complex marked section markup and will describe how you can toggle the versions to have only the relevant ones showing on the screen. What this means in practice is that the software takes the IGNORE keyword very seriously.

Common Section Title

Marked sections are a powerful feature which, by coincidence, are also great fun to use. This paragraph, which deals with the topic in general, will be common to all versions.

The third paragraph will appear only in the tutorial version of this description, and will very carefully avoid promotion of anyone's software. Of course, it may not always be the third paragraph.

◆ APPENDIX B

SGML Users, Start Here

If you've been using SGML for any length of time at all, chances are good that the Web/HTML phenomenon hit you very hard indeed. You've been slaving away over complicated cost justifications, you've carefully built implementation plans, analyzed existing and potentially useful SGML applications from your own and related industries — all in all, you've done a conscientious, serious job of ensuring that SGML makes sense for your operation, can be justified, can be implemented without untoward surprises, and generally makes sense.

Suddenly, as if with no forethought at all, your neighbor in the next department has bought a handful of personal computers, tied them into the Internet, downloaded some free software and is publishing Web pages — and getting a great deal of enthusiasm both internally and outside for his or her foresight, willingness to embrace new technologies, and so forth.

It doesn't seem quite fair somehow. After all, you're the one who actually had the foresight to investigate this SGML stuff in the first place, you're the one who has discovered this valuable "new" technology, you're the one who's been going to the conferences, reading the newsletters and the thick books, *you're the one who deserves the real credit here!*

The Overlap between Art and Science: HTML Implementations Aren't At All Like SGML Implementations — Yet!

Ever since Marcel Duchamp mounted a bicycle wheel on a stool, art has been pretty much a matter of opinion. Interestingly, the only opinion that seems to count in the end is that of the artist. If the artist says "this is art", then it is. Your opinion and my opinion — as audience to the art — matter less. Science turns out to be somewhat similar. One hears arguments that sociology and psychology are not sciences, but by and large people agree that certain areas are scientific.

Where does SGML come in? If we approach it from the point of view of computing, it's based on a near-rational approach to computing languages, it involves parsing streams of data and it seems pretty scientific. However, if we approach it from its historic roots — and even its major practitioners today — it acts, much of the time, as a publishing tool. And publishing, as part of the creative processes of writing and design, is certainly an art.

One could convincingly argue both sides of this debate, but none of it would matter — except that SGML today is at a crossroads and crisis: More people are using SGML today than ever before. Tens of thousands of them are working with the World Wide Web's HTML application — and they don't even know that they're using SGML.

Naturally, we, the traditional SGML crowd, are deeply offended. *How can someone use SGML and not even know it?* And, even more dramatic news — *there are more of them than us.* Let's look for the silver lining in this cloud.

A few years ago it seemed clear that no one wanted to type raw text markup. We had to go off and create context-sensitive editing tools to insert tags automatically. Today there are some tens of millions HTML documents on the Web and probably less than 30 per cent were created with any editorial assist tool. It seems some people are willing to type tags — lots of people, in fact, and lots of tags.

Fine, the pessimists say, but HTML is just about the simplest DTD imaginable and most of those documents are inconsistent, messy and basically badly done. The optimists point to the silver lining then: *Hundreds of thousands of people know a little about element and attribute markup.* Not much perhaps, but enough that maybe they can be swayed a little towards more interesting and more useful and more accurate markup.

Now let's approach a discussion of art and science from a different direction — *simplicity*.

Here's where I'm completely baffled: Over the last decade, a lot of people have said that the reason they like SGML authoring and editing software is because it's such a simple way to create SGML. Another group of people say that the SGML revolution can't really happen until all SGML tools are easier to use. Sometimes they say "as easy to use as word processing tools". At the same time there are people who say that word processing software is too complicated and they never use more than a fraction of the functionality.

Meanwhile back in the Web world, we hear people say that HTML is simple, in fact so simple they can type in the markup. "*Why*," they ask, "*can't SGML be as simple as* HTML?" Some of these people go on to say that HTML would be fine, if only it had SUPERSCRIPT and SUBSCRIPT element types. Or if only it had an APPLET element type in which to encapsulate little specialized applications. Or BLINK or MARQUEE or FONT. Or if you could define your own element types. Or maybe use the HTML element types with any attributes so that HTML becomes completely extensible.

"Wait a minute," you say. "Surely that extensibility is what SGML is all about! This is what DTDs are for!"

"That's true," comes back the argument, "but we want to do this in the framework of HTML so it'll be simpler."

This then is part of the art.

HTML with its constraints on how to establish hypertext links, its rules for building forms, and some esoteric attributes in the document head, has complexities that rival many other applications. But with only a few dozen element types in the standardized HTML 3.2, it seems simpler than DTDs with less sophistication, but more element types.

There's another very important piece of the puzzle, which is *sizzle*. With HTML, there's a lot of "bang for your buck", "pizzazz for your pound", "drama for your Deutschmark". (Welcome to the internationalized edition of this book.) That is, a number of element types have been interpreted by the Web browsers to do very exciting things — build an electronic form, open any other Web page in the world, and so forth.

There are compelling, dramatic capabilities to show for your work doing markup. You insert a few elements and attributes, open your file in a Web browser, and presto! Stuff happens. There is a sense of digital gratification people normally get only from computer games and the recalculate command in a spreadsheet.

Typical SGML applications are not normally like this. Traditionally SGML has been a part of a production system, where the real rewards come from cost savings, or time reduction, or reusability. The immediate compelling excitement of something like the Web isn't there.

So there's art in this part too. Tim Berners-Lee and his colleagues at CERN designed a mechanism for short-term gratification on an enormous scale. Authors, like most humans, still think of the world as being fairly big, and the idea that their files can be read by anyone anywhere on the World Wide Web is very appealing. There's science hidden in this part too, of course, because the mechanisms do actually work.

Most big SGML systems are rationalized on the basis of cost savings or return on investment. How does this relate to the euphoria about the Web? This is very interesting and very fuzzy. *No one understands the economics of the Web.* This helps a lot. People give it the benefit of the doubt and believe intuitively that they must exploit this medium — be seen to be doing it, exploit its newness, exploit its reach, invest in some completely unpredictable gold rush to follow. Rarely do other SGML implementations have such benefits of the doubt.

Let's summarize the characteristics of the world's most popular SGML application and see what we get:

1. Simplicity, or at least a high ratio of functionality to tag.
2. Compelling capability.
3. An appealing, or even gratifying, scale.
4. At the same time very personal: a relationship, primarily between one person and the Web.
5. Extensibility, either real or illusory.
6. An irrational urge on the part of its adherents to participate, coupled in some cases with greed.

Isn't this an interesting list? Compare it with the top six characteristics of or reasons behind the majority of SGML applications:

1. Conformance to a standard or mandated compliance.
2. Savings of time and/or money.

3. Reusability of information.
4. Impersonal: Part of a production process or a document or information management system.
5. Actual extensibility, using internationally standardized methods and capabilities.
6. An irrational belief that things are more complicated than they really are.

Of course, it is the responsibility of this book to encourage full-blown SGML capabilities to appear on the Web, at which point this fairly straightforward pair of lists gets intertwined, and considerably muddier.

HTML Shows Us There's a Trade-off between Payoff and Work

Markup is generally treated as a burden — as some onerous tough task that is required of users and that they must suffer through. Two comments on this:

First: The success of HTML tells us that the real question, in all complex or apparently complex tasks, is "Is there a payoff?" With HTML, the answer is instant and exciting: I type in a handful of markup codes, fire up any Web browser and I have a formatted publishable-on-the-Web document. The pay-off is personal.

In general, till now, SGML has been used as part of major publishing production systems, and the reward for using it has been restricted to:

- easier revision — the next time a document is revised, when suddenly that process becomes much easier and faster
- lower costs
- re-use — the moment someone wants to re-publish in a different medium or different style, it's simpler
- retrieval — when someone else wants to find richly-encoded text within some massive database of information.

All of which add up to one critical fact: Someone else gets the reward, most of the time, not the person who went to the trouble of ensuring a well marked up document.

HTML is the opposite. Others may take advantage of the value of the HTML markup too, but the near-immediate satisfaction goes to the person who did the markup. This is the real step forward. (And by making full SGML browsers available for the Web, SGML companies are hoping to create the same kind of incentive for richer markup too — with even more fun, two-way traversal of links, one-to-many linking, links into documents in which you cannot insert markup of any sort, typed links, all the richness one would hope for from an extensible markup language.)

Second: You are an expert. Whoever you are. From the point of view of SGML markup, at the moment you're writing something, you know what is a title, what is a list item, what is a part number, and so forth. The job of well-defined SGML markup is to reflect the way documents really are, and, one hopes, to reflect the way people work with those documents.

At that point it should be a simple task to pick out an element type from a dialog box pick list (just like a list of styles in a wordprocessor or desktop publishing program), click on it, have the markup automatically inserted and be grateful for not having to type in the codes by hand! This cannot be done magically. If you're only interested in markup that a computer can insert automatically, then all you'll obtain is the simplest possible markup. It may seem a bit of a truism, but it's worth saying anyway: *What makes a marked-up document valuable is the added value that the markup brings.* Without markup, the computer can't tell that This is Emphasized and This is a Book Title. A human can, and needs to let the computer know.

There will never be an easier method of acquiring this added value than the act of asking some author what he or she is up to: What is this thing you've just typed in? What did you mean by that? Part of the job description for good software is to extract that value in as natural and unobtrusive a manner as possible. It cannot read the author's mind, but it can get as close as can be modelled: The DTD gives you a chance to model the constructs that the author *expects* to use. This, in turn, means that those constructs are likely, even anticipated, and the job of extraction of the author's added value should therefore be easy.

The advantage one gets with the good SGML editing tools is that a pick list of possible markup can be context sensitive: It offers you only the element types that make sense (and are therefore allowed by the DTD) at that point in the document. In the best of all worlds, in fact, there is a subtle compromise at work: The software is offering a pick list of plausible markup given what the author is now doing, and the author is choosing — perhaps from a longer list — the construct that he or she really wants. Good software will do its best to ensure that the element type that's wanted can be made valid at that point in the document.

If You're Part of the SGML Literati, How Best to Use This Book?

It would be foolish to pretend that the slow, step by step building up of interesting DTDs from either plain ASCII text or from basic HTML offers much to people who have done serious document analysis and built raw DTDs from scratch, before breakfast. Nonetheless, I do hope this book will serve you well in several regards:

- Most people who are implementing SGML need additional tools to help them teach their colleagues the value of what they're up to, as well as specific exercises to teach neophytes the rudiments of the language. More and more, you may find that people who are learning about SGML already know something about HTML. You may find that the approach in this book can serve to give your colleagues with an HTML background points of comparison with the new world to which you are introducing them.

- You may also find that the approach in this book can serve to give you an understanding of the value in their HTML experience, and introduce you painlessly to specific HTML constructs. These, in turn, may usefully be migrated to some of your other SGML applications.

- The example files — especially towards the end of the book — are gathered from a small variety of existing projects and applications. You may find in them useful models for your own work, or at least simplified versions of techniques that may be extended to meet more sophisticated requirements.

- The book tries its best to use correct SGML terminology at all times. There is a kind of laziness in all modern language, and computer jargon — and even SGML jargon — is just as lazy as any other. You may find it useful to refresh your use of SGML terms from the text herein.

- Finally, there is one underlying moral lesson that I've learned from my work with HTML that I would like to share with you, although it is somewhat obvious: *Never underestimate the value of simple approaches to markup.* We in the SGML community have been accused on occasion, and perhaps justifiably, of being a priesthood, of making markup unnecessarily complex, either for commercial reasons, or, less rudely, out of a sense of fascination with the possibilities of the language itself. HTML shows us that simple markup that gets the job done can be its own reward.

Naturally, this short chapter is addressed to a great degree to those people to whom I am closest, the ones I've been working with in this community since the early 1980s, the ones who are as guilty as I of making SGML sometimes seem overwhelming. We now have the opportunity to embrace HTML as we would any other major public SGML application, as we have the aerospace, the computing, the publishing, the defense, the semiconductor and other industries. As with any other public application, the generalized tools and techniques we have developed make sense for HTML implementations; indeed one could argue, realistically, that because SGML implementations have traditionally been so big and so complex, we have a great deal to teach the Web world about document management, document databases, and production electronic publishing environments. While this is certainly true, we also have a great deal to learn about the joy of implementing quick, compelling solutions; or getting marked up pages out there with vigor for people to read, comment on, disagree with, and link to.

My hope is that this book begins to bridge the gap.

How Do We Put SGML on the Web?

A model of how the World Wide Web works would show a continuum of activities that are accomplished, and a division of labor between what happens on the "server side", the computer hosting the published pages and running server software, and the "client side", the browser and querying tool or tools that are on the reader's/user's machine.

One way in which HTML is simple is that most Web documents are, at this time, written in HTML, posted on the server, and read by HTML browsers on the client machines. But the underlying premise of this book is that there is added value in offering full-blown SGML across the Web, and the fact is that there are many HTML browsers deployed in the world. There is a temptation to publish SGML to the Web in some fashion that takes advantage of those browsers. On the other hand, a handful of Web SGML browsers have already appeared, and more will appear.

Accordingly, we have an opportunity to figure out the scenarios under which SGML might work in the Web model:

- **SGML on the Server converted to HTML on the fly at the Server:** The "Down Translation" mechanism allows owners of information to preserve or build up an investment in data stored as SGML but publish it to the Web in such a way that the existing pool of browsers can read it. That is, the information provider designs a "mapping" from an SGML application's element types into what is likely to be a much smaller set of HTML element types. This has advantages in that it may be fairly simple to achieve, but it does suggest that there is no value in having the richness of SGML markup made available to the readers.

- **SGML on the Server converted to HTML on the fly on the Client:** On some of the Internet newsgroups, it has been suggested that owners of SGML data treat HTML as a pure "display architecture", essentially a little language of formatting capabilities that browsers share. In this model, an SGML application might carry around a set of formal mappings in FIXED attribute values, for instance, to tell an HTML browser which HTML element a hitherto unknown SGML element maps to. Browsers would need to be rewritten to read attribute values of SGML documents instead of element type names.

- **SGML on the Server converted to HTML in batch mode on the Server:** This approach is fairly straightforward to implement, and indeed has been implemented on the Web today. It implies that an information provider will make available parallel SGML and HTML version of a Web site, perhaps by running a program overnight to perform a down translation from the richer SGML marked-up documents to a parallel HTML universe. At the Home Page level, users would be offered a choice of universe.

- **SGML on the Server with SGML on the Client, HTML as the Front Door:** I admit to a certain bias, having been working on a book devoted to the notion of full SGML on the Web, but it seems to me that if you've made an investment in rich markup, you've done it for a reason: Either your data is of a complexity that the subtlety of available display in HTML is not enough, or your information users can exploit those structures in some way. All in all, I'm nervous about the fact that in any down translation, inevitably, you lose important distinctions between types of information that *must* be important to you — otherwise you've wouldn't have built the application in the first place.

In the debate about how much work to do on the server, and how much on the client, here are the top ten reasons to have full SGML capabilities on both the server and the client:

1. For speed in Web delivery, you want to download as much work as possible onto the client.

2. Based on either physical constraints or customization criteria, you want to further process the content on the reader's desktop.

3. You, as publisher, want on-screen formatting according to *your* idea of what the important structures are, as embodied in the markup declared in your DTD.

4. You want formatting beyond HTML's capabilities, in particular based on containers. In HTML, you can't make formatting distinctions based on an element type's full parentage, for example, you can't say "I want a paragraph in a list item in a ordered list to be displayed differently than in an unordered list". SGML browsers can and do.

5. You want navigation beyond HTML's capabilities, one-to-many linking, two-way linking, graphic-to-graphic linking, automatic generation of tables of contents, figures, and so on. These are all supported by SGML structures and SGML software.

6. The markup determined by your SGML application is likely to be the markup that makes sense for the paper publishing you or your readers need to do. Accordingly, you are likely to want the markup available for rich formatting on paper at the client side of a Web relationship.

7. You want commands sensitive to markup, perhaps new menu items to appear if the text includes a specific element type.

8. You want to exploit SGML's inclusion capabilities, its ability to say "Anywhere within this structure, I'd like to be able to use the following constructs."

9. Using SGML's entity referencing capabilities, you may want to store reusable portions of your content, either text or graphic, on the client desk, and call them in locally for faster display.

10. You want the possibility of extensive user interaction tracking, where the software recognizes how often someone clicks on a PARTNUMBER element, for example, or a PRICE.

❧ Appendix C
A Good Time to be Using SGML

1. New Products

This seems at first glance to be obvious, to have an obvious user-oriented advantage: more choice. But there's more to it than this: The arrival of new products forces old products to get better. They start leapfrogging each other at an exhilarating pace and at any particular moment, when you stop to catch your breath, things look healthier and healthier. And new products, inevitably, increase the size of the market. Now you could argue that new products and new companies actually dilute the market, dividing up the pool of potential sales into something smaller and smaller chunks. If a market's not growing this is certainly true, but in the case of SGML, I think we can safely say that the market is growing faster than it is being divided.

Why is this good news for you?

In the first place: Less risk. This idea has particular resonance for SGML users because you can switch. If you have a great whopping database of wordprocessed files all stored in proprietary ways, and you've built up a large production system predicated on moving into that proprietary format, and better software comes along that uses its own proprietary format, then how likely are you to want to change? Darn unlikely.

This is why the old generation wordprocessing vendors make such a big deal about how easy it is to read each other's formats. They want to take your mind off the real crux of the problem. Which is: in serious production environments, switching wordprocessors is not the issue — disrupting production systems is the real problem. And simply having a converter filter from one proprietary system to another doesn't help with the real problem.

This is, in part, why it's so interesting that *Adobe*, *Corel* and *Microsoft* have announced SGML software, with Frame+SGML, WordPerfect SGML Edition, and Microsoft Internet Explorer. They are actually, for the first time in their corporate lives and product lines, selling software that makes it easy for you to switch to someone else's software.

You — the large scale "**YOU**" SGML users around the world — made them do this.

Microsoft and *WordPerfect* knew they couldn't ignore the requests — *demands* would be more like it — of the entire airline industry, of the hardware and software documentation industry, and so forth.

This has the interesting immediate impact of actually raising the clout of users. Because SGML software makes it easier to switch, there is a great deal of pressure on all creators of SGML products to compete on capability alone, since they can't count on proprietary formats any more as a kind of metaphorical ball and chain on the user. Now exactly what "capability" means among this group of competitors is very interesting.

- For some, capability means fitting in as closely as possible, with how you work already — extending your regular wordprocessor, for example, to support SGML, in a reasonable fashion, without sacrificing the look and feel of the existing software of the document.
- For others, competing on capability means supporting SGML as richly as possible, giving users access to, and therefore full use of, all the powerful constructs that make up this international standard.
- For some, competing on capability means blending in, tying directly in to database or publishing environments in such a way that the SGML tools become the window onto the entire information environment.
- For others, the competitive capability may mean offering a complete replacement for existing database or production systems, building a system on a solid SGML foundation, and exploiting SGML at every stage in information's life cycle.

These are all sound approaches and never before have all of them been available to you. Being a newcomer to SGML today is simultaneously less risky and more exhilarating because of all that's going on. I say this in this odd way because we often associate risk with exhilaration. I can tell you that if you're new to SGML, while you may never enjoy the exhilaration of that moment back around 1989 when many of us realized that this SGML stuff really was going to work, I'd gladly trade it for the slightly less exhilarating but monumentally less risky position you find yourselves in today.

2. Spread of SGML to new industries

In 1990, there were six industry or cross-industry groups building SGML applications. Today there are a minimum of 16 in manufacturing, aerospace, telecommunications, railways, computer systems software, humanities and sciences, product descriptions information, military, automotive, consumer electronics, print publishing, pharmaceuticals, electric utilities, government, legal, and multimedia entertainment.

This statistic stands for an extraordinary growth because every single one of those 16 groups is comprised of not just one or two companies, but often, dozens, around the world, working together to create an SGML application which none of them controls individually.

These are consensus standards — and all that that means, including blood, sweat and tears, hard work, compromise, as well as the thrill of tackling an important subject cooperatively, and making it work. Why should this matter to you if you're not part of one of these industries? We started the SGML conferences in 1988. At every one we have what I've called "Reports from the Front", news from each initiative, with a description of the technical approaches, with addresses for getting copies of their public documents and so forth. They have been very forthcoming and quick to share their insights and the details of what they've done.

The SGML community, worldwide, is enough like a small town that everyone gets to learn from every one else. Because so much attention and energy gets focussed on these major public applications, participants have a lot to both learn and teach. In a similar vein, SGML *Open*, the industry consortium, through its technical working committees, is out there solving real-world interoperability issues that are related to but go beyond the scope of SGML itself.

From your point of view as users, then, the growth of industry initiatives means a boost to the general level of SGML experience and expertise.

3. The World's Largest SGML Application

It's an exciting time to be involved with SGML because of the phenomenal growth of the World Wide Web. There's about 100,000 networks connected to the Internet — that's nodes on the Internet, including some individual computers, but also huge corporations with only a handful of front doors onto this network of networks. Some estimates say that as many as 30 to 50 million people have used a browser to get documents across the World Wide Web, the very, very simple SGML application that sits on top of the Internet providing shared documents to an astonished world.

Since 1993, when the NCSA Mosaic browser left the lab at the US *National Center for Supercomputing Applications*, the Web has become a completely viable medium for publishing, sparking more vigor and imagination than CD-ROM, the previous new medium, and being taken as seriously in corporate publication planning as paper, the third oldest medium.

Why is this good news for you?

If you're a supplier of information to any industry you're likely to look seriously at a medium with no incremental cost of delivery for your parts catalog, up-to-the-minute maintenance information and promotional materials. If you're one of their customers you'll want the timeliness of the information. All those people who don't use SGML are busy trying to figure out how to do conversions into SGML, or if they haven't yet heard about the SGML Web browsers, into HTML. You, either as part of the SGML crowd or by becoming part of it, are way ahead of them.

So the really good news is that if you're interested in this medium, and if you have SGML files, you are ready to publish on the Web now. Instantly. By the end of 1996 there will be five or six full-blown SGML browsers available for the Web. (There's one included with this book from *SoftQuad Inc.*, called SoftQuad Panorama. A gift of SGML software! Aren't you glad already that you bought this book?!)

4. Appearance of SGML in Mainstream Magazines and on Bookstore Shelves

And I mean really mainstream magazines. And not just the computer mainstream magazines like *Byte*, and *MacWeek* and PC *World* and PC *Computing*. I mean *Forbes* and *Business Week* and *The New York Times*.

Admittedly, this is kind of funny, because usually we think of these people as reporting the news. But in this case, *they are the news*. The fact that they've finally smartened up and started talking about SGML is a big deal for several reasons.

1. The subject is worthy of coverage, on its own merits.
2. The subject is worthy of coverage because readers want to know about what's going on here, about new products, new adoptions, new initiatives.
3. They build a stronger, more informed market. As someone who spent the better part of the last decade, it seems, explaining SGML to people who had never heard of it, I can't tell you what a pleasure it is to talk to people who have not only heard of it, but want to learn more.
4. This kind of interest snowballs. When one important magazine talks about SGML as a solution to interoperability issues, or document management, or streamlined production, or multiple media output, or accessibility, then before long it looks silly if some other magazine doesn't include it.
5. Knowing there's potential coverage means vendors are keen to talk about new products and users are keen to talk about new applications or installations. Which in turn, I think, has the subtly subversive effect of encouraging people to do the kind of work that they would want to have written about — and that can't be a bad thing.

On the book side, it is indeed the case that mainstream publishers are producing more and more SGML books. Several are listed in the *Bibliography* (p. 449) at the back of this book, along with other sources of information, both on- and off-line.

5. Attendance at SGML conferences is nearly doubling each year.

Anywhere from 100 per cent to 180 per cent growth in each of the last two years. Why is this good for you? It's the summary of all the previous reasons: The creators of new products see, at these conferences, everything that's going on with industrial, commercial, educational and scientific SGML development. As you can imagine, the pressure on all of them to do better, to create more powerful and useful software, is great. At the same conferences, implementors of SGML systems — the users — have the opportunity to boast about what they're doing, to show interesting solutions to interesting problems. Others in the audience say to themselves, "Our system is as interesting as that one. We have ideas to share too." And the following year, they do. In this way, quickly but surely, we build a richer and richer foundation of shared expertise and common knowledge in the field.

That, in turn, leads to growth in efficiencies back at the home office, which leads to more boasting, which leads to more people creating SGML systems. Somewhere along the way, people like me come along and say: "This information needs to be spread even more widely. I'll try to synthesize some of what I've learned into a book."

❧ Appendix D
Just Enough History

In a hallway in CERN

Legend has it that a pivotal event in the story of the World Wide Web took place in 1989 in a hallway at CERN, the European nuclear research facility. At that time, Tim Berners-Lee was a young researcher struggling with the question of how to link high-energy physics researchers around the world. As a result of a brief hallway conversation, Anders Berglund (the pragmatist) introduced the concepts of SGML to Berners-Lee (the visionary), Tim's problem was solved, and he went on to create the hugely successful computer communications tool now known as the World Wide Web and its document representation standard: HTML.

The history, like most histories, is somewhat messier and more convoluted than the legend. The World Wide Web and HTML may appear to be overnight successes, but the tools and concepts that made their creation possible have long and independent evolutions. Even more important, these tools and concepts represent the legacy of a large number of individuals who were all trying to solve very specific problems. The World Wide Web represents the convergence of three principle technology trends: hypermedia, the Internet, and the concept of generalized markup. Understanding their history is the key to understanding the future of the World Wide Web and SGML's evolving role within it.

The Roots of the World Wide Web

Hypertext and hypermedia

Even before there was an Internet, there was the search for hypertext, a concept first identified in a famous article by Vanevar Bush, one of Franklin Roosevelt's science advisors. In the July, 1945 issue of *Atlantic Monthly*, Bush predicted that modern technology would soon give people the power to retrieve knowledge from throughout the world and the ability to link or connect bits and pieces of that knowledge in both new and personal ways.

As early as 1951, Douglas Engelbart begun to envision using computers, not just for crunching numbers, but as a collaborative tool that would help mankind deal with urgent and complex issues. In 1962, he developed a "Conceptual Framework for Augmenting Human Intellect" that set the stage for his tool-development activities at the *Stanford Research Institute* during the 60s and his more famous work at *Xerox's Palo Alto Research Center* (PARC). These tools include the hypermedia-based oN-Line System (NLS), which later evolved into the commercial product AUGMENT, synchronous distributed shared-screen conferencing, windowing systems, outlining tools, and the mouse.

To Engelbart, however, hypermedia and the other innovations that he has nurtured have been secondary derivatives of his conceptual framework, which emphasizes such concepts as the co-evolution of tool-systems, and human-systems and the Concurrent Development, Integration and Application of Knowledge (CoDIAK). Engelbart's current call for an open hyperdocument system (OHS) echoes his real interest in providing an infrastructure for collaboration. The seamlessly integrated, multi-vendor architecture that OHS represents would provide "interoperability among knowledge domains."

In the early 1960s, Ted Nelson extended Bush's concepts, coining the terms *hypertext* and *hypermedia* along the way. Nelson's efforts grew from his interest in film-making and what he saw as the need to link multiple, related abstractions in order to organize complex projects. At the core of Nelson's approach is a concept he now calls *transclusion*. Transclusion refers to the fact that the same piece of information can have meaning in a variety of contexts and that each context should be able to reference the shared data without duplicating it.

In 1967, Nelson started using the term "Xanadu" to describe a networked publishing system based on these concepts. Xanadu is a broad and complex vision that is as much a financial model as a set of technical specifications. It is designed to maximize the impact of the individual by providing an infrastructure for complete works to be distributed, pieces of these works to be referenced (or transcluded), and royalty fees to be handled automatically. Despite years of work and considerable investment (especially those by *Autodesk, Inc.*) Xanadu has not been implemented and many consider the Web to be the closest, existing implementation of the Xanadu concept.

Today, hypermedia is a mainstream commodity, available in a wide variety of commercial software products. Hypermedia is inherently a visionary concept, however, and its champions are often disappointed with real-world implementations. As Ted Nelson states in a recent issue of *Communications of the* ACM, "Like Doug, I have had a unified vision, of which today's popular attainments are only centerless shadows of the edge."

The Internet

The Internet was also born in the 1960s, not from a desire to link the world's knowledge, but from the desire to survive nuclear attack. The Internet was designed from the beginning to be a communications network that would survive the bomb. The characteristics that gave the Internet its ability to survive — its lack of central control, its "standards-by-consensus" approach to technical specifications, and its ability to bypass malfunctioning parts of the system — are the very things that make it difficult today to provide security, protect financial data, or limit access to pornography.

Generalized Markup, SGML, and HyTime

While the stories of how the Internet and hypertext developed over time are relatively well known, the story of the third major root of the World Wide Web is probably less familiar. People have been struggling with the idea of "generalized markup" for almost as long as they've been connecting computers to local, national, and international networks. By the time Tim Berners-Lee decided to adapt some of the key features of the movement for this generic markup for use in HTML, researchers and publishers had been working with the tools for nearly 20 years.

Generic Coding

The concept of generic coding traces its origins back to the 1960s. As computers started being used for document production, many organizations encountered a major roadblock: the different software and file formats used by their individual computers were fundamentally incompatible with each other. The electronic exchange of documents was more than difficult, The different conceptual approaches that each system took to documents, and how to represent them inside the computer, made conversions all but impossible. This was in contrast to the document processing industry of today, when individual software vendors compete in terms of function but share similar approaches to document formatting — similar enough that conversions are possible, if not 100 per cent reliable.

In 1967, William Tunnicliffe, then chairman of the *Graphics Communications Association* (GCA) Composition Committee, introduced the concept of generic coding in a meeting with the *Canadian Government Printing Office*. His idea was to separate the information content of a document from the formatting codes which are used to describe its visual appearance (e.g., "heading" instead of "format-17"). This would allow documents to be exchanged electronically and then converted into whatever format-specific version was needed on the individual computer systems. A similar concept was being developed by Stanley Rice, a book designer in New York. Rice was proposing the development of a catalog of universal tags that would reflect editorial structures.

As a result of these developments, Norm Scharpf launched a generic coding project as part of the GCA's Composition Committee. This effort formed the basis of what became known as the *GenCode Committee*. The GenCode Committee introduced a number of important concepts: different tag sets for different classes of documents, the idea of constructing documents out of sub-documents.

Generalized Markup Language at IBM

In 1969, Charles Goldfarb led a research project at IBM that focused on how to apply computers to legal work. The system that he had in mind would do the following for lawyers: retrieve information to help them figure out the subject matter of the case and do research on past cases in the relevant jurisdiction that may have bearing on the current case; combine excerpts of the retrieved documents with new text to prepare legal briefs; and typeset the resulting documents.

Initially, Goldfarb was told to choose the IBM system that worked best, but it turned out that such a system didn't exist. Instead, Goldfarb was sent from product group to product group, finding only partial solutions. As a result, Goldfarb, along with Edward Mosher and Raymond Lorie, in 1969, created a way to allow the different computer systems used for text editing, formatting, and information retrieval to share the same documents. Using the same initials as their own names, the three men called their solution the Generalized Markup Language (GML). GML was based, in part, on the generic tagging ideas of William Tunnicliffe, Stanley Rice and others. But GML introduced the concept of formally-defined document types, with a clearly defined element structure for each document type.

The difference is that, instead of trying to create a single set of tags that would serve for all possible kinds of documents that an organization might wish to publish, GML introduced the concept of a *document type definition*, or "DTD". A DTD provided a specific set of tagged element types for a particular type of document.

In GML, DTDS were only for humans to read, a sort of contract between the authors of the documents and the programmers who wrote the procedures that formatted them. Goldfarb went on to invent SGML, which, among other things, introduced the concept of a program called a *validating parser*. An SGML parser could read a DTD and validate markup without going to the expense of formatting the document.

IBM's need to distribute information about its products made it one of the world's largest publishers. It has used GML (and later, SGML) almost exclusively, ever since the late 1970's. In 1978, Goldfarb was asked to join a committee of the *American National Standards Institute* (ANSI) that was working on computer languages for processing text information. This committee worked with the GenCode committee of the *Graphic Communications Association*. The two groups worked together to convert Goldfarb's basic language design into a standard that could be used by publishers, authors, computer software vendors, and others.

Standardizing the DOD

By 1980, early working drafts of a proposed International Standard for SGML had been developed by the ISO. Other drafts followed, and by the time the sixth version had been developed and reviewed, the Graphic Communications Association was able to publish it as an industry standard. Several large organizations, including the

U.S. Internal Revenue Service and the Department of Defense, began using the standard, even though it continued to evolve. Goldfarb continued to serve as the technical leader of the movement as the project editor for both ISO and ANSI committees working on the development of SGML. Anders Berglund, a particle physics researcher at CERN served on the ISO committee preparing the SGML standard.

A final draft of the SGML standard was issued in October of 1985. After a year of review, ISO approved the draft and it was officially published as ISO 8879 in 1986. *Information processing — Text and office systems — Standard Generalized Markup Language* (SGML).

At the same time, during the mid-1980s, the U.S. *Department of Defense* was pioneering in the application of SGML to real-world problems, under the banner of CALS, the Computer-aided Acquisition and Logistics Support effort (now known as "Comerce at Light Speed"). As one of the largest purchasers of goods and services in the world, the DoD had powerful incentives to automate its procurement paperwork. To make it easier for companies and the government to exchange information about products and billing, DoD has established a common set of information standards and tools for electronic data interchange. These tools and standards rely heavily on SGML. Other industries with high needs for information exchange, such as aerospace, automotive, and pharmaceuticals, have adopted SGML as the vehicle for industry-wide collaboration and information exchange.

SGML *at* CERN

The man whose meeting with Tim Berners-Lee gave Tim the key to creation of HTML, was Anders Berglund. Berglund, was working at the time at the CERN, and was heavily involved with the on-going development of an international effort to create tools for the exchange of information in electronic form. He learned of the SGML efforts at the offices of ISO near CERN in Geneva. He and Eric van Herwijnen attended the second European conference on SGML that was held in Heidelberg in 1985.

Berglund and van Herwijnen developed a publishing system at CERN that was based on SGML and used the sample DTD from an annex of the standard, which was in turn based on the original GML DTD. Although their publishing system was not the only one at CERN, its use was fairly common and set the stage for the Web's HTML specification.

ASCII and Angle Brackets: What the Web got from SGML

Tim's Problem: Markup and Metadata

By inventing the World Wide Web, Tim Berners-Lee solved one of the basic problems of electronic publishing: How do you deal with the unanticipated? How do you let a piece of software know what it should do when it opens a file and tries to display the contents on a screen?

Let's begin by seeing how a wordprocessor accomplishes this. Say you've typed, "Why Use SGML on the Web?" and clicked on a command that makes this title appear in boldface. You save the file. Next time you open the file, the phrase is still in boldface. Obviously, there's more in the file than just the six words. There are codes — normally invisible — that let the software know what to do.

- In Microsoft Word's "Rich Text Format", for example, this phrase would appear as: {\b\f4 **Why Use SGML on the Web?**}
- In WordPerfect's internal language, it would appear in codes that can't even be reproduced in print because they include special computer control codes that do not have an equivalent letter or symbol. These control codes are used because they aren't likely to be misinterpreted as content.
- The codes that permeate the content of *this* file, and which indicate how it is to appear, are called markup.

Berners-Lee wanted both much more and much less than what one gets with a standard wordprocessor: much less because he didn't want incomprehensible codes cluttering up the file in ways that humans would find difficult both to understand, and, more importantly, to write; much less too because he didn't care whether the forms of communication he was establishing for the first version of the Web would have all the fancy display capability of a standard wordprocessor.

At the same time, he wanted much more: He wanted anyone to be able to create documents for the Web. That is, he wanted anyone to understand and be able to employ the form of markup he was about to create.

The Solution: SGML

In his conversations at CERN with Anders Berglund and others, Berners-Lee picked up several of the most important aspects of SGML, and built them into HTML:

1. Identifying markup using standard characters, in particular the angle bracket (delimiter in SGML) allows any system to know that whatever follows the angle bracket, up to a close angle bracket (>) will be markup that the system must use as an instruction, rather than as content. In HTML, for example, TITLE indicates that the text that follows is the title of the file, and in many Web browsers should be treated specially (displayed in a small box at the top of the software window rather than in the text window, for example).

2. Marking the end of something with an angle bracket followed by a slash. A twin pair of tags, the start-tag <A>, followed by text, followed in turn by an end-tag </A>, indicates to Web software that the content in between is an anchor, something that a user could click on in order to initiate a link to another file.

3. Transmitting across computer networks in the basic set of keyboard characters, the so-called ASCII character set, so as not to cause the unexpected. In practice this means no "control" or "alt" characters, and gives rise to the need for ...

4. Identifying special characters (such as accents, or bullets) using the SGML technique of entity references. In practice this means that such a character is referred to in text using an a delimited entity reference: & begins the entity reference and a semi-colon ends it. é for example, in a file produces an é on the screen or printed page.

He also got some other characteristics of SGML that he hadn't planned on:

1. The use of ASCII files has a number of important implications. It means that individuals can use any text editor and are not required to use specialized HTML editors. It also lowers the perceived learning curve. Together, these two phenomena rapidly sped acceptance of the Web, by avoiding barriers that would have existed if Berners-Lee had designed a proprietary, binary file format.

2. It is not difficult for individuals to design and apply their own "HTML tags" to documents. This, too, offers benefits to users, but at the expense of compromising portability. The *Netscape* <BLINK> tag is an example of this.

Mosaic makes the Web explode (1993)

Hardin, Andreesen, and NCSA...

Across the ocean from CERN, a team of people at the U.S. *National Center for Super-computing Applications* (NCSA) at the *University of Illinois* followed Tim Berners-Lee, by building on defined standards, and writing a freeware graphical browser. The program, which they called Mosaic, allows people to interact with pages written in the HTML language. Because NCSA is a government-supported agency, the program was made available on the Internet for free.

This powerful, visual, and free tool gave large numbers of people the means to view, and incentive to publish, their own Web pages. At first there were only a few hundred or a few thousand people publishing on the Web, but there are now hundreds of thousands of people publishing for themselves, their companies, their community organizations, schools, governments, and so on.

The Revolutionary Aspects of HTML Browsers

Mosaic made the World Wide Web very popular very quickly for two principal reasons:

1. It's simple to use. It follows a page model for display — that is, the unit of what you see on the screen roughly matches what we think of as a page. It uses a selection of typefaces, point sizes and emboldening that appears automatically from the markup.
2. It's visual. It displays graphic images and supports powerful cross-network linking. A phrase can reference another document, and a click opens that other document, wherever it is, on another computer, in another country.

The Web Today

Architectural overview

How do Web Browsers fit into the continuum of document delivery systems?

Display tools come in several varieties, each optimized for different capability, and each recognizing different levels of complexity in the information structures it can successfully process:

1. ASCII or Text Readers take the simplest way out: They assume everything in an incoming data stream will be an ASCII code, and display it accordingly. If the input turns out to have been more complex or non-text, the system breaks — everything displays as text, sometimes therefore as gibberish. Text viewers have a great advantage: Many and various tools can read, write, search through and manipulate ASCII text. It is the lingua franca of most North American and European computer operating systems and can be considered *a great leveler*. Unfortunately the level is very low. There is no *added value* information in an ASCII text stream, no way to tell where a picture should go, what should be displayed at a particular point size, how to distinguish someone's name from a part number.

2. Raster viewers, at the next level of display, take the same approach, but with a finer degree of visual capability: They can display what appear to be more complex documents than ASCII display, with illustrations, and bold face, and big type, but in reality the input is very simple indeed — a collection of dots. This type of display cannot be searched, is not machine processable into, for example, a database or a spreadsheet, and its only value is that it can closely match a printed page. One cannot transmit a data stream that is anything but raster images.

3. In the next category are Page Viewers such as Adobe Acrobat, Common Ground or Envoy. Acrobat, for example, knows that the data stream being received by the software is encoded in *Adobe's* "Portable Document Format" and it offers sophisticated functions to present that file with a visual presentation closely matching the printed page on any monitor, irrespective of the font capabilities of the receiving computer. The others use similar techniques. To differing degrees, these products may allow the content to be searched for words and phrases, but they are based on the premise that there is one desired presentation

of the page. Like raster encoded pages, these are not machine processable and cannot be re-designed to suit the requirements of the reader. More importantly, one cannot send a data stream to them that is anything but page images in their preferred proprietary encoding without the use of "helper" applications.

4. Moving up the ladder of complexity in content handling are HTML browsers, software associated with display on the World Wide Web. Netscape Navigator, Microsoft Internet Explorer, and various versions of Mosaic are among the most popular examples. The key to their success is HTML, which is an SGML application with its own set of specific information element types. The HTML element types are essentially the paragraph, the title, the list, the graphic image and others in a small but powerful fixed set of recognizably useful content objects. Because they're ASCII-based, HTML files may be searched for words and phrases, and a new generation of tools has appeared that can use the defined elements of HTML markup for restricted searches, for example, to "Smith" only when it appears in a title. Significantly, World Wide Web browsers, by virtue of the encoding and transfer protocols they support, can be sent data in non-HTML formats to be passed off to appropriate tools for display or processing.

5. Browsers that understand full SGML offer the next level of capability. In fact, SGML is a meta-language, a set of conventions to allow users or groups of users to design a set of structural element types that establish the markup for a *class* of documents (training materials, for example, or maintenance manuals, or memos). That markup can be anything that is meaningful in the domain of those documents. In practice, HTML is simply one of an infinite number of possible SGML applications, optimized, in this case, for World Wide Web display. In HTML browsers, the units of information come from a fixed set. Browsers built on full SGML can provide that capability (paragraphs, tables, titles, and so forth) plus "model year", "part number", "required tool" or any other information structure that makes sense for the tasks to which the information will be put. Full SGML offer machines processability, re-definition of display based on individual needs or whim, search restricted to any arbitrary information element, and, perhaps of primary importance, conformance to an international standard supported by a variety of nations, industries and software products.

What makes the Web important?

Three things:

1. Simple point–and–click interface.
2. A very straightforward application of the Standard Generalized Markup Language, the international standard for document interchange.
3. The idea that a complex set of protocols layered atop the Internet can mask complicated, clunky machine names and addresses.

The Revolutionary Component

The idea that a file in Switzerland or Japan or Canada opens as readily as a file on a local machine — simply by following a link — may be commonplace today, but it's fairly revolutionary compared to the olden days of 1992.

The Social Value

It gets us on the road. It enables anyone to publish anywhere, knowing that the display will take care of itself. Access to technology is only part of democratization; not worrying about the technology is what makes it relevant.

The Economic Value/Saving or Making Money

Yes in some cases, almost in a lot of others. Web technologies make us believe that real value is right around the corner. This is prototypical technology, opening the imagination to new possibilities. In the end, it may even be about giving away technology so that the money is made by selling the content. This is one of the reasons that the real focus of attention needs to be on the content.

Public, Private, and Personal Characteristics

It's deliriously public: Anyone with access to the Internet can download a browser for most kinds of computers. More importantly, the major browser makers make copies of the software available very early, and yes, it gets, feedback, early and often. They participate in the public activities helping to shape the World Wide Web, and they listen closely.

The World Wide Web is also private. In 1994, a team of developers left NCSA and founded the company that became *Netscape Communications*; after a record-breaking public share offering, some of them are now "Netscape millionaires." Since then many companies, such as *Microsoft, SoftQuad, Spyglass, Sun* and others have entered the market with browsers of their own.

On the personal side, Tim Berners-Lee continues to take his role as shepherd and steward of the World Wide Web very seriously. Far from being a millionaire, Tim is now the Director of the *World Wide Web Consortium* where he leads a global team. The rest of the world, it seems, is busy trying to make its fortune on the World Wide Web.

⚜ APPENDIX E

Licence Agreement and Limited Warranty

READ THE FOLLOWING TERMS AND CONDITIONS CAREFULLY BEFORE OPEING THIS CD PACKAGE. THIS LEGAL DOCUMENT IS AN AGREEMENT BETWEEN YOU AND PRENTICE-HALL, INC. (THE "COMPANY"). BY OPENING THIS SEALED CD PACKAGE YOU ARE AGREEING TO BE BOUND BY THESE TERMS AND CONDITIONS. IF YOU DO NOT AGREE WITH THESE TERMS AND CONDITIONS, DO NOT OPEN THE CD PACKAGE. PROMPTLY RETURN THE UNOPENED CD PACKAGE AND ALL ACCOMPANYING ITEMS TO THE PLACE YOU OBTAINED THEM FOR A FULL REFUND OF ANY SUMS YOU HAVE PAID.

1. GRANT OF LICENCE: In consideration of your purchase of this book, and your agreement to abide by the terms and conditions of this Agreement, the Company grants to you a nonexclusive right to use and display the copy of the enclosed software program (hereinafter the "SOFTWARE") on a single computer (i.e., with a single CPU) at a single location so long as you comply with the terms of this Agreement. The Company reserves all rights not expressly granted to you under this Agreement.

2. OWNERSHIP OF SOFTWARE: You own only the magnetic or physical media (the enclosed CD) on which the SOFTWARE is recorded or fixed, but the Company and the software developers retain all the rights, title, and ownership to the SOFTWARE recorded on the original CD copy(ies) and all subsequent copies of the SOFTWARE, regardless of the form or media on which the original or other copies may exist. This licence is not a sale of the original SOFTWARE or any copy to you.

3. COPY RESTRICTIONS: This SOFTWARE and the accompanying printed materials and user manual (the "Documentation") are the subject of copyright. The individual programs on the CD are copyrighted by the authors of each program. Some of the programs on the CD include separate licensing agreements. If you intend to use one of these programs, you must read and follow its accompanying license agreement. You may **not** copy the Documentation or the SOFTWARE, except that you may make a single copy of the SOFTWARE for backup or archival purposes only. You may be held legally responsible for any copying or copyright infringement which is caused or encouraged by your failure to abide by the terms of this restriction.

4. USE RESTRICTIONS: You may **not** network the SOFTWARE or otherwise use it on more than one computer or computer terminal at the same time. You may physically transfer the SOFTWARE from one computer to another provided that the SOFTWARE is used on only one computer at a time. You may **not** distribute copies of the SOFTWARE or Documentation to others. You may **not** reverse engineer, disassemble, decompile, modify, adapt, translate, or create derivative works based on the SOFTWARE or the Documentation without the prior written consent of the Company.

5. TRANSFER RESTRICTIONS: The enclosed SOFTWARE is licensed only to you and may **not** be transferred to any one else without the prior written consent of the Company. Any unauthorized transfer of the SOFTWARE shall result in the immediate termination of this Agreement.

6. TERMINATION: This license is effective until terminated. This license will terminate automatically without notice from the Company and become null and void if you fail to comply with any previous or limitations of this license. Upon termination, you shall destroy the Documentation and all copies of the SOFTWARE. All provisions of this Agreement as to warranties, limitation of liability, remedies or damages, and our ownership rights shall survive termination.

7. MISCELLANEOUS: This Agreement shall be construed in accordance with the laws of the United States of America and the State of New York and shall benefit the Company, its affiliates, and assignees.

8. LIMITED WARRANTY AND DISCLAIMER OF WARRANTY: The Company warrants that the SOFTWARE, when properly used in accordance with the Documentation, will operate in substantial conformity with the description of the SOFTWARE set forth in the Documentation. The Company does not warrant that the SOFTWARE will meet your requirements or that the operation of the

SOFTWARE will be uninterrupted or error-free. The Company warrants that the media on which the SOFTWARE is delivered shall be free from defects in materials and workmanship under normal use for a period of thirty (30) days from the date of your purchase. Your only remedy and the Company's only obligation under these limited warranties is, at the Company's option, return of the warranted item for a refund of any amounts paid by you or replacement of the item. Any replacement of SOFTWARE or media under the warranties shall not extend the original warranty period. The limited warranty set forth above shall not apply to any SOFTWARE which the Company determines in good faith has been subject to misuse, neglect, improper installation, repair, alteration, or damage by you. EXCEPT FOR THE EXPRESSED WARRANTIES SET FORTH ABOVE, THE COMPANY DISCLAIMS ALL WARRANTIES, EXPRESS OR IMPLIED, INCLUDING WITHOUT LIMITATION, THE IMPLIED WARRANTIES OF MERCHANTABILITY AND FITNESS FOR A PARTICULAR PURPOSE. EXCEPT FOR THE EXPRESS WARRANTY SET FORTH ABOVE, THE COMPANY DOES NOT WARRANT, GUARANTEE, OR MAKE ANY REPRESENTATION REGARDING THE USE OR THE RESULTS OF THE USE OF THE SOFTWARE IN TERMS OF ITS CORRECTNESS, ACCURACY, RELIABILITY, CURRENTNESS, OR OTHERWISE.

IN NO EVENT, SHALL THE COMPANY OR ITS EMPLOYEES, AGENTS, SUPPLIERS, OR CONTRACTORS BE LIABLE FOR ANY INCIDENTAL, INDIRECT, SPECIAL, OR CONSEQUENTIAL DAMAGES ARISING OUT OF OR IN CONNECTION WITH THE LICENSE GRANTED UNDER THIS AGREEMENT, OR FOR LOSS OF USE, LOSS OF DATA, LOSS OF INCOME OR PROFIT, OR OTHER LOSSES, SUSTAINED AS A RESULT OF INJURY TO ANY PERSON, OR LOSS OF OR DAMAGE TO PROPERTY, OR CLAIMS OF THIRD PARTIES, EVEN IF THE COMPANY OR AN AUTHORIZED REPRESENTATIVE OF THE COMPANY HAS BEEN ADVISED OF THE POSSIBILITY OF SUCH DAMAGES. IN NO EVENT SHALL LIABILITY OF THE COMPANY FOR DAMAGES WITH RESPECT TO THE SOFTWARE EXCEED THE AMOUNTS ACTUALLY PAID BY YOU, IF ANY, FOR THE SOFTWARE.

SOME JURISDICTIONS DO NOT ALLOW THE LIMITATION OF IMPLIED WARRANTIES OR LIABILITY FOR INCIDENTAL, INDIRECT, SPECIAL, OR CONSEQUENTIAL DAMAGES, SO THE ABOVE LIMITATIONS MAY NOT ALWAYS APPLY. THE WARRANTIES IN THIS AGREEMENT GIVE YOU SPECIFIC LEGAL RIGHTS AND YOU MAY ALSO HAVE OTHER RIGHTS WHICH VARY IN ACCORDANCE WITH LOCAL LAW.

ACKNOWLEDGEMENT

YOU ACKNOWLEDGE THAT YOU HAVE READ THIS AGREEMENT, UNDERSTAND IT, AND AGREE TO BE BOUND BY ITS TERMS AND CONDITIONS. YOU ALSO AGREE THAT THIS AGREEMENT IS THE COMPLETE AND EXCLUSIVE STATEMENT OF THE AGREEMENT BETWEEN YOU AND THE COMPANY AND SUPERSEDES ALL PROPOSALS OR PRIOR AGREEMENTS, ORAL, OR WRITTEN, AND ANY OTHER COMMUNICATIONS BETWEEN YOU AND THE COMPANY OR ANY REPRESENTATIVE OF THE COMPANY RELATING TO THE SUBJECT MATTER OF THIS AGREEMENT.

Should you have any questions concerning this Agreement or if you wish to contact the Company for any reason, please contact in writing at the address below:

> Robin Short
> Prentice Hall PTR
> One Lake Street
> Upper Saddle River, New Jersey 07458

✒ BIBLIOGRAPHY

Other Books About SGML

Alschuler, Liora. ABCD... SGML, International Thomson Computer Press, (1995) ISBN 1-850-32197

Bryan, Martin. SGML: An Author's Guide to the Standard Generalized Markup Language, Addison-Wesley, (1988) ISBN 0-201-17537-5

Donovan, Truly. Industrial-Strength SGML: An Introduction to Enterprise Publishing, Prentice Hall PTR (1997). ISBN 0-13-216243-1

Ensign, Chet. SGML: The Billion Dollar Secret, Prentice Hall PTR (1997). ISBN 0-13-226705-5

Goldfarb, Charles F. The SGML Handbook, Oxford University Press, (1990) ISBN 0-19-853737-9

Maler, Eve; ElAndaloussi, Jeanne. Developing SGML DTDs from Text to Model to Markup Prentice Hall, (1995) ISBN 0-13-309881-8

Smith, Joan. SGML and Related Standards. Chichester, West Susses: Ellis Horwood, Ltd., (1992).

Travis, Brian; Waldt, Dale. The SGML Implementation Guide, Springer-Verlag, (1995) ISBN 3-540-57730-0

Turner, Ronald C., Douglass, Timothy A., and Turner, Audrey J. Readme.1ST: SGML for Writers and Editors, Prentice Hall, (1995) ISBN 0-13-432717-9

Van Herwijnen, Eric. Practical SGML, Second Edition, Kluwer Academic Publishers, (1994) ISBN 0-7923-9434-8

Other published SGML works by Yuri Rubinsky

Rubinsky, Yuri. "Can Inanimate Objects Have Intentions? This Column Does, and So Can a DTD". <TAG>: The SGML Newsletter **10** No. 11 (July 1989). ISSN: 1067-9197.

Rubinsky, Yuri. "Comments on an SGML Application for Hypermedia and Multi-Media Interchange". SGML Users' Group Newsletter **15** (January 1990) 16-17. ISSN: 1067-9197.

Rubinsky, Yuri. "Comments on an SGML Application for Hyper- and Multi-Media Interchange: Informal Report from the GCA Hypertext/Hypermedia Standards Forum." <TAG> **11** (October 1989) pp. 5–6.

[by Mark A Crook]. "Yuri Rubinsky Explores Use of SGML to Generate Text for Sight-impaired." OCLC Newsletter **212** (November/December 1994) pp. 16–17

Rubinsky, Yuri. "Copy of Letter to NIST [on Conformance Testing Program] Dated January 20, 1994." SGML Users' Group Bulletin Newsletter **26** (February 1994) pp. 4–6. ISSN: 0952-8008.

Rubinsky, Yuri. "Implementation Development and Surprise." SGML Users' Group Bulletin **2** No. 2 (1987) pp. 113–115. ISSN: 0269-2538.

Rubinsky, Yuri. "Life Beyond Cross-Roads." <TAG> **9** No. 2 (February 1996) p. 5. ISSN: 1067-9197.

Rubinsky, Yuri. "In Praise of Shelf Life and SGML." InterConsult's Corporate Publishing Newsletter (October 19, 1987).

Rubinsky, Yuri. "The Screen is Deeper than the Page." InterConsult's Corporate Publishing Newsletter (April 25, 1989)

Rubinsky, Yuri. "SGML to Braille, Large Print, and Audio." In Part 4: Distinguished Seminar Series Annual Review of OCLC Research, 1994. Dublin, OH: OCLC Online Computer Library Center, 1995. approximately 6 pages, 1 reference.

Rubinsky, Yuri. "SGML in the Realm of the Desktop." GCA Conference Highlights Variety of Possibilities for SGML, Including Dictionaries. <TAG>: The SGML Newsletter **1** No. 8 (January 1989) pp. 12–13.

Rubinsky, Yuri. "SGML Year in Review [1991]." SGML Users' Group Newsletter 21 (December, 1991) pp. 3–6.

Rubinsky, Yuri. "SGML Year in Review [1990]." SGML Users' Group Newsletter 18 (November, 1990) pp. 5–6.

Rubinsky, Yuri. "SGML Year in Review [1991]." <TAG> 20 (December, 1991) pp. 1–5.

Rubinsky, Yuri. "Electronic Texts The Day After Tomorrow." In SCHOLARLY PUBLISHING ON THE ELECTRONIC NETWORKS. Edited by Ann Okerson. Washington, DC: Association of Research Libraries, Office of Scientific & Academic Publishing, 1993. ISBN: 0-918006-61-9

Rubinsky, Yuri; Lehman, Philip. "Markup Language Creates Blueprint for Style, Format." Government Computer News 7 No. 13 (June 24, 1988) pp. 73–74.

Rubinsky, Yuri. "The SGML Year in Review [Being the Text of a Speech Given at the GCA's SGML '92 Conference]." SGML Users' Group Newsletter 23 (November 1992) pp. 2–8.

Rubinsky, Yuri; Usdin, Tommie. "The SGML Year in Review –1993." SGML Users' Group Bulletin Newsletter 26 (February 1994) pp. 8–15. ISSN: 0952-8008.

Rubinsky, Yuri. "Standards for Hypertext Interchange." SGML Users' Group Newsletter 15 (January 1990) pp. 14–15.

Rubinsky, Yuri. "Standards for Hypertext Interchange Need Not Come out of Thin Air." <TAG> 11 (October 1989) pp. 4–5.

Rubinsky, Yuri; Usdin, B. Tommie. "The [1994 SGML] Year in Review." <TAG> 7 No. 12 (December 1994) pp. 1–4. ISSN: 1067-9197.

❧ Glossary

The sources of definitions in this glossary are identified as follows:

ISO 8879	International Standard ISO 8879: Standard Generalized Markup Language (SGML)
ISO/IEC 10744	International Standard ISO/IEC 10744: Hypermedia/Time-based Structuring Language
Charles F. Goldfarb Series	Charles F. Goldfarb Series on Open Information Management. These definitions are not part of an ISO standard but are consistent with the standardized terminology and have been adopted as "standard" for this Series.
HyperText Markup Language	HyperText Markup Language — 2.0. IETF RFC 1866.
HyperText Transfer Protocol	Hypertext Transfer Protocol — HTTP/1.1. An Internet Draft from the IETF HTTP Working Group (12 August 1996).
Uniform Resource Locators	Uniform Resource Locators (URL). IETF RFC 1738

anchor   An object (or aggregation of objects) that is linked by a hyper-link.

> Note   The term "object" is not a formal construct in HyTime; an anchor could be a document, an element, an arbitrary chunk of data, or any other thing.
>
> (ISO/IEC 10744)

application   Text processing application.
See also SGML application   (ISO 8879)

application convention   Application-specific rule governing the text of a document in areas that SGML leaves to user choice.

> Note   There are two kinds: content conventions and markup conventions.
>
> (ISO 8879)

architectural form   Rules for creating and processing components of documents. There are four kinds: element form, attribute form, data entity form, and data attribute form.   (Charles F. Goldfarb Series)

ASCII   American Standard Code for Information Interchange.
                                        (Charles F. Goldfarb Series)

attribute (of an element)   A characteristic quality, other than type or content.   (ISO 8879)

attribute definition   A member of an attribute definition list; it defines an attribute name, allowed values, and default value.   (ISO 8879)

attribute definition list   A set of one or more attribute definitions defined by the attribute definition list parameter of an attribute definition list declaration.   (ISO 8879)

attribute (definition) list declaration   A markup declaration that associates an attribute definition list with one or more element types.   (ISO 8879)

attribute form   An architectural form that applies to attributes of elements.
                                         (ISO/IEC 10744)

attribute specification A member of an attribute specification list; it specifies the value of a single attribute.   (ISO 8879)

attribute value The value assigned to an attribute, whether specified or defaulted.   (Charles F. Goldfarb Series)

attribute value type One of the fifteen types of value that can be defined for an attribute.

    Note   They are: character data, general entity name, general entity name list, id value, id reference value, id reference list, name, name list, name token, name token list, notation name, number, number list, number token, number token list.

                           (Charles F. Goldfarb Series)

attribute value literal A delimited character string that is interpreted as an attribute value by replacing references and ignoring or translating function characters.   (ISO 8879)

browser A program used to read documents in electronic form.

    Note   It is sometimes called a "viewer" or "reader" program.

                           (Charles F. Goldfarb Series)

catalog See *entity catalog*.

character data Zero or more characters that occur in a context in which no markup is recognized, other than the delimiters that end the character data. Such characters are classified as data characters because they were declared to be so.   (ISO 8879)

character set A mapping of a character repertoire onto a code set such that each character in the repertoire is represented by a bit combination in the code set.   (ISO 8879)

clink See *contextual link element form*   (Charles F. Goldfarb Series)

comments	A portion of a markup declaration that contains explanations or remarks intended to aid persons working with the document. (ISO 8879)
comment declaration	A markup declaration that contains only comments. (ISO 8879)
concrete syntax (of SGML*)*	A binding of the abstract syntax to particular delimiter characters, quantities, markup declaration names, etc. (ISO 8879)
conforming SGML *application*	An SGML application that requires documents to be conforming SGML documents, and whose documentation meets the requirements of this International Standard. (ISO 8879)
containing element	An element within which a subelement occurs. (ISO 8879)
content	Characters that occur between the start-tag and end-tag of an element in a document instance. They can be interpreted as data, proper subelements, included subelements, other markup, or a mixture of them.

> Note   If an element has an explicit content reference, or its declared content is EMPTY, the content is empty. In such cases, the application itself may generate data and process it as though it were content data.
>
> (ISO 8879)

content model	Parameter of an element declaration that specifies the model group and *exceptions* that define the allowed content of the element. (ISO 8879)
contextual hyperlink	A hyperlink that occurs "in context", meaning that one anchor of the link is the link element itself. In an interactive application, the self anchor can be accessed externally from adjacent elements or data in the document hierarchy. (Charles F. Goldfarb Series)

contextual link element form	An element form that represents a binary contextual hyperlink having the fixed anchor roles reference mark (REFMARK) for the self anchor and reference subject (REFSUB) for the other anchor. (Charles F. Goldfarb Series)
data character	An SGML character that is interpreted as data in the context in which it occurs, either because it was declared to be data, or because it was not recognizable as markup. (ISO 8879)
data content	The portion of an element's content that is data rather than markup or a subelement. (ISO 8879)
data content notation	An application-specific interpretation of an element's data content, or of a data entity, that usually extends or differs from the normal meaning of the document character set.

> Note   It is specified for an element's content by a *notation attribute*, and for a data entity by the notation name parameter of the entity declaration.
>
> (ISO 8879)

dataloc	Data location address. (Charles F. Goldfarb Series)
data location address.	A location address that addresses the string and token data objects resulting from tokenization. (Charles F. Goldfarb Series)
declaration subset	A delimited portion of a markup declaration in which other declarations can occur.

> Note   Declaration subsets occur only in document type, link type, and marked section declarations.
>
> (ISO 8879)

declared value	The attribute value type that is defined for an attribute. (Charles F. Goldfarb Series)

declared value parameter	The parameter of an attribute definition that defines the attribute value type. Its value is either a name token group, in which case the attribute value type is name token, or a keyword that identifies the attribute value type.

Note	The keywords are: CDATA, ENTITY, ENTITIES, ID, IDREF, IDREFS, NAME, NAMES, NMTOKEN, NMTOKENS, NOTATION, NUMBER, NUMBERS, NUTOKEN, NUTOKENS.

(Charles F. Goldfarb Series)

default value	A portion of an attribute definition that specifies the attribute value to be used if there is no attribute specification for it. (ISO 8879)
delimiter characters	Delimiters are normal characters which are assigned special roles in SGML to allow humans and computers to easily distinguish markup and content. (ISO 8879)
delimiter (string)	A character string assigned to a delimiter role by the concrete syntax. (ISO 8879)
descriptive markup	Markup that describes the structure and other attributes of a document in a non-system-specific manner, independently of any processing that may be performed on it. In particular, SGML descriptive markup uses tags to express the element structure. (ISO 8879)
document instance	Instance of a document type. (ISO 8879)
document element	The element that is the outermost element of an instance of a document type; that is, the element whose generic identifier is the document type name. (ISO 8879)
document type	A class of documents having similar characteristics; for example, journal, article, technical manual, or memo. (ISO 8879)

(document) type declaration	A markup declaration that formally specifies a portion of a *document type* definition.

> Note   A document type declaration does not specify all of a document type definition because part of the definition, such as the semantics of elements and attributes, cannot be expressed in SGML. In addition, the application designer might choose not to use SGML in every possible instance — for example, by using a data content notation to delineate the structure of an element in preference to defining subelements.
>
> (ISO 8879)

document (type) definition	Rules, determined by an application, that apply SGML to the markup of documents of a particular type.

> Note   Part of a document type definition can be specified by an SGML document type declaration. Other parts, such as the semantics of elements and attributes, or any application conventions, cannot be expressed formally in SGML. Comments can be used, however, to express them informally.
>
> (ISO 8879)

DTD	Document (Type) Definition	(ISO 8879)

element	A component of the hierarchical structure defined by a document type definition; it is identified in a document instance by descriptive markup, usually a start-tag and end-tag.

> Note   An element is classified as being of a particular element type.
>
> (ISO 8879)

element array	A repeatable sequence of elements of the same type, or of a fixed sequence of types. (Charles F. Goldfarb Series)

element declaration   Element type declaration

> Note   "Element declaration" is the standardized term for
> what the Charles F. Goldfarb Series calls an "element
> type declaration". The latter term is clearer because
> the declaration defines an element type, not just a
> single element. The SGML standards committee
> intends to replace this term with "element type dec-
> laration" when the standard is revised.
>
> (Charles F. Goldfarb Series)

element form   An architectural form that applies to elements.

(Charles F. Goldfarb Series)

element type declaration   A markup declaration that contains the formal specification of the part of an *element type definition* that deals with the content and markup minimization.   (Charles F. Goldfarb Series)

element set   A set of element, attribute definition list, and notation declarations that are used together.

> Note   An element set can be public text.
>
> (ISO 8879)

element type   A class of elements having similar characteristics; for example, paragraph, chapter, abstract, footnote, or bibliography.

(ISO 8879)

element (type) definition   Application-specific rules that apply SGML to the markup of elements of a particular type. An element type definition includes a formal specification, expressed in element and attribute definition list declarations, of the content, markup minimization, and attributes allowed for a specified element type.

> Note   An element type definition is normally part of a doc-
> ument type definition.
>
> (ISO 8879)

end-tag	Descriptive markup that identifies the end of an element. (ISO 8879)
entity	A collection of characters that can be referenced as a unit.

        Note

- Objects such as book chapters written by different authors, pi characters, or photographs, are often best managed by maintaining them as individual entities.
- The actual storage of entities is system-specific, and could take the form of files, members of a partitioned data set, components of a data structure, or entries in a symbol table.

(ISO 8879)

entity catalog	Information existing outside a document that can be used by an SGML system when locating the storage objects in which entities declared by that document are stored. An entity catalog typically associates public identifiers with *system identifiers*.

        Note   SGML Open Technical Resolution TR001-1994 is acommonly used specification for an entity catalog.

entity declaration	A markup declaration that assigns an SGML name to an entity so that it can be referenced. (ISO 8879)
entity reference	A reference that is replaced by an entity.

        Note   There are two kinds: named entity reference and short reference.

(ISO 8879)

entity structure	The organization of a document into one or more separate entities.

        Note   The first entity is an SGML *document entity*; it contains entity references that indicate where the other entities belong with respect to it.

(ISO 8879)

exceptions	A parameter of an element declaration that modifies the effect of the element's content model, and the content models of elements occurring within it, by permitting inclusions and prohibiting exclusions. (ISO 8879)
exclusions	Elements that are not allowed anywhere in the content of an element or its subelements even though the applicable content model or inclusions would permit them optionally. (ISO 8879)
external entity	An entity whose replacement text is not incorporated in an entity declaration; its system identifier and/or public identifier is specified instead. (ISO 8879)
external identifier	A parameter that identifies an external entity or data content notation.

Note
- There are two kinds: system identifier and public identifier.
- A document type or link type declaration can include the identifier of an external entity containing all or part of the declaration subset; the external identifier serves simultaneously as a declaration of that entity and as a reference to it.

(ISO 8879)

formal public identifier	A public identifier that is constructed according to rules defined in this International Standard so that its owner identifier and the components of its text identifier can be distinguished. (ISO 8879)
fragment identifier	In HTML, the value of the NAME attribute of an A or LINK element, when used in a URL to address the element. (Charles F. Goldfarb Series)
general entity	An entity that can be referenced from within the content of an element or an attribute value literal. (ISO 8879)

462

general entity reference	A named entity reference to a general entity. (ISO 8879)
generalized markup	Markup that is free of system and processing dependencies because it describes a document's information content rather than its presentation. (Charles F. Goldfarb Series)
Generalized Markup Language	A notation for generalized markup. *Note* It is the precursor to SGML. (Charles F. Goldfarb Series)
generic identifier	A name that identifies the element type of an element. (ISO 8879)
GML	Generalized Markup Language *Note* It is the precursor to SGML. (Charles F. Goldfarb Series)
http protocol	The Hypertext Transfer Protocol (HTTP) is an application-level protocol for distributed, collaborative, hypermedia information systems. It is a generic, stateless, object-oriented protocol which can be used for many tasks, such as name servers and distributed object management systems, through extension of its request methods. A feature of HTTP is the typing and negotiation of data representation, allowing systems to be built independently of the data being transferred. (HyperText Transfer Protocol)

Hypermedia/Time-based Structuring Language	A standardized hypermedia structuring language for representing hypertext linking, temporal and spatial event scheduling, and synchronization. HyTime provides basic identification and addressing mechanisms and is independent of object data content notations, hyperlink types, processing and presentation functions, and other application semantics. Hyperlinks can be established to documents that conform to HyTime and to those that do not, regardless of whether those documents can be modified. The full HyTime function supports "integrated open hypermedia" (IOH) — the "bibliographic model" of referencing that allows hyperlinks to anything, anywhere, at any time — but systems need support only the subset that is within their present capabilities. (ISO/IEC 10744)
HyTime	Hypermedia/Time-based Structuring Language (ISO/IEC 10744)
HyperText Markup Language	A simple markup language used to create hypertext documents that are platform independent. HTML documents are SGML documents with generic semantics that are appropriate for representing information from a wide range of domains. HTML markup can represent hypertext news, mail, documentation, and hypermedia; menus of options; database query results; simple structured documents with in-lined graphics; and hypertext views of existing bodies of information (HyperText Markup Language)
ID	Unique identifier. (ISO 8879)
ID *reference list*	An attribute value that is a list of ID reference values. (ISO 8879)
ID *reference value*	An attribute value that is a name specified as an id value of an element in the same document instance. (ISO 8879)
inclusions	Elements that are allowed anywhere in the content of an element or its subelements even though the applicable model does not permit them. (ISO 8879)

464

information-content markup	Descriptive markup in which markup names are based on the subject matter of the document type.

> Note   Information-content markup is sometimes called "content tagging", although that term is a poor one because all non-empty SGML elements have content and elements in content can be tagged regardless of the connotation of the markup names.
>
> (Charles F. Goldfarb Series)

instance (of a document type)	The data and markup for a hierarchy of elements that conforms to a document type definition. (ISO 8879)
internal entity	An entity whose replacement text is incorporated in an entity declaration. (ISO 8879)
keyword	A parameter that is a reserved name.

> Note   In parameters where either a keyword or a name defined by an application could be specified, the keyword is always preceded by the reserved name indicator. An application is therefore able to define names without regard to whether those names are also used by the concrete syntax.
>
> (ISO 8879)

location address	An element form that represents the address of one or more objects. A reference to a location address is treated as a reference to the objects addressed by the location path that it begins.

> Note   A location address can be the location source of another location address, thereby forming a location ladder.

> Note   A location address is the HyTime representation of what is commonly known in computing as an "indirect address".
>
> (Charles F. Goldfarb Series)

location ladder   A set of location addresses, known as "location rungs", in which each rung is the location source of the rung below it.

> Note   A location ladder is visualized as running from top to bottom. A rung that is a step in a location path is considered to be the bottom rung with respect to that path.

> Note   A location ladder represents a progressive culling of the set of addressable objects as one proceeds downward.

(Charles F. Goldfarb Series)

location path   A set of location addresses, known as "location steps", in which the first step references the second and so on. A location path can have branches, created when a step addresses two or more objects, at least one of which is a location address. A branch terminates when its last step references only objects that are not location addresses. The objects addressed by a location path are all those, other than steps, that are addressed by any of the steps in the path.

> Note   A location path is visualized as running from left to right. Each step is the bottom rung of a location ladder.

> Note   A location address can be a step in more than one location path, but can be the first step in only one.

(Charles F. Goldfarb Series)

location source   The set of objects from which a location address selects the objects that it addresses.

> Note   For example, the location source of a treeloc is the tree in which the node addressed by the treeloc is found.

(Charles F. Goldfarb Series)

marked section	A section of the document that has been identified for a special purpose, such as ignoring markup within it. (ISO 8879)
marked section declaration	A markup declaration that identifies a marked section and specifies how it is to be treated. (ISO 8879)
mark up	To add markup to a document. (ISO 8879)
markup	Text that is added to the data of a document in order to convey information about it.

> Note   There are four kinds of markup: descriptive markup (tags), references, markup declarations, and processing instructions.
>
> (ISO 8879)

markup character	An SGML character that, depending on the context, could be interpreted either as markup or data. (ISO 8879)
(markup) declaration	Markup that controls how other markup of a document is to be interpreted.

> Note   There are 13 kinds: SGML, entity, element, attribute definition list, notation, document type, link type, link set, link set use, *marked section*, short reference mapping, short reference use, and comment.
>
> (ISO 8879)

(markup) A feature of SGML that allows markup to be minimized by
minimization feature shortening or omitting tags, or shortening entity references.

> Note Markup minimization features do not affect the doc-
> ument type definition, so a minimized document
> can be sent to a system that does not support these
> features by first restoring the omitted markup.
> There are five kinds: SHORTTAG, OMITTAG, SHOR-
> TREF, DATATAG, and RANK.
>
> (ISO 8879)

model group A component of a content model that specifies the order of
occurrence of elements and character strings in an element's
content, as modified by exceptions specified in the content
model of the element and in the content models of other open
elements. (ISO 8879)

name A name token whose first character is a name-start character.
(ISO 8879)

name character A character that can occur in a name: name start characters,
digits, and others designated by the concrete syntax. (ISO 8879)

named location A location address that addresses objects by their unique
address names.

> Note For example, a named location address can address
> elements and entities in the same document as itself
> and in other documents.
>
> (Charles F. Goldfarb Series)

nameloc Named location address. (Charles F. Goldfarb Series)

name start character A character that can begin a name: letters, and others designated by the concrete syntax. (ISO 8879)

name token   A character string, consisting solely of name characters, whose length is restricted by the NAMELEN quantity.

> Note   A name token that occurs in a group is also a token; one that occurs as an attribute value is not.

(ISO 8879)

name token group   A group whose tokens are required to be name tokens.

(ISO 8879)

*non-*SGML *character*   A character in the document character set whose coded representation never occurs in an SGML *entity.*   (ISO 8879)

*non-*SGML *data entity*   A data entity in which a non-SGML character could occur.

(ISO 8879)

notation attribute   An attribute whose value is a notation name that identifies the data content notation of the element's content.

> Note   A notation attribute does not apply when there is an explicit content reference, as the element's content will be empty.

(ISO 8879)

notation declaration   A markup declaration that associates a name with a *notation identifier.*   (ISO 8879)

notation identifier   An *external identifier* that identifies a data content notation in a notation declaration. It can be a public identifier if the notation is public, and, if not, a description or other information sufficient to invoke a program to interpret the notation.   (ISO 8879)

notation name   The name assigned to a data content notation by a notation declaration.   (ISO 8879)

number   A name token consisting solely of digits.   (ISO 8879)

number token	A name token whose first character is a digit.
	Note A number token that occurs in a group is also a token; one that occurs as an attribute value is not.
	(ISO 8879)
parameter	The portion of a markup declaration that is bounded by ps separators (whether required or optional). A parameter can contain other parameters. (ISO 8879)
parameter entity	An entity that can be referenced from a markup declaration parameter. (ISO 8879)
parameter entity reference	A named entity reference to a parameter entity. (ISO 8879)
parsed character data	Zero or more characters that occur in a context in which text is parsed and markup is recognized. They are classified as data characters because they were not recognized as markup during parsing. (ISO 8879)
procedural markup	Processing instructions that are embedded within a document and executed in the order in which they are encountered. The document components affected by procedural markup are normally determined by the position of the processing instructions in the document.
	Note In contrast, the document components affected by a style sheet are normally identified explicitly.
	(Charles F. Goldfarb Series)
procedure	Processing defined by an application to operate on elements of a particular type.
	Note A single procedure could be associated with more than one element type, and/or more than one procedure could operate on the same element type at different points in the document.
	(ISO 8879)

processing instruction Markup consisting of system-specific data that controls how a document is to be processed. (ISO 8879)

prolog The portion of an SGML document or SGML subdocument entity that contains document type and link type declarations. (ISO 8879)

publication-structure markup Descriptive markup in which markup names reflect the structure of publications, such as divisions, headings, lists, and paragraphs.

> Note For example, when publication-structure markup is used for an automobile maintenance manual, the procedure for removing a tire might be marked up as an "ordered list" element, with each step tagged as a "list item". In contrast, when information-content markup is used, the element types could be "procedure" and "procedure step".

> Note Publication-structure markup is sometimes called "structural markup", although that term is a poor one because all SGML markup is structural regardless of the connotation of the markup names.

> (Charles F. Goldfarb Series)

public identifier A minimum literal that identifies public text.

> Note
> • The public identifiers in a document can optionally be interpretable as formal public identifiers.
> • The system is responsible for converting public identifiers to system identifiers.

> (ISO 8879)

471

public text	Text that is known beyond the context of a single document or system environment, and which can be accessed with a public identifier.

Note

- Examples are standard or registered document type definitions, entity sets, element sets, data content notations, and other markup constructs (see *Annex D of ISO 8879:1986*).
- Public text is not equivalent to published text; there is no implication of unrestricted public access. In particular, the owner of public text may choose to sell or license it to others, or to restrict its access to a single organization.
- Public text simplifies access to shared constructs, reduces the amount of text that must be interchanged, and reduces the chance of copying errors.

(ISO 8879)

reference	Markup that is replaced by other text, either an entity or a single character. (ISO 8879)
reference concrete syntax	A concrete syntax, defined in this International Standard, that is used in all SGML declarations. (ISO 8879)
replacement text	The text of the entity that replaces an entity reference. (ISO 8879)
required attribute	An attribute for which there must always be an attribute specification for the attribute value. (ISO 8879)
reserved name	A name defined by the concrete syntax, rather than by an application, such as a markup declaration name.

Note   Such names appear in the International Standard as syntactic literals.

(ISO 8879)

separator A character string that separates markup components from one another.

Note
- There are four kinds: **s**, **ds**, **ps**, and **ts**.
- A separator cannot occur in data.

(ISO 8879)

SGML Standard Generalized Markup Language (ISO 8879)

SGML *application* Rules that apply SGML to a text processing application. An SGML application includes a formal specification of the markup constructs used in the application, expressed in SGML. It can also include a non-SGML definition of semantics, application conventions, and/or processing.

Note
- The formal specification of an SGML application normally includes document type definitions, data content notations, and entity sets, and possibly a concrete syntax or capacity set. If processing is defined by the application, the formal specification could also include link process definitions.
- The formal specification of an SGML application constitutes the common portions of the documents processed by the application. These common portions are frequently made available as public text.
- The formal specification is usually accompanied by comments and/or documentation that explains the semantics, application conventions, and processing specifications of the application.
- An SGML application exists independently of any implementation. However, if processing is defined by the application, the non-SGML definition could include application procedures, implemented in a programming or text processing language.

(ISO 8879)

SGML *character*   A character that is permitted in an SGML entity.   (ISO 8879)

SGML *declaration*   A markup declaration that specifies the character set, concrete syntax, optional features, and capacity requirements of a document's markup. It applies to all of the SGML entities of a document.   (ISO 8879)

SGML *document*   A document that is represented as a sequence of characters, organized physically into an entity structure and logically into an element structure, essentially as described in this International Standard. An SGML document consists of data characters, which represent its information content, and markup characters, which represent the structure of the data and other information useful for processing it. In particular, the markup describes at least one document type definition, and an instance of a structure conforming to the definition. (ISO 8879)

SGML *document entity*   The SGML entity that begins an SGML document. It contains, at a minimum, an SGML declaration, a base document type declaration, and the start and end (if not all) of a base document element.   (ISO 8879)

SGML *entity*   An entity whose characters are interpreted as markup or data in accordance with this International Standard.

Note   There are three types of SGML entity: SGML document entity, SGML subdocument entity, and SGML text entity.

(ISO 8879)

SGML *parser*   A program (or portion of a program or a combination of programs) that recognizes markup in SGML documents.

                Note   If an analogy were to be drawn to programming language processors, an SGML parser would be said to perform the functions of both a lexical analyzer and a parser with respect to SGML documents.

                                                                  (ISO 8879)

SGML *system*   A system that includes an SGML parser, an entity manager, and both or either of:

1. an implementation of one or more SGML applications; and/or
2. facilities for a user to implement SGML applications, with access to the SGML parser and entity manager.
                                                    (ISO 8879)

Standard Generalized Markup Language   A language for document representation that formalizes markup and frees it of system and processing dependencies.
                                                    (ISO 8879)

start-tag   Descriptive markup that identifies the start of an element and specifies its generic identifier and attributes.   (ISO 8879) *style sheet*   A set of procedures and processing instructions that is maintained separately from the documents to which it is applied. The document components affected by a style sheet are normally identified explicitly, either by instructions within the style sheet or by an external association, such as an SGML link process definition.

Note   In contrast, the document components affected by procedural markup are normally determined by the position of processing instructions in the document.

Note   A style sheet could itself be a document with the style specifications represented as descriptive markup that is interpreted by a rendition process.

(Charles F. Goldfarb Series)

subelement   An element that occurs in the content of another element (the containing element) in such a way that the subelement begins when the containing element is the current element. (ISO 8879)

system declaration   A declaration, included in the documentation for a conforming SGML system, that specifies the features, capacity set, concrete syntaxes, and character set that the system supports, and any validation services that it can perform.   (ISO 8879)

system identifier   System data that specifies the file identifier, storage location, program invocation, data stream position, or other system-specific information that locates an external entity.   (ISO 8879)

tag   Descriptive markup.

Note   There are two kinds: start-tag and end-tag.

(ISO 8879)

token   The portion of a group, including a complete nested group (but not a connector), that is, or could be, bounded by **ts** separators.
(ISO 8879)

treeloc Tree location address. (Charles F. Goldfarb Series)

tree location address A location address that addresses a single node of a tree in the classical manner by selecting a node from an addressable range at each level of the tree, starting at the root.

(Charles F. Goldfarb Series)

Uniform Resource Locator A compact string representation for a resource available via the Internet. The generic syntax for URLs provides a framework for new schemes to be established using protocols other than those defined in this document. URLs are used to *locate* resources, by providing an abstract identification of the resource location. Having located a resource, a system may perform a variety of operations on the resource, as might be characterized by such words as "access", "update", "replace", "find attributes". In general, only the "access" method needs to be specified for any URL scheme. (IETF RFC 1738)

unique identifier A name that uniquely identifies an element. (ISO 8879)

URL Uniform Resource Locator (IETF RFC 1738)

validating SGML parser A conforming SGML parser that can find and report a reportable markup error if (and only if) one exists. (ISO 8879)

ᨠ INDEX

B

C

E 🐛

F

G

H

I

J

W

Y

X

❧ COLOPHON

This book is available in several published forms, each of which is published one set of text and graphics files. Naturally, it an SGML document. Yuri Rubinsky started writing the book using a stripped down version of the ISO 12083 DTD. Murray Maloney added hyperlinking and an assortment of small structural and phrase-level element types. As you might have expected, both Yuri and Murray used *SoftQuad* products to create the SGML file, DTDS, navigators and style sheets. To create DTDS, we used SoftQuad RulesBuilder. To create the contents of this book and the sample files, we used SoftQuad Author/Editor. We used SoftQuad Panorama PRO to print early drafts, and to create style sheets and navigators

The images of screens in this book were captured by Cheryl Simpson, using Paint Shop Pro and edited using SoftQuad MetalWorks, ImageMagick and xv. The graphical tree views of DTDS are from Near and Far Designer, a product of Microstar Corporation. The pencil drawings were created by Colin Moock.

The printed book was designed by Liam Quin in the summer and typeset by him in the early fall of 1996. The software used included James Clark's NSGMLS SGML parser, Larry Wall's Perl 5 programming language, together with David Megginson's SGML.pl package, producing sqtroff input for SoftQuad Publishing Software, which generated the PostScript file that was sent to a publisher who produced the printed book you might be reading now.

The typeface used for the body text is FontHaus Celestia, designed by Mark von Bronkhurst; Adobe Caslon is used as a companion bold face.

AFTERWORDS

It's Over... But It Goes On

Yuri Rubinsky was taken from us suddenly and tragically on January 21, 1996. He was 43 years old.

I first heard of Yuri Rubinsky around 1987 because a new company called *SoftQuad* was circulating a history of SGML — and it was thoroughly inaccurate. At a technical documentation conference that year Yuri was introduced to me as the author of that history. I liked him immediately; as far as I know, so did everyone who ever met him.

I wasn't even annoyed about the bogus history — which gave the U.S. *Defense Dept.* the credit for my invention. I knew that Yuri and his company were very special because they were like the chess-playing dog. It didn't matter that the dog lost every game — it was amazing that it even tried to play! Yuri may have gotten the history wrong, but the fact that he made the effort to give credit — outside his own company — for the technology that SoftQuad was exploiting, marked him as a rare and caring individual.

That respect and appreciation for the people who created the technology of his industry continued for as long as I knew him. On the day before he died he telephoned to tell me of the look of surprise and pleasure on the face of Doug Engelbart — inventor of the mouse and pioneer of many of the techniques used in today's World Wide Web — on receiving a tribute organized by Yuri and a cash award provided by SoftQuad.

Yuri also had an unflagging belief that anything that ought to be done *could* be done. He also had the drive and commitment to back up that belief. I benefited personally from that commitment not long after I met Yuri. I had had to stop working on *The* SGML *Handbook* because of neck surgery and it was unclear when I would be able to type again. Yuri thought it important that I finish the book. His solution to my keyboard incapacity was to organize a production team — largely conscripted from SoftQuad. — the mainstay of which was an expert transcriber for my taped dictation. Yuri himself acted as editor of the tapes, as well as indexer, cross-referencer, designer, and production manager. He also introduced me to Murray Maloney, who did the programming and production of the index. As a result of these efforts, the Handbook got into print in 1990 and has been there ever since.

And something else resulted as well. My relationship with Yuri, which started with the occasional phone call to discuss the book, quickly blossomed into a close personal friendship and professional collaboration.

Yuri liked to refer to SGML as the "quiet revolution", because of the profound change it makes in the way information is managed. Yuri was a leader in that revolution, inspiring everyone with his vision of how the technology could be applied and his idealism that it should be used to benefit humanity at large as well as the corporate sector. Like all good revolutionaries, he and I used to conspire a lot — planning which committees to join, what papers to write, and which speeches to give. At his memorial service, I was delighted to learn from his wife and parents that Yuri had thought of me as his "SGML guru." I always thought of him as my counsellor.

In 1993, when Mark Taub and Phyllis Bregman approached me to edit this series, one of their compelling arguments was that they had already signed some top authors. One of them was Yuri Rubinsky. I loved the idea of helping Yuri with his book as he had helped with mine. I'm sorry I couldn't have completed the project with him, of course, but I was pleased to see how well his vision and ideals had rubbed off on his posthumous co-author, Murray Maloney.

Yuri was always good at that.

Charles F. Goldfarb
September 29, 1996

Afterwards

I first met Yuri Rubinsky when I applied for a job at his fledgling software company just over 10 years ago. He and one of his partners, David Slocombe, interviewed me in a donut shop. I couldn't tell from that meeting how important Yuri would become to me. But one thing I recall very clearly: It was the most unusual interview ever. Yuri called to offer me the job a few days later, and I became SoftQuad employee number eight on March 3rd, 1986.

Yuri Rubinsky died suddenly on the evening of January 21, 1996. The SGML world took a collective gasp, paused at the enormity of the loss and then, of course, carried on. For many of those close to Yuri, though, his death remains unreal. The loss we feel is tremendous. There's a continuing sense of obligation to talk about him to those who didn't know him personally and a continuing need to share Yuri stories, ideals and vision.

I was honored when I was approached to complete this work in progress. I met with my family to discuss the commitment required but there was never really any question that I wouldn't try to complete Yuri's last project. My wife and children gave me their support, but none of us fully understood how overwhelming and consuming the task would be. This project provided me with a new understanding and respect for just how truly remarkable Yuri's achievements were. As I was going through his notes I got a renewed sense of his intelligence, insight, humor and his delightful style. I found so many ideas, any one of which could have been the subject of a book. We have no way of knowing what he would have envisioned, would have brought to our world.

Being with Yuri was always an adventure. It seemed as if he knew how to get the most out of every second. He had a way of looking at things that made you reach for a higher understanding or meaning, to go beyond the ordinary. He never said you should think about something in this way or that, or look, I'm going to teach you something here. He just led by example. He was the kind of person who wouldn't let you get away with "absolute" statements. He'd want to know why that was so. Not in a challenging way but out of genuine curiosity. Certainly, "it's always been that way" was never a reasonable response from his point of view.

Yuri made the impossible seem not only possible but even probable. He had a way of looking at things, of breathing life into ideas, of providing a spark, of building fires, of creating something extraordinary from the ordinary. He was sensitive, caring, thoroughly enlightened. He had character and compassion and intelligence and a quality of humbleness and gentleness that drew people to him. It was these traits and his drive which helped him achieve so much in his short life.

 This summer I was honored again when I was invited to participate in a workshop of the Yuri Rubinsky Insight Foundation. A dozen of Yuri's colleagues gathered at an island retreat to discuss the goals of the foundation and to set out a plan for the foundation. During one of our discussions — in the middle of a hot summer day — something very unusual happened: A bat flew up to the bay window and landed on a spider's web to feed on an insect that was trapped there, and it got caught in the web. The conversation stopped as people stood to observe this bizarre occurence. And just as voices of concern were raised, the bat suddenly broke free of the web and flew away. This incident has left a lasting impresion on me.

Completing this book was an enormous task for me, but for Yuri it was only one of the many things in which he was involved. I'm sure Yuri would have seen this particular project as just another small step forward. Sometimes, I thought I would never be finished, and now, I am reluctant to close the final chapter. In some way, I think I was hoping to hang on to Yuri, to stay connected, just a little while longer, in much the same way as those who admit they're still reluctant to delete Yuri's email address from their files. I feel privileged to have been able to work with him, share ideas and take part in the exciting ride. Somewhere along the way, though, I've come to understand that while this particular connection with Yuri is passing, in so many other ways he will always remain a part of us.

I just can't imagine having lived in a world without Yuri.

Murray Maloney
September 1996

Yuri Rubinsky

Yuri was born in Tripoli, Lebanon on August 2, 1952. His family moved to the Toronto, Canada area when he was three. He graduated from Brock University and studied architecture at the University of Toronto. After a stint of odd jobs in the Yukon, Yuri decided to focus on publishing. He attended the Radcliffe publishing course at Harvard University in the summer of 1978 and was so impressed that he decided that  Canada needed a similar course. Two years later, he convinced the Banff Centre for the Arts to sponsor the Banff Publishing Workshop. In Canada, he is probably best known as founding co-director of the influential Banff Publishing Workshop and for his work in applying technology to help visually impaired people.

Yuri Rubinsky is best known in a great many parts of the world as a co-founder of SoftQuad Inc. and as co-founder and chairman of the SGML Open consortium. Along with partners David Slocombe and Stan Bevington, he founded SoftQuad to develop and sell tools for SGML. Almost from the beginning, he was instrumental in bringing the SGML community together and spreading the SGML gospel. In recent years, he has also been involved in helping to shape standards for HTML and the World Wide Web.

Yuri was an author, publisher, visionary — a man of amazing energy and talent. His books (as co-author) include A History of The End of The World (1982), The Wankers' Guide to Canada (1986) and Christopher Columbus Answers All Charges (1993). He was editor of Charles F. Goldfarb's The SGML Handbook (1990) and SoftQuad's The SGML Primer (1991). Most recently, Yuri was finishing two books on SGML and the Internet, as well as an historical comedy on Vergil, Mesmer and Neil Armstrong.

In addition to books, Yuri co-authored and produced the play "Invisible Cities" in 1981, authored a one-edition newspaper spoof, *Not The Globe and Mail* (1984), created and edited *Yorker* magazine (1985-86), and co-authored and produced SGML: *The Movie* (1990).

But anyone who knew him will remember Yuri most of all as a marvelous person — the kind of person who brightened every room he was in and made you feel better and more noble for being with him. Yuri was bright, witty, original, insightful and, most of all, human in the very best sense. He was never concerned with technology for its own sake, but always concerned with what it could do to help people.

We will never forget him.

Jonathan Seybold
January 1996

Yuri Rubinsky Insight Foundation

The *Yuri Rubinsky Insight Foundation* is dedicated to commemorating the genius of the late Yuri Rubinsky by bringing together workers from a broad spectrum of disciplines to stimulate research and development of technologies that will enhance human access to information of all kinds. Recognizing that all human capabilities are limited in various ways, it seeks to achieve, to the fullest extent possible, equality of access for all.

The Foundation provides a focal point for those honoring the life and work of Yuri Rubinsky, an industry leader, inventor, entrepreneur, author, humanitarian, and friend.

For more information, contact *yrif@yuri.org.*

Murray Maloney

Murray Maloney was born in Montreal in 1955. He attended
Stanstead College in Quebec, *Santa Barbara City College* in California, and graduated from *Seneca College* in Toronto. He
began his career in 1975, as a test technician for consumer and
industrial cable, video, radio and television systems. He
worked in the electronics and computer hardware fields until
September, 1982, when he was hospitalized for burns and
temporary blindness following the crash of a DC-10 aircraft in Malaga, Spain. After
his release from hospital, he bought his first computer and took time off to study
computer electronics, programming, networking, and technical communications.
These events led to his later interest in accessibility for the sight-impaired.

Murray joined SoftQuad in 1986, where he wrote, designed and typeset several
award-winning books, and worked with Yuri Rubinsky and Charles Goldfarb to produce the index for *The SGML Handbook*. From 1991 until 1995, he was a manager and
publishing systems architect with the *Santa Cruz Operation*, where he helped design
and develop the world's first HTML-based context-sensitive help and online documentation system in 1993. In 1995, Murray re-joined SoftQuad to work with Yuri
Rubinsky as a spokesperson for the company. Murray is a technical director with
SoftQuad today.

Murray is a sponsor of the *Davenport Group*, a member of SGML Open's technical
committee, a founding member of the IETF HTML Working Group and the W3C
HTML Editorial Review Board, a member of the W3C Advisory Committee, and an
advisor to the *Yuri Rubinsky Insight Foundation*.

Murray Maloney lives in Pickering, Ontario with his wife Joan and his three
children: Andrea, Brendan and Christopher.

NOTES